CW01177331

MOVE OVER BROKERS HERE COMES THE BLOCKCHAIN

Dr Keir Finlow-Bates

Published by Thinklair TMI 2020

♀**think**lair

While every precaution has been taken in the preparation of this book, the publisher assumes no responsibility for omissions or errors, or for damages resulting from the use of the information contained herein, the accuracy of which is suspect at best. Readers should note that the author subscribes to an extreme fallibilist philosophy which posits that nothing can ever be rationally supported or justified in a conclusive way, that even mathematics cannot show us what is true, and that everything is therefore subjective.

In other words, *Here Be Dragons*.

MOVE OVER BROKERS HERE COMES THE BLOCKCHAIN

First hardback edition: 11 December 2020

Text and cover:
Copyright © 2019-2020 Keir Finlow-Bates

Strawberry on front cover:
Derivative work based on an image submitted to pexels.com by Ylanite Koppens, and used under the Pexels license

Character image on back cover:
Copyright © 2017 Markus Lehtokumpi, used with permission

Trademarks: All trademarks are the property of their respective owners. Good luck with that guys!

ISBN: 978-1-716-47972-4

Acknowledgments

Edward Nawotka published an article back in 2011 in which he suggested that publishers should "credit the editors, proofreaders, agents, publicists and others inside the books"[1]. It is notable that in the film industry the name of almost everyone who had an influence on the movie produced is listed at the end, whereas books are typically presented as the work of only the author and the cover illustrator.

I would therefore like to acknowledge the following people, who all, in their own way, had a profound effect on this book:

Many thanks to Jon Callan, Diana Hildebrandt, Anthony Day, and Brigitte Custard for their sterling efforts as beta readers.

Further thanks to Andy Martin for never hesitating to question my assumptions, and John Kost for clicking 'like' on pretty much everything that I have ever written. Also, Ken Bodnar for being my Latin consultant, Tamra Groff for suggesting the strawberry and razor image on the cover, and Trekk for prompting me to set a deadline by pointing out how many people were writing books – there is nothing like a bit of competition to get you moving.

I am deeply indebted to everyone who commented on or clicked in response to my LinkedIn posts, thereby providing me with encouragement and insight for my personal ongoing blockchain explorations. I have manually collected the names of every person who reacted to any blockchain post I submitted in the last five months (up to and including the infamous pseudonymous Spider-Man post). On the next page have listed all who clicked five times or more – I couldn't fit any more in, but I sincerely thank all of you for your support!

And last, but not least, I would like to express my eternal gratitude to Satoshi Nakamoto, wherever and whoever you may be.

Anita Kalergis, Luc Detemmerman, Greg Phillips, Marius Corneliu, Robin Carre, William L. Foster II, Kimmo Rouhiainen, Kerry Allen, Christine Fahey, Sean Brizendine, Maurício Magaldi, Thomas Edde, Geoff Marr, Sri Krishna Charan Viswanathan, Aaron Tobias, Robert Young, J. Brian Hennessy, Pratik Sanjay Patil, Shalini Paul, Samson Williams, Benjamin Sangwa, Vladyslav Kurmaz, Jason Van, Daniel Delaney, Miguel Benavent De B.

Odin O, Martijn Van Veen, Remesh Sartani, Noel Wilamowski, Deshan Kuruvita - Aratchy, Daniel Doiron, Allister Frost, Phil Doyle, Nicholas Zahabizadeh, Kevin Maguire, Drew Frierson, Haresh Jani, Tommy Cooksey, Jean-Marc Goossens, Matthew Cartwright, Chad C. Martin, Armando Castellano Jr, Steve Tendon, Guilherme Maia, Athanasios Pournaras, Brian Nammari, Ian T. Staley, Chris Evoy, Sean Finlay, Vincent Luchtenberg, John Lee, Andries Viljoen, Vidith Kim, Mohamed Youssef, Damien Wan, Richard Durham, Erik Hjalmar Emillon, Joan M., Nikola Lazic, Audry Polanco, Annemarie Monschein, Kris Vette, Chris Butler, Gio Almuarrawi, Robert Rongen, Jahu Coleman, Kristi Hightower, Bruno Schneider - Le Saout, David De Vriesere, Leos Stehlik, Philipp Redlinger, Mikko Valjakka, Brandon Kerzner, Jeremey Bush, Alexander Dinershtein, Kristine Mallari, Peter Jalkotzy, Yash Rana, John Macleod, Neeraj Badaya, Jari Mitro.

Craig Wedge, Kate Suominen, Shadman Hossain, Jorge Santos, Paulo Jacinto Rodrigues, Irina Heaver, Kris K, Neeta Chougule, Ivan Vujic, Richard Piacentini, Bjorn Bjercke, Brian Sherrell, Konrad Hurren, Sufyan Al-Hassan, Koenraad Janssens, Scott Taylor Firp, Nick Waters, Craig Jacobs, Predrag Nikolik, Tim Rainer, Luis Javier Costa Giraldo, Kaustubh Padakannaya, Kevin Koo, Matias Romo, Steve Safronoff, J. Given, John Migid, Mikko Rieger, Henry Swift, Rafael Edelmann, Robin Roy Thomas, Demetrios Dolios, Rohit Tripathi, Pablo Zanetta Ferraro, Robert Valli, Kuldip Singh Nijjar, Marko Järvelin, Harman Puri, Jason Price, Douglas Bodden, Danish Siddiqui, Gottfried Szing, Florin Ghimici, Arif Mustafa, Nihal Pathan, Ina O' Murchu, Jérôme G., Liam Machin, Duncan Cameron, Vasily Hall, Jordan Fengel, Ana Paula Picasso, Tanya Matveeva, Vikram Anand Bhushan, Devi Prasad Choudhury, Miloš Milosavljević, Patrick Jones, Max Thake, Oluwatobi Joel, Mark Treleaven, Matt O'Neill, Pertti Reponen, Nicolae Ghibu, Robert Bakker, Prevoo, Magnus Westerlund, Joseph Royal, Travis Logue, Kris Kalwij, Thierry Gribeauval, Daniel Caner Alkan, Sabit Kshetri, Sharon Hartung, Alexander Samarin, Whit Gallimore, Denis Petrovcic, Jun Hyuk Ahn, Tom B, Ryan "Coop D'ville" Cooper, Alexandre Blanc, Manuel Kotoucek, Koushik Annapureddy, Saul Tarazona, Charlie Northrup, Susan Brown, Paul Emmanuel, Charmaine Yan, Vinay M., Omar K., Ragunath A., Max Luck, John Rigler, Marcel Thiess, Julian Fifield, Rob Falla, Irfan Khan, Victor Cucos Mba, David Braybrooke, Juan Usandizaga, Chirag Popat, Samar Abdelhameed, Philip Bossonney, Scott Olson, Kevin O'Malley, Luis M Garcia, Dr Jane Thomason, Stephan Missura, Dave Villeneuve, Sergio Mazzarella, Lesly Machorro, Paul F. Dowding, Harrison McQueen, John Mckenzie, Mohammed Naquib, Steve Clarke, Joanne Thornton Gaicd, Julio Fernández, Victor Romain, Marquis Allen, Ron Reichert, Sumit Bakshi, Markus Laatikainen, Christopher Dalton, Asmita David.

Table of Contents

Preface..11
Introduction...15
   Doing it yourself...18
   Origins of the crises..18
   That's entertainment...20
   Summing up...23
Three Chords...25
   Playing in the band...25
   Coding up a blockchain..28
Weltanschauung!...31
   Disintermediated digital assets...33
   Triple-entry ledgers...34
   Consortium enablement..36
   Data ownership..37
   The frictionless marketplace...38
Blockchain City...41
   Unpacking the analogy..42
   Who can get on the bus?...45
   When is a bus not a block?..48
Buying Trust..49
   The manufacture of consensus..54
   All your database are belong to us......................................57
   Not my CAP of T...59
   What is trust?...59
Hash Functions...63
   That never happened!..64
   Shorter is better...65
   The fingerprint of a file..66
   Cryptographic hash functions...68
   Magical elves under toadstools...69
   Oh the wonderful things that a hash can do.......................71
Part One on Identity: Who Are You?.......................................83
   The problem of identity..84

Pseudonymity..86
The right to privacy...88
Tainted coins..89
Mixing...90
Ring signatures..92
The hunting of the zk-snark...95
Summary...98

Passwords are the Worst..99
On a train...101
Connecting to a server...103
The problem with categories..105
The lines of communication...107
Make mine a double..112
One-way tickets...116
What could go wrong?..118

Part Two on Identity: Self-Sovereignty................................121
The ship of Theseus..122
The network of our identity..124
Some definitions..126
These truths are not self-evident..130
But ... why blockchain?...139

Cryptocurrencies and the User Experience..........................143
Tales from the crypto..143
The sum of the parts...144
The failure of analogies..150
What's in your wallet?...150
The parable of the panicking cryptocurrency owner.......152
The engineer and the aristocrat...153
Model transference..153

The Network Effect..155
The worst network diagram ever.......................................157
Blockchains and networks..160
The handshake problem...160
The birthday paradox..164
Erdős numbers...165

On Value...167
Elementary, my dear Watson..168
Where does the money come from?..................................173

- Bartering is inefficient...176
- Fixed prices..178
- Rounding up..179

The Truth is a Harsh Mistress.................................181
- Truth tables...182
- On meaning..187

Clever Covenants...189
- Scripts and balances..190
- The lone and level sands...192
- Turing completeness..195
- How to stop going round in circles.............................196
- What can these smart contracts do?............................199
- Dishwasher warranties..200
- Summary..201

Government Without Leaders.................................203
- Checks and balances..204
- Corporate hierarchies...206
- Blockchain and governance.....................................207
- Voting with your virtual feet...................................214
- On-chain governance...215

Knives, Forks, and Spoons....................................217
- Blockchain forks..218
- A Minecraft analogy..219
- Split those coins!...226
- Identical Banks...227
- How to store your cutlery.......................................230

Fair Gambling...233
- Born to lose..234
- The weak law of large numbers................................235
- Proving fairness..236
- Hash functions to the rescue (again)..........................237
- Entropy...238
- Strong passwords and private keys............................245
- How to choose a winner...246
- The arrow of time...253

Rise of the Autonomous Machines..........................255
- Back to the ship of Theseus....................................256
- An IoT overview...256

The relevance of markets..258
Putting it all together...260
The automatic bazaar..260

Independent Sacrificial Offerings..263
Definitions...264
The flip side of the coin..266
Insecurities..267
Futility...267
Ask yourself the hard questions......................................268
In summary...270
The centralized IOU..271
So what now 271

DeFining Finance...273
Underlying Assets..275
Derivatives...276
Decoupling...277
Centralized exchanges..277
Crypto-capitalism..278
Crypto-loans...280
Stablecoins...281
Automated Market Makers..285
Flash loans...288
Automated pyramid schemes..290
Risks..292
Evolution or Revolution?..293

Selling Out..295
The great treasure hunt..296

References..299

Discography..317

About the Author...321

Figures

Figure 1: Three chords - now form a band[12].................26
Figure 2: The long tail...27
Figure 3: Three computer concepts: Now launch a blockchain......28
Figure 4: Transaction Town comparison table..........................43
Figure 5: Creative thinking assessment test...........................50
Figure 6: Creative results...52
Figure 7: The labeling response..53
Figure 8: An example of a hash function..............................66
Figure 9: Grid representation of a SHA-256 hash output...........68
Figure 10: A hash function-generated one-time password pad....73
Figure 11: SHA-256 hashing of a phrase with an added nonce...76
Figure 12: People and their fruit selections..........................93
Figure 13: The closing of the loop....................................95
Figure 14: An example of a false claim about the author, who was never arrested for a traffic violation as a young man.........141
Figure 15: Ford on his Quadricycle in 1896.........................146
Figure 16: Some familiar numbers.....................................148
Figure 17: Some (probably) unfamiliar numbers...................149
Figure 18: Centralized, decentralized and distributed networks...157
Figure 19: Decentralized distributed network......................159
Figure 20: The sum of the first 5 numbers..........................162
Figure 21: The sum of the first 5 numbers represented twice....162
Figure 22: Quadratic growth of network connections..............163
Figure 23: A section of the periodic table...........................169
Figure 24: A bartering matrix of comparative values of items....177
Figure 25: A price table...178
Figure 26: Truth table for logical NOT...............................182
Figure 27: Truth table for logical AND..............................183
Figure 28: Truth table for logical OR................................183
Figure 29: Truth table for logical XOR (exclusive OR)............184
Figure 30: Truth table for logical IMPLIES.........................184
Figure 31: Truth table for the contrapositive......................186
Figure 32: Do-it-yourself truth table for double negative.........187
Figure 33: A 5 bitcoin unspent transaction.........................192
Figure 34: A transaction in progress.................................193
Figure 35: Transaction complete......................................194

Figure 36: Illustrating Minecraft blocks suitable for mining........220
Figure 37: My great new cutlery arrangement.............................230
Figure 38: Wins and losses in a "fair" game................................236
Figure 39: XOR table using binary arithmetic.............................251
Figure 40: Four people generating a random number..................252
Figure 41: The internal balance of the machinery........................285
Figure 42: If Bitcoin were to replace other value storing entities.296

Preface

> I hope you know that this will go down
> On your permanent record
> *Gordon James Gano, 1983[a]*

Sometimes the simplest ideas have the most profound influence on the way humanity progresses.

This may sound like a peculiar way to start a book about blockchain, which is seen as a complicated and convoluted invention that you may believe it is really hard to get your head around. Am I truly implying that blockchain is a simple idea?

Okay, so the mechanics of blockchain are indeed complicated, but it is not the mix of cryptography, game theory, and peer-to-peer networking that matters here. Cars are incredibly complicated machines too. Do you know what the solenoid or alternator in your car does? They are both there in the engine bay, and without them, you won't be going anywhere soon, but you don't need to know their function to drive a car.

The key point of blockchain can be found on the next page.

A blockchain allows you to create a unique, unforgeable and unalterable digital item, on a computer network, with clearly defined ownership.

And a blockchain doesn't require trust in a broker or third party to do so. This is what lies at the core of blockchain's power. I think the subconscious grasp that people have of this matter is what explains the current buzz and interest surrounding the technology.

There is something we take for granted in the real world. If I own and live in a house, you can't own it, and you can't live in it without my permission. My car is my car, and not yours, because I have the key and the registration documents to it, and it sits on my driveway. If I'm fortunate enough to amass enough wealth, I can buy and hang a Mondrian painting on my wall that no one else can have access to, and if I'm not wealthy I can pick up a rock on the beach or a stick in the forest and take it home, and it's mine (all mine) and not yours.

Some of these concepts of possession are even backed up and enforced by governments, especially when the items in question are considered extremely valuable. That's the essence of ownership. Even my three-year-old twins understand this. They spend hours arguing with each other who this block of Plasticine clay or that soft toy belongs to. It seems that ownership is a really intrinsic concept to human beings.

But in the digital world, it's a different matter. It's trivial to generate an identical copy of a video, e-book, picture, music file, or piece of software, and send it around the world at no cost. This makes it really hard to enforce intellectual property rights – you have to resort to litigation, which only makes sense if the entity you're suing is large, centralized, wealthy, and cumbersome. Thousands of tiny and relatively poor people copying and using your stuff can't be prosecuted using traditional legal methods in any way that will result in regaining profits to the litigant. So strangely enough, given its origins, I don't think the crypto-anarchists of the future are going to look back too fondly at the rise of blockchain.

Here's the root of the root and the bud of the bud: blockchain allows you to make digital objects that are as distinct, entity-wise, as the five-pound note you got in your change from the chip shop, or the signed copy of a Sex Pistols album you picked up at a trade fair, but they exist on a computer network rather than in the real physical world. Think about it:

Digital objects that are as real as physical objects. That's an extremely significant technological revolution.

I'm sure when the wheel was first invented, a lot of the rest of the tribe thought it was over-hyped because after all: you can still just carry the stuff you foraged, or hunted, to the cave on your back, or with a few simple journeys to and fro. However, with a bit of refinement, and by building the right things around it, the wheel has proved to be an unparalleled game-changer for society. With a cursory inspection I've counted over twenty in my kitchen, and nothing in my kitchen really moves anywhere other than round in circles. Wheels are a significant invention – no one would deny that.

Forget drones, IoT, 3D printing, the cloud, 5G, RFID tags, VR, fog computing, or whatever else is riding the Gartner hype-curve this month. Like double-entry bookkeeping, limited liability companies, the internal combustion engine, or even the wheel, I truly believe blockchain is eventually going to bring along huge changes that will impact all of our lives in all sorts of unpredictable ways.

In this book, I am going to explain to you why I hold this belief, and a lot more. Some of it may even make sense.

Keir Finlow-Bates, Finland 2020

Introduction

> Right here we go now
> A sociology lecture
> With a bit of psychology
> A bit of neurology
> A bit of fuckology
> John Lydon, 1977[b]

You may be asking yourself, what on Earth could punk rock and blockchain have in common? One involves sneering band members swaggering around on stage spouting profanity and spitting at the audience, and the other involves esoteric cryptographic concepts, computer code, and nerds. I'm pulling your leg, right?

So I'll get straight to the point: both arose due to severe economic pressures, a desire to "do it yourself", and to regain *control* and *ownership* over something that was being exploited, mismanaged, and appropriated by middlemen more interested in turning a profit than providing a service to those supplying and/or consuming a product. And what's more, the desire to do it yourself coincided with the means of production becoming available to anyone who was interested.

Punk provided any musician, songwriter, or vocalist with an opportunity to control the means of production and distribution of their *product* – the music. Whereas blockchain provides the opportunity for anyone with access to a computer and a bit of financial and technical knowledge to control the means of *transaction* – the holding or trading of value. As such, both "movements" share remarkable parallels in terms of their origins, triggering events, and even in the profiles of some of the characters involved in each social space.

Punk was ultimately re-appropriated by the music industry; as to whether blockchain will be fully co-opted by the software, tech, finance, and banking industries, or even our slow-moving governments, with the independent open blockchains supporting cryptocurrencies closing down over time … well, that remains to be seen.

At least, that's my argument. And even if I'm wrong, it makes for a much more entertaining book than yet another dry treatise starting with a sentence like: "Blockchain comprises a time-stamped hash-linked list distributed over a peer-to-peer network with a consensus algorithm for incentivizing data consistency and utilizing asymmetric key cryptography for identity and access management". Try putting a soundtrack to that.

So here's the problem: articles, books and tutorials generally fall into one of two camps. Either they discuss the *how* of blockchain in excruciating detail, but barely touch on the *why* part. Or they cover the *why* part, but completely skip the underlying details as to how it all functions (and as a result, they usually contain plenty of misconceptions and unrealistic predictions). Really, we should be focusing on both the *why* and the *how*, with some *what* but as little *how* as possible – this is because the *how* is not only the hardest part to grasp, but it also distracts those of us with a penchant for the technical from the real-life applications of blockchain. For most people the question is, "given its properties, why would you use blockchain?" rather than how it actually works under the hood. You don't need to know how an internal combustion engine works in order to drive a car. But it helps to know a bit more than just how the steering wheel, gas pedal, and break need to be operated in order to drive – for example, when your car breaks down or won't start in the morning.

But no matter how cool the algorithms may seem, how clever and beautiful the combination of computer software and mathematical constructs are, and how amazing the emergent technical properties of the system turn out to be, all those things really don't matter, unless you're mainly in it for the elegance of the technology (which is fine – after all, that's what got me hooked on blockchain).

Exploring stuff for the simple crystalline magnificence of it all is for academics. People like G. H. Hardy, a mathematician researching number theory in Cambridge University back at the start of the 20th century, can say stuff like:

> *I have never done anything "useful". No discovery of mine has made, or is likely to make, directly or indirectly, for good or ill, the least difference to the amenity of the world.*
>
> *— G. H. Hardy*[2]

Similarly, mathematical geniuses such as Paul Erdős get (or rather, got) to amble around the world, living out of a suitcase and popping amphetamines like candy while ignoring the practicalities of how to open a carton of orange juice in favor of conducting mathematical research, or more accurately, engaging in glorious mathematical play[3].

(Incidentally, my Erdős number is 6. That's surprisingly high, and there will be more on what an Erdős number means in a later chapter on "network effects" to illustrate the power of networks, social or otherwise.)

But back to the main thrust of this chapter: the rest of us actually want or need stuff that does stuff. And ironically, Hardy's and Erdős's work provides much of the mathematical foundation required to enable public key cryptography, one of the developments on which blockchain is built. That's not to say that some of the underlying theory is not worth examining, but don't worry – this book will not be overwhelming you with equations and code.

Instead, my aim is to explain how things function mainly through analogies (a fancy way of saying "entertaining yet illuminating stories"), and only to examine the actual mathematics and computer science when a deeper understanding of the mathematical and cryptographic engines driving blockchain furthers an understanding of why blockchain does what it does, and why it matters.

There will be moments were we do have to get our hands dirty, and actually grapple with technical and mathematical concepts. But don't be afraid – these things are not as difficult as your school experiences may have conditioned you to believe they are. At worst, you may have to go back and re-read a few of the paragraphs. I promise to make it as simple and grounded as possible.

So, let's roll up our sleeves and get started.

Doing it yourself

In this section, we begin by time-traveling through the magic of fonts. Anything in this font concerns the 1970s and punk, and anything in this font concerns 2008 onward, and blockchain. So now I am going to fire up that typographical time machine.

Origins of the crises

In the mid 1970s punk rock started gaining more and more influence over the music scene in the United Kingdom, traveling over from the United States, and New York in particular. Although it had been simmering underground for at least a decade before, larger and larger groups of young adults finally started to turn away from over-produced navel-gazing progressive rock and pop. Music created, managed, and run for fat profits by the industry, with the middlemen consisting of record labels, producers, studios, and advertising agencies, all familiar with taking large cuts for their services. Instead, the youth turned towards a movement that seemed authentic and genuine, and within the reach of anyone with a guitar and something (or even nothing) to say.

The United Kingdom was in the throes of social unrest due to an economic crisis. Stagflation struck: inflation rates of 20% combined with a reduction in productivity in the economy, topped off by the 1973 oil crisis in which petrol prices rose by 400%[4], led to worsening conditions for almost everyone, especially for the working classes. That brought on strikes, anger, and hardship. Youth unemployment was on the rise[5], and understandably many young people saw no real future on the horizon for themselves.

Fast forward to the global financial crisis of 2007-2008. This time the culprit was not an oil embargo threatening the prosperity of the energy-hungry First World states. Instead, the economic collapse was due to a systemic failure in the financial systems[6]. Banks, ever eager to find new ways to sell "financial products" invented new *securities* backed by packages of mortgages – the loans ordinary people use to be able to buy their own home. Sounds harmless, right?

Securities, simply put, are monetary contracts with something "backing them" that is supposed to give them underlying value. The problem was that these new securities sliced, diced, and repackaged large numbers of mortgages in such a way that it wasn't possible for anyone to determine how risky they were. Some of the mortgages were owed by financially solvent, reliable people. Many were, unfortunately, "subprime mortgages" - loans marketed to buyers clearly unable to afford them in the long term and that should therefore never have been issued, with the borrowers relying on ever-increasing house prices and a steady economy in order to be able to continue servicing the loan.

But the financial world wasn't worried, because a new product – the "credit default swap" – allowed them to purchase insurance against these securities going bad. Except a) the financial institutions offering this insurance weren't able to pay out (and some of them were the very institutions issuing the sub-prime mortgages, which is exactly like being your own insurer) and b) no one knew that there was a problem brewing, because the ratings agencies that ranked how reliable and financially secure the various banks were, had been producing their credit reports for money, money which came from the very organizations issuing the risky loans in the first place.

In summary, everyone involved had been lying to everyone else, including themselves.

As a result, the world's fourth-biggest investment bank, Lehman Brothers, went bankrupt after 158 years of existence, the other banks got scared, and the global financial system ground – well, not to a halt, but to a crawl. And as it turns out, the banks are the lubricant in the engine that keeps the global financial system running.

Governments of the world responded by throwing cash at the banks in order to save them under the "too big to fail" doctrine, whilst instituting austerity programs on ordinary citizens to cover some of the costs.

Understandably, this made a lot of people *unhappy* and *angry*. As the punk poet Alexei Sayle put it, "Austerity is the idea that the world-wide financial crash of 2008 was caused by Wolverhampton having too many libraries".[7]

The financial crisis of 2008 also drove a lot of people to look at how money is created, who controls its creation, and what they do with it.

And one person actually launched some software to try to do something about it, and I'll talk about that person later.

Surprisingly, it turns out that the mechanics of ensuring fast reliable transfers of money or value are easier to replicate than three and a half minute pop songs.

That's entertainment

With a lack of resources and an apparently bleak future, it is not surprising that youth culture in 70s UK turned to a do-it-yourself approach in generating their own scene. The hippies of the sixties, and the beat generation of the decade before them, laid the groundwork for changes in fashion with a devil-may-care attitude, or at least some tie-dye t-shirts and other cheap clothing. Other youth sub-cults like the Teddy Boys from the fifties and the Mods of the sixties chose expensive tailored suits as their uniforms, but as a punk, simply buying a Pink Floyd t-shirt and scrawling "I hate" in marker pen on it, or ripping the sleeves off an old denim jacket was enough to make a fashion statement, and remarkably cheap to boot.

However, punk did not spring up overnight like mushrooms in a forest after an autumnal rainfall. A number of different factors aligned themselves at just the right time for it to happen. I mentioned some of the societal factors above, but there were also technical changes that impacted the whole scene:

1. The rise of cheap copy shops or printing shops meant that punk fanzines (fan magazines) with irreverent names such as *Sideburns* and *Sniffin' Glue,* could be self-published affordably and easily, and in quantity, in comparison to the limitations of spirit duplicators or expensive publishing houses[8].

    The fanzines were often handed out for free at pubs and clubs, helping to push awareness of the music and advertising new releases.

    In other words: punk had access to a means of promotion.

2. Advances in recording technologies in the early 70s meant that recording studios were upgrading their equipment, and this flooded the market with high-quality second-hand multi-track recorders.

    As a result, bands like the Buzzcocks were able to self-record and self-produce their own album.

    Furthermore, record pressing plants now accepted small-batch orders, which not only reduced risks but lowered the initial entry cost. This allowed something close to "on-demand" fulfillment.

3. Clubs and pubs allowed amateurs to come in and play their new music to the emerging scene, just like the New York jazz clubs of the 1920s and 1930s. Punk had a place to "happen".

In summary, with a relatively small cash outlay, punk artists could control the means of production[9], and advertise what they had written and recorded.

Meanwhile, forty years on, the pieces were slotting into place to allow the emergence of possibly the greatest financial revolution since the popularization of double-entry bookkeeping back in 1494 by Luca Pacioli[10]. And those pieces were:

1. The most significant development, undoubtedly: the Internet and the World Wide Web. Information that was previously only available in university libraries could be obtained with a few simple clicks.

    Furthermore, the Internet enabled cheap and easy advertising of what you were doing.

    Finally, the Internet allowed like-minded people all over the globe to connect, discuss, and develop together. A network of bits and bytes enabled a network of human brains.

2. Add to that: the emergence of open-source software, allowing anyone to obtain and deploy well-tested sophisticated cryptography libraries written by experts.

    No one should ever roll their own cryptography code without years of experience and third-party scrutiny. However, software libraries such as OpenSSL allow even a lowly system administrator to write scripts that do very clever super-secure things.

3. To top it off: the rise of "do it yourself" publishing through blogs, online articles, and knowledge sharing, thereby providing walk-through tutorials on how to ... well ... do stuff. And of course, it wasn't just text that could be published. Source code and software could be distributed equally easily over the network.

Suddenly you didn't have to be the world's most remarkable computing polymath working in an elite group of coders in a research department of a large corporation to be able to put together some really interesting computer software and get other people to take note.

As a side note, it is interesting to see that Github and Stack Overflow were both launched in 2008, the same year that Satoshi Nakamoto published the seminal blockchain paper "Bitcoin: A Peer-to-Peer Electronic Cash System" that started it all[11]. In the next chapter I will be looking at the above points in more detail, both from a historical and technical point of view: examining both "how" and "why" Nakamoto went about creating Bitcoin, and inadvertently launched what is now the blockchain industry.

Summing up

During the financial troubles of the seventies, some people expressed their dissatisfaction by making a new kind of music – punk. And at the end of the first decade of the new millennium, a person or some people expressed their dissatisfaction by kicking off a new kind of money – cryptocurrency.

As it turns out, both the music industry and the finance industry are not really as complicated as the insiders pretend they are. We now have evidence that there are enough talented and dedicated people out there outside the system, who can step in, and possibly shake things up.

Of course, only time will show us how successful they will be.

Three Chords

> Artistic freedom, do what you want
> But just make sure that the money ain't gone
> *Paul Weller, 1978[c]*

After you realize that recording a record or writing a new form of cryptocurrency doesn't require a large operation with a crowd of highly skilled technicians and lots of corporate or venture capital funding, it's easy to flip the other way and think that anyone can do it.

Unfortunately, you'd be wrong.

Playing in the band

The iconic punk manifesto (the "Three Chords" diagram, reproduced below) formed a rallying call to hundreds or possibly thousands of young hopefuls, encouraging them to pick up a guitar and start strumming.

Although plenty of trash was produced by most of them, long since resigned to the dustbin of forgotten music, you only have to listen to what still lives on in order to realize that the best classic punk music is not trivial: the drummer John Maher's rhythmic illusion in the beat of *Orgasm Addict* by the Buzzcocks, or Steve Jones's middle eight riff on *Anarchy in the UK* by the Sex Pistols, for example.

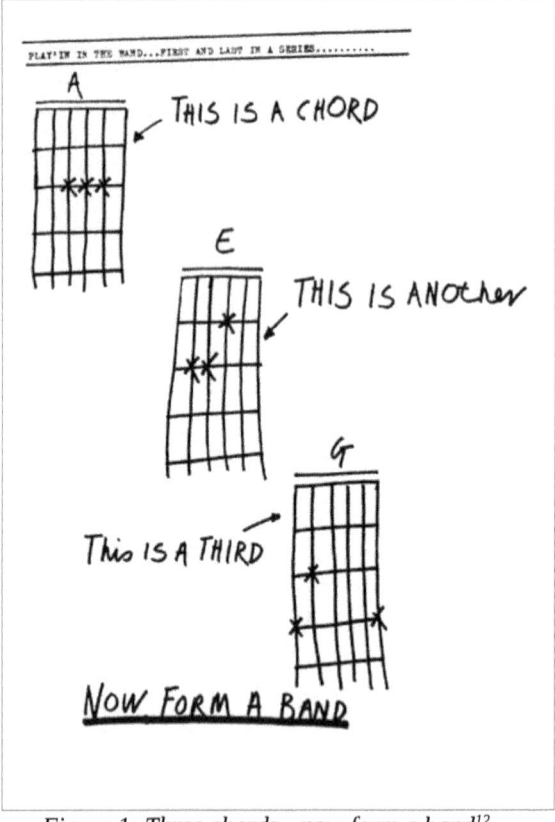

Figure 1: Three chords - now form a band[12]

I was the bass player in a punk covers band called the Punkstains, back in the early 2000s, and I promise you: this stuff is not trivial to play.

What punk did reveal is that among the flotsam and jetsam of society there are many more skilled lyricists, drummers, guitarists, bassists, and singers than you would at first think. The head of the demand curve promoted by the mainstream music industry creates an illusion that creativity and capability are in scarce supply. That's not actually the case.

The long tail theory[13] was conclusively demonstrated to be true by punk music, namely that access to instruments, advertising, recording studios, and record production was all that was required, and that there was actually no shortage of talent out there. The same applies to computer software.

Hang on – that sounds like a contradiction. Let me back up, and summarize it differently: there are lots of remarkable and capable people out there; many more than you would think by looking at the traditional institutions that promote talent. The bad news is: the odds are that you and I are not among them. (That doesn't mean that we can't contribute though. Every little bit helps.)

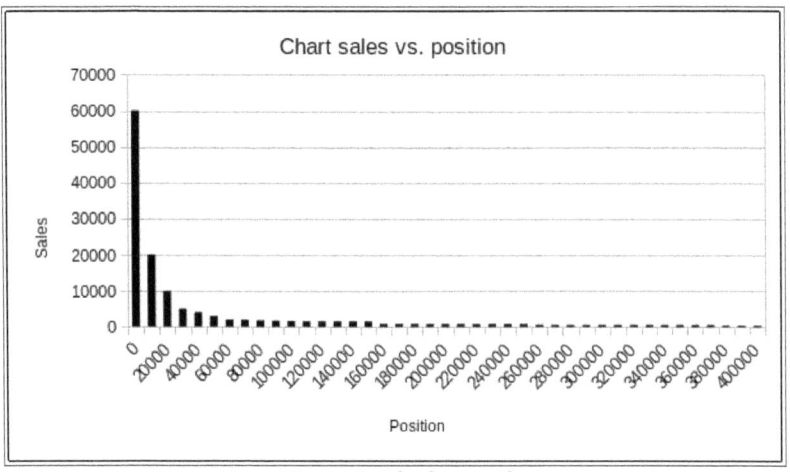

Figure 2: The long tail

Back to the story though: when plotting the *number of sales* against each music track's *chart position* on a graph, the area under the product tail past the top one hundred hits turns out to be just as great (if not greater) than the area under the first one hundred. These areas equate to profits, and what's more, those profits are distributed in a more egalitarian manner between all those artists in the second half.

Once the record labels, managers, and promoters have all taken their cut, of course.

Coding up a blockchain

The figure below is a tongue-in-cheek summary of the components you need for a blockchain:

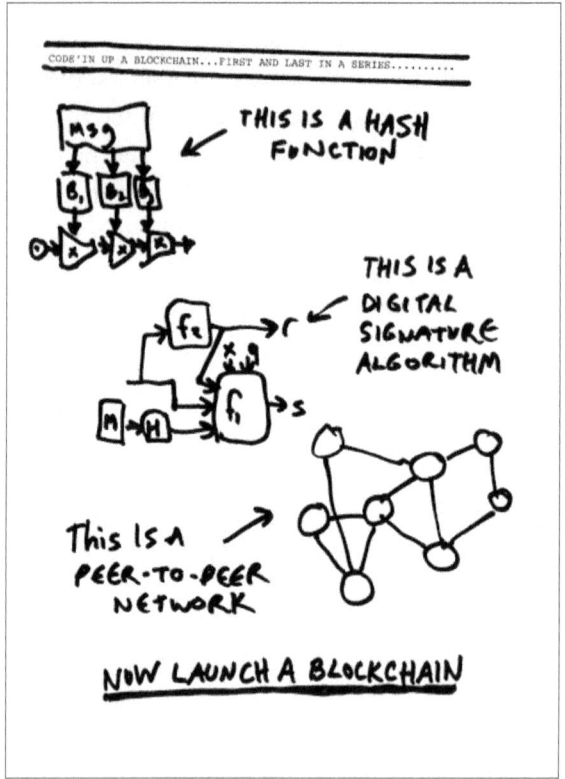

Figure 3: Three computer concepts: Now launch a blockchain

Actually, I've missed out one final important part, namely the consensus system, so I'll put an example of one here:

```
if sha256(sha256(block_header)) < target_difficulty:
    submit(block) # print("work proven") if you want to gloat
```

Those two lines of code are the basis of the "proof-of-work" system for Bitcoin, and indeed most other proof-of-work systems. See, for example, Jakobsson's paper, in which the term was first coined[14]. We'll be digging into that in more detail later.

I'm now going to attempt to explain the architecture of what are called open permissionless blockchains with a restaurant analogy. Working up the diagram we have:

A peer-to-peer network: this is a bunch of computers on the Internet communicating directly between each other, and in which each computer acts both as a server (a computer "serving up" stuff) and as a client (a computer "receiving stuff"). If we use the analogy of a computer server being a waiter, and a computer client being a diner, then a peer-to-peer network is like an Uberified restaurant that anyone can visit, and in which anyone can be a waiter, or a diner, or both, as they see fit.

In a peer-to-peer network, the participating machines are peers – literally, in that no one computer is more special or more powerful in its capabilities on the network than the others (of course some machines may have more RAM, CPU power, disk space, or network bandwidth, but that's by-the-by), and they act both as waiters and diners.

A digital signature algorithm: this is what participants on the blockchain use to prove they are who they are, and that they are allowed to do what they are asking to do. So, for example, if a quantity of bitcoin cryptocurrency is associated with a Bitcoin address, only the person with the private key for that address can sign a transaction that transfers it somewhere else. This is like the diner handing over their credit card, and then signing the bill. Except that the diner got to create that card in the first place.

A hash function: technically this should actually be labeled as a "cryptographic hash function", and it is one of those computer science concepts that it is not trivial to get your head around, but you do have to understand it in order to really grasp what is going on a lot of the time in blockchain. Therefore there is a whole chapter on hash functions later on, and they keep cropping up throughout the story. Unfortunately, I can't come up with a restaurant analogy for hash functions. Fortunately that later chapter I mentioned will provide a better one. Hang in there for now.

So, there you go – three things (or four things if you're dealing with a public open system) that you need to build a blockchain.

How hard can it be? Let's find out...

Weltanschauung!

> So if our schools won't teach us,
> We'll teach ourselves to analyze and understand
> *Chris Hannah, 1996[d]*

It takes time for society to understand how to apply the most significant inventions that are dreamed up. The reason for this is probably because, in a fundamental sense, they change not just the way we do things but also the way we see and understand them. And this is not just a recent thing – it has been going on for a long, long time.

For example, a couple of millennia ago, Hero of Alexandria described (and possibly invented) the wonderfully named *aeolipile*, a primitive steam engine[15]. At the time it was seen as a curiosity or a toy, and it was only far, far later, in 1712, that the first commercially-viable steam engine was invented (or rather improved upon) by Thomas Newcomen, and was then put into use at the start of the industrial revolution in the United Kingdom[16]. Even though further improvements were made, there were still engines based on Newcomen's design running up until 1900, so it is his device that really marks the start of the steam-power era.

But why did it take so long for steam power to take hold? Even after production-worthy cost-cutting steam engines were draining the mines in Cornwall, England, it still took another 64 years for James Watt to produce the first truly efficient, versatile steam engine, and even so, by 1800 there were 1500 Newcomen engines and only 450 Watt engines in operation.

A combination of factors apply including the main point that, initially, the demand for mined ores was just about being met by horses and people, combined with the indisputable fact that people don't like change. At least, that's what is often claimed.

Personally, I think above all it's the fact that a vision of what an industrial society could look like did not yet exist. A hundred years later the first steam trains were operating, able to run on tracks made from iron that could be plentifully mined through the assistance of those very same pumps, and smelted by the coal also being retrieved with – yes, you guessed it – those steam pumps. For most people, looking at those inefficient bulky infernal engines churning away in Cornwall, ideas of steam powered trains were not just ludicrous, they were inconceivable. Horses worked perfectly well for travel and work.

And so, it's not possible to point to one single inventor of the steam engine. Hero, Thomas Savory, Thomas Newcomen, James Watt – all have a partial claim to the title, as do many others. The bigger picture is that everyone else around started to understand what the point of these engines was, and as a result, they took off. To us, it now seems intuitively obvious, but back then a mine operator or factory owner was probably just as happy, if not happier, with human labor and possibly water-wheel power. The infrastructure wasn't there, the transportation network wasn't there, and above all, the vision wasn't generally accepted.

The same applies to the printing press. After it was invented by Johannes Gutenberg in 1440, two hundred or so were manufactured and sold to the aristocracy over the next decades. But when the novelty wore off, most were shut down. Aristocrats didn't need multiple copies of books – they could pay scribes and monks to make them their own bespoke volumes. The printing press had no market, and no real purpose, which seems absurd to us now. But the device simply did not fit the world view of the time. Ordinary people didn't buy books. They worked in the fields, and many of them couldn't read. The rich, who did buy books, could afford to have them made on-demand.

By the time Martin Luther found a genuine societal use for the printing press, namely the publication of significant quantities of "seditious" pamphlets, it was 1517, over three-quarters of a century later[17].

Truly great inventions have wide applicability and open up all sorts of new possibilities beyond their initial purpose, but it takes a while for their moment to arrive. A small number of people will have a feeling that those possibilities are there, but most don't. That's why it takes so long for inventions to have an impact.

Blockchain has a surprising number of emergent properties and depending on the property that is focused on, the relevance to a particular use case shifts. It would be a lot simpler for the industry if blockchain had one clear simple use case (but a lot less interesting).

Some of the categories, or "camps" have been identified by Caruso[18], in order to examine these various emergent properties and how they inform particular blockchain use cases. It is worth looking at them in more detail because perhaps they can help us place this peculiar beast into a particular world view and, for once, actually accelerate the process of adoption.

Disintermediated digital assets

The initial purpose of the first blockchain (Bitcoin, of course) was to solve the double-spend problem in a disintermediated data store by creating digital assets with clear ownership, that can be transferred or transacted without requiring an intermediary. That's worth reiterating in a simpler form - it's all about digital entities that:

- cannot be duplicated
- have clear ownership, and
- can be transferred *directly* from one party to another

This is more revolutionary than it first seems, probably because we are used to physical objects having these properties, and it is more the fact that digital objects *don't* have these properties that is counter-intuitive.

This results in Bitcoin behaving like gold that can be emailed, or blockchain providing shares in a company that can be issued and traded without requiring brokers or stock exchanges.

And when a business development manager grasps this, they immediately start thinking about loyalty point schemes or transferable computer game objects, which is about as trivial as you can get. But more on that later.

Triple-entry ledgers

Double-entry bookkeeping is a recurring accounting method that reduces errors and fraud, and its final wide adoption was one of the developments that is now credited with being a driving force behind the Italian Renaissance back in the fifteenth and sixteenth centuries.

The problem with modern accounting is that it is costly - as anyone who runs a company in Finland will know, your accounting costs and auditing can easily eat up 5% or more of your revenues. And yet fraud still happens.

Many blockchains use the concept of transaction inputs and outputs rather than a straight-up balance tallied against an owner. In fact, some of you may be surprised to hear that there is actually no such thing as a "bitcoin". Rather there is a chain of transactions from owner to owner, starting with the creation of the asset due to mining (this is called the *coinbase input*), through to the current holder, with each input to an owner having a corresponding output from the previous owner. Bitcoins are a chain of credit and debit records, except that the ledger is across all participants in the Bitcoin economy, and not just for one specific company or organization.

Carried over into accountancy, the blockchain model allows the books for one company to be cross-referenced with the books of all the other parties the company has transacted with. Ian Grigg[19] described this with the (in hindsight obvious and yet highly insightful) name of "triple-entry accounting". Whereas double-entry accounting labels mismatches in the books as "either error or fraud", triple-entry accounting actually enables the clear determination of which of the two possibilities is the truth.

Take a moment to think about that (actually, you don't have to, because I'm going to drone on about it for the next few paragraphs).

Innovation in accountancy comes along about once every five hundred years. And blockchain should be able to provide an improved system that can immediately establish whether there has been a mistake or someone has been fiddling the books. That is if technologists and accountants can eventually communicate properly with each other (in both directions) and enable it to be adopted as a standard in accountancy. Then again, although double-entry bookkeeping is now considered an essential part of accountancy, it did not get adopted globally overnight. These things take time.

In summary, distributed ledger technology will enable us to:

- link transactions across the books of different companies,
- enhance transparency in the financial world, and
- reduce errors and fraud

Blockchain may well be the new accounting ledger technology that pushes this development forward, and although it is possibly the greatest financial invention since double-entry bookkeeping (which took hold half a millennium ago) you should not be too optimistic. If a field of human activity that has had an immense impact on our lives only sees such major advancements every five hundred years and takes decades to be adopted then it's not worth holding your breath.

But, if you happen to be alive when one of those innovations pops up, surely it's worth sitting up and paying attention, especially if you are a qualified accountant? After all, five hundred years is at least sixteen generations of people. Do you really want to be the accountant who just missed out on that?

But the flow of transactions and the recording of those transactions is not just limited to finance.

Consortium enablement

Consortia involve groups of companies, not necessarily fully aligned and sometimes even in competition, getting together to create something of greater value for all. An example is the supply chain - which at it's most basic involves goods (i.e. stuff) flowing in one direction, and money flowing in the opposite direction. In its more complicated form, raw materials may be processed into products or processed along the way, but ultimately there is supposed to be an end consumer. As a result, the various parties have to trust that each participant will play their part, deliver on time, and not replace supplies with inferior materials or simply abscond with the money.

Manifests, waybills or bills of goods, purchase orders, invoices: the list of paperwork involved goes on and on in order to ensure the smooth running of the supply chain. If something goes wrong it can take weeks, months, or years of forensic effort to determine the actual cause of the breakdown in a supply chain, followed by further months or even years of litigation to get compensation. That is, if the compensation arrives at all.

Thinking back to the section on triple-entry accountancy: what if all the supply chain activities and transactions were recorded on a blockchain? Wouldn't that be the equivalent of multiple-entry bookkeeping, with added details such as location, quantity and quality, temperature, damage and goods mistreatment, warranties and insurance, and payment all folded into one? It is the logistics manager's dream!

To draw out the essential parts: with blockchain there is the hope that we can:

- track transactions down the chain, and payment up the chain
- trigger the automatic release of payment on completion
- tag transactions with metadata covering transportation and production events
- enable automated audits using the tamperproof nature of the records

Supply chain is one specific example, but all the above equally applies to e-commerce sites (which currently rely on centralized commerce hubs like Amazon, eBay or Alibaba).

The key here is linking data to real objects, which deserves a book all to itself. However, what about considering just the data, which many people are describing as "the new oil"[20]?

Data ownership

The next step for the Internet is thought by some to be about raising it up from just moving data around and providing tools for filtering and accessing that data across the network (with associated credit card payments), into a totally new sphere of activity.

It may become possible to tie "value", represented by digital assets, to the data flowing around the internet. And decentralization could move that value from the large Silicon Valley data aggregators back to the actual original generators and supposed owners of said data. Data is being created at a phenomenal rate, and new data mining techniques mean that all sorts of previously unthought-of interpretations, analytics, and correlations can be extracted from it.

And so blockchain has a part to play on the Internet of Value as well, due to its potential for identity and access management (IAM):

- securely identified parties of data ownership
- automated micro-payments (for example with sidechains)
- granting and revoking of permissions through public key infrastructures

In this concept, blockchain acts as an underlying protocol layer to handle identity, access, and ownership requests, in the same manner that the HTTPS protocol for the web handles the identification, submission and retrieval of data. See, for example, Henry He[21].

This is going to be particularly significant when everyone has a large collection of internet devices, from phones to fridges to cars, all generating information at phenomenal rates. Public sentiment is slowly moving more and more towards individual control and ownership, and every data breach or misuse of personal information by the large players is another nail in the coffin of centralized management.

We may be unable to avoid a data-permeated future where every last detail about our lives is recorded online for the analysis of specific gatekeeper companies, but it just might be possible to put in place an integrated system where governments and large corporations are computationally unable to access and use (or misuse) that data without permission.

Blockchain could even allow such systems to arise organically, rather than through central planning and control.

The frictionless marketplace

Whether you are talking about digital gold or cash, goods on a supply chain or in an e-commerce network, or data from a user-base or IoT devices, the bottom line is the same:

Blockchain may enable a digital marketplace with less transaction friction, fewer middlemen and rent-seekers, less centralized unaccountable authoritarian domination, less censorship, more cohesion and interoperability, and ultimately more individual control.

Well anyway, that's the dream for us ordinary folks. As is always the case with dreams and visions, there have been a lot of occurrences of words such as "maybe", "perhaps", and "possibly" turning up, so in the next chapter, I will try to be more definite about my statements.

Blockchain City

> The bloody train is bloody late
> You bloody wait you bloody wait
> John Cooper Clarke, 1980[e]

Imagine there's a place called Transaction Town. The people living there need to travel to Blockchain City in order to record their financial transactions permanently. Yes, it's a pain in the neck, but fortunately, the town has a lovely bus stop, and a bus comes every ten minutes to take them to the city. And transactions are important, so everyone puts up with the extra effort to ensure that they don't lose all their money.

Unfortunately, as is often the case with buses, although they are usually on time – the schedule is one bus every ten minutes – sometimes you can stand at the bus stop for twenty or thirty minutes. If you're really unlucky it might even take an hour or more for a bus to come by. Other times, three come along almost all at once!

The interesting thing about these buses is that you buy your ticket at the bus stop, and you pay as much or as little as you like. Of course, each bus has a fixed capacity – it can only take so many people on board. If there are not many other people waiting, then paying very little for your ticket is a smart move. But if there are a lot of people in the queue, well, the bus drivers are paid according to the cost of all the tickets they accept. So when a bus finally arrives, the driver usually selects the passengers who paid the most. That means that if you decided to be a cheapskate during busy times, you have to wait for the next one, and the next one, and possibly even the one after that.

The good news is that you can ditch your ticket, get a refund, and buy a more expensive one if you decide that you actually really need to get to Blockchain City quickly, and you made a mistake by trying to cut costs. But once you've bought a ticket and are standing at the bus stop, you have to go to Blockchain City. You can't change your mind when it comes to that decision.

And that's an analogy as to how Bitcoin and other proof-of-work blockchains partially function. It doesn't cover the actual proof-of-work part (which I'll address later), but it does provide some insight into a lot of other supposedly tricky parts of blockchain.

Unpacking the analogy

I am now going to talk about how some of the underlying components that make blockchain function. As I pointed out, you can drive a car without knowing anything about internal combustion engines or electric motors. However, if you want to hang out with the enthusiast crowd and have a modicum of authority, you have to know something about the tech. Even if you're a business development manager.

The good news is that in this chapter I use the above analogy of Blockchain Town to discuss blockchain features and functionality in a manner that doesn't rely on mathematics or computer science, or anything technical at all. There is a lot of power in *analogies*, namely using familiar concepts in everyday life to illustrate what is going on and to grasp the underlying concepts. Provided the analogy is a good one.

So all you have to do is learn what technical term corresponds to the familiar concept, swap out the words, and before you know it you'll be talking just like a blockchain software engineer. Or at least you will be able to talk to one.

A Comparison Table

In the table below, the left column presents a Transaction Town term, and the right one shows the corresponding blockchain term.

Transaction Town	Blockchain
Bus	Block
Passenger	Transaction
Ticket price	Transaction fee
Bus driver	Miner
Driver's wages	Block reward
Bus stop queue	Mempool
Blockchain City	Hash linked list

Figure 4: Transaction Town comparison table

Blocks, transactions and fees

So why is a bus transporting fee-paying passengers like a blockchain block?

- Both a block and a bus are discrete entities with a clear start and finish,
- They both have a fixed capacity, so you can't fit more passengers (or transactions) on board than the imposed limit,
- They both come along at fairly regular intervals but aren't totally predictable – in mathematics they both match something called a Poisson Process (well, in the bus case

only if you're waiting at a stop near the middle of the bus route)[22],

- There's a bit at the front that, although not forming part of the passengers or transactions, is required as a kind of "engine" to make the whole thing work,

- You have to pay a fee to be admitted onto the bus (or have your transaction accepted), unless the driver (or miner) takes pity on you,

- The driver is paid for providing the service.

Join the queue

I mentioned that there is this concept called "the mempool" in blockchain, which I compared to a bus stop in Transaction Town. When you submit a transaction to a blockchain, you are actually only submitting it to one or two nodes. A node is a computer that is running the core blockchain software and is connected to other nodes also running the same software, to form what is known as a peer-to-peer network. The Blockchain City analogy doesn't cover this aspect.

When the transaction arrives at a node, it is checked to see that is valid (that's like examining someone's bus ticket to make sure it's not a forgery), and that it hasn't been seen before (that's like verifying that the ticket hasn't been used once already).

If the transaction passes all the checks, then the node forwards it on to further nodes, who perform the same checks, and continue forwarding on, until the transaction is present on pretty much every node.

So each node has its own mempool, or store of unprocessed valid transactions, and the contents of those mempools, although not identical, are almost the same. The whole system is extremely dynamic, as new transactions are arriving all the time and percolating their way through the system.

And then at some point, a new block is mined. Remember, this is like a bus finally arriving at the Transaction Town bus stop to take away some of the waiting passengers.

In a real blockchain system each node, on detecting a new block, forwards it on to the other nodes that it is connected to, just like the unprocessed transactions were. And furthermore, the node deletes any transactions in its mempool that are detected in that new block.

Who can get on the bus?

In the blockchain world, you will see a lot of people talking about private versus public blockchains, and permissioned versus unpermissioned or permissionless blockchains. And there are a lot of strong opinions about these terms, to the point that some people will argue vehemently that particular blockchains are not really blockchains at all. (And to be fair, they may have a point.)

So what do these terms actually mean? Well, the first blockchain, namely Bitcoin, is both a public and a permissionless blockchain. Simply put, this means that anyone can find and download the software required to create a Bitcoin address, mine blocks and obtain block rewards if they are lucky, look at the code that makes the whole system run, write further software that builds upon or automates Bitcoin transactions, or even participate in the future development of the whole system (provided you can convince the current development gang that you have something to contribute).

Bitcoin is about as open and indiscriminate as a computer system can be. So what about the other extreme types of blockchain? Time for another analogy.

Public and permissionless

In real life, a park is an example of something that is both *public* and *permissionless*. Anyone can go into a park – after all, they are public spaces. They are also permissionless: you don't have to have a membership card in order to have a go on the swings or slides or look at the ducks swimming in the lake.

There are probably rules about whether you can have a barbecue or play loud music, but if you stick to those rules, you're welcome to come and go as you please. Anyone can use a park as it was intended, without having to fill in any forms or be vetted or assessed in any way.

Public but permissioned

A public library is a good example of a public yet permissioned institution. It's there on the street, visible to all, and anyone can walk in and have a look around. But what you can't do is actually use it without permission – you can't check out a book without a membership card. You have to request one of those and be approved for it through some formal process applied by an authority (usually the chief librarian). So, for example, if you're not a local resident you might be turned down.

A library is a public institution, but full access to its services has to be granted by an authority. That authority may be a government institution, or a private corporation, or some kind of co-operative, but the fact remains that there is a gatekeeper.

Private and permissioned

The first example I came up with for a private and permissioned blockchain was that of a secret society. You need to know the location of a nondescript door in an ordinary city street in order to locate the society, and when you knock on the door, you are only let in if you are a member and know the secret passphrase.

Some people pointed out to me that this analogy sounds quite creepy. So another example is a company intranet, access to which can only be gained if you are a) in the building or logged in over a

VPN, and b) a company systems administrator has set up an account for you, with a username and password.

That's a lot less exciting as a parallel than mysterious secret societies though, isn't it?

Private and permissionless

Initially, the idea of a private yet permissionless blockchain may sound a bit far fetched. Why would you have a system which is kept secret, but if discovered allows anyone to participate. However, I have found an analogy that gives us a handle on potential use cases.

Consider a secret rave, like the ones that used to take place in remote locations such as forests or farm fields back in the early nineties in the United Kingdom. These parties were private, in that the fact that there were large groups of people gathering in order to dance to bleepy beat-laden electronic music while consuming designer drugs was not advertised publicly. The organizers didn't want the police to find out about them and raid the event.

Instead, the notification for the parties was by word of mouth. However, if you managed to find out about one, and subsequently turned up with a six-pack and a smile on your face, you were more than welcome to join in.

So a private yet permissionless blockchain is basically an open blockchain operating under the radar, and I would predict that any such system if it gains enough traction, will naturally evolve into a true public permissionless system.

Hybrid systems

In the above four sections, I have described four fundamental structures for blockchains, which have different applications in various areas of life. Public permissionless systems work well for cryptocurrencies, for example, whereas private permissioned blockchains are finding more traction in the corporate world. This is because companies don't want random teenage hackers around the world signing up to their blockchains and clogging them up with all sorts of mischievous activities.

However, a blockchain does not need to neatly fit into just one of those categories. You can have hybrid blockchain systems, where parts of the system are public and permissionless, and other parts are permissioned. To extend the library analogy – you can walk in and sit down at a reading desk to read a particular book that you have taken off the shelves (so that's a public permissionless activity), but if you're not a member you can't check out the book and take it home (because that is a public permissioned activity). And the library might have a hidden room somewhere out back storing valuable antique tomes and manuscripts that the general public is not aware of, and that can only be browsed and handled by a few specific individuals (a private permissioned activity).

When is a bus not a block?

There is one key aspect of blockchain missing from the analogy I presented. A bus is not hash-linked to the bus that came before it. Unfortunately, no analogy can be perfect, but don't worry, in a couple of chapters I'll explain what hash-linking is, and how something called a "hash-linked list" forms the very backbone or spine of a blockchain system. For added fun, we will also cover directed acyclic graphs (DAGs), and Merkle trees, neither of which are as intimidating as they may first sound.

But for now, let's take a break from the more technical side of things. Blockchains are sometimes described as "building trust" and at other times as being "trustless". So the next chapter will look at what "trust" is in the context of blockchain.

Buying Trust

> Antisocial, tu perds ton sang-froid
> Repense à toutes ces années de service
> Antisocial, bientôt les années de sévices
> Enfin, le temps perdu qu'on ne rattrape plus
> *Bernie Bonvoisin, 1980[g]*

As anyone who has worked on setting compensation plans for a sales force or a performance award scheme for employees knows, you get what you measure and what you reward. And if what you're measuring is not in alignment with progress or profitability for your company, then the company will suffer.

Furthermore, no matter how much effort you put into preventing the system from being gamed, there are going to be people out there who find unexpected ways of maximizing their return while minimizing their effort, often by performing pointless or even counter-productive tasks.

A central authority can mitigate this by stepping in and declaring "that's not what we wanted", but it comes at a cost – the most severe being disillusionment in the minds of those who are being managed. Let me give you an example from my school days.

Back in the mid-eighties, when I was about fifteen, the school made all the "fourth-formers" (or sophomores as they're called in the USA) sit a General Reasoning Test. The test contained sub-tests for verbal, mathematical and logical reasoning, spatial awareness, and so on. An outside expert was even brought in to administer and mark the whole thing, presumably at significant cost. Because there were about fifty of us sitting through this, the administrator made us review each other's tests and performed spot examinations to ensure we weren't cheating. The individual components of the tests were extremely difficult, in that it was hard to get even ten out of twenty-five points. But we all struggled along.

It was all going fine for me until the following was placed on my desk:

Figure 5: Creative thinking assessment test

The verbal instructions were simple: "Convert as many squiggles as you can into animals within one minute."

Here's a bigger copy, so you can have a go yourself (and if you want to do so, don't turn the page until you've finished, because my spoiler answers are on the next page):

CREATIVE THINKING ASSESSMENT TEST
SECTION 3B : 60 SECONDS

DRAWING: ___ / 25   LABELLING: ___ / 25

The administrator started the timer, and off we went. After the minute was up, the administrator asked the group, "So, how many did you manage to create?"

"Eight", "Three", "Seven" ... and so on, and then it was my turn. "All of them. Twenty-five."

The administrator raised one eyebrow. "Really? Let me see."

And so I showed him my efforts:

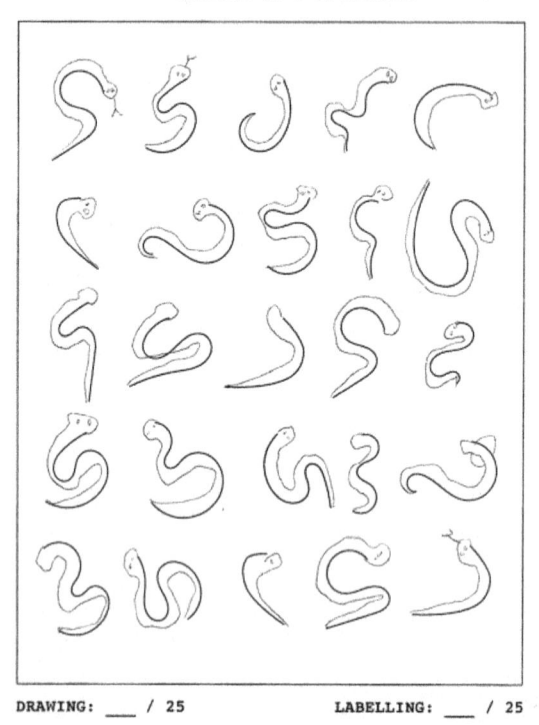

Figure 6: Creative results

You will notice that I was running out of time, so I stopped adding eyes and tongues half-way through.

"What on earth is this?" he asked.

"They are snakes," I replied.

"The animals were all meant to be different," he sniffed.

Apparently, although it wasn't included in the instructions, just drawing lots of creatures from the sub-order *serpentes* was not acceptable.

And so the test moved on to the second part, in which we were instructed, by the administrator (who was barely able to hide his glee), to label each *different* animal to identify it. Fortunately, I had been playing the recently released computer game *Elite*[23], in which the various spacecraft were named after ... you guessed it ... snakes. So here was my final result:

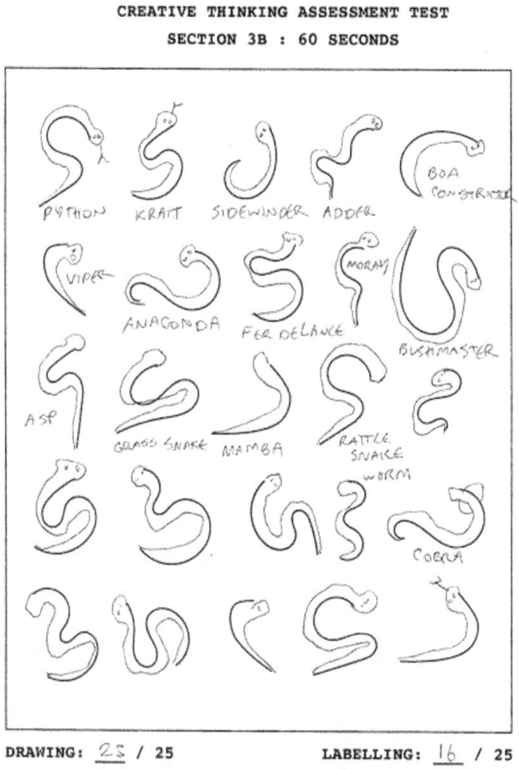

Figure 7: The labeling response

At this point, the administrator was furious, and I was marched off to the headmaster's office, where I was reprimanded for being a smart-aleck. The result was that my creative thinking score was not added to my total, and presumably, there was a black mark put against my name for causing trouble.

I can laugh about it now, but at the time it was terrible. My traumatic childhood aside, what can we learn from this episode?

> Lesson 1: Specifying rules is really very hard, especially when you have a particular outcome in mind. People will – either unintentionally or intentionally – subvert, re-interpret, redirect or otherwise radically alter any rules or restrictions you impose on them to maximize their personal gain.
>
> Lesson 2: A central authority can compensate for lesson 1, but often at the cost of breeding resentment, dissatisfaction, and disillusionment, which may ultimately bring down the system.

Now imagine trying to set up such a rule/incentive system in which anyone can join in, no one has omnipotence or oversight, and the whole shebang is meant to run along smoothly year after year without any problem for decades or even possibly centuries. Oh, and the system involves moving around large amounts of money.

What could go wrong?

The manufacture of consensus

Nakamoto decided to tackle the following accountancy problem:

How to ensure an <u>open public</u> ledger of balances is maintained in a reliable and trustworthy manner, with a "single view of the truth" as to those balances, while preserving some level of anonymity.

If you re-read that sentence, you'll realize that this core problem contains quite a few tricky sub-problems. Unpicking each in turn helps explain the end solution that Nakamoto came up with. For now, I'll summarize, but throughout this book, various fundamental aspects of blockchain are examined, because ultimately Nakamoto's achievement was to identify the problems hiding beneath the big problem and then finding existing solutions from the worlds of cryptography, computer science, mathematics, and networking, and finally combining them in such a way that the sum of the parts became substantially larger than the individual bits.

In other words, trying to explain blockchain is like trying to explain the magic of a band – you need a driving bass line, catchy drum beat, the poetry of the lyrics, the power of vocals, some good guitar riffs, and a dash of charisma in the lead singer, but it's the synthesis of all of the aforementioned that makes for a classic song with lasting impact.

You can't explain it by looking at the individual components in isolation, other than noting that the best bands and the best inventions have all of them in abundance.

Double spending

The double-spending problem is: how to prevent someone from using the same cash twice to buy two different things.

In the real world, double-spending is prevented automatically by the fact that physical objects only have a singular existence. Or in simple terms, the same five-pound note can't be in my wallet and your wallet at the same time.

In the digital world, historically, we have prevented double-spending by using a trusted central authority. When you spend five pounds using your credit card, both you and the coffee shop accepting your money rely on the fact that the payment processor will debit my account by five pounds, and increment the coffee shop's account by five pounds. We need the payment intermediary because the digital world doesn't observe the "conservation of mass" in the way that the real world does, and so it has to be artificially imposed*.

---

*   To be fair, quantum mechanics and special relativity show us that even the real world doesn't properly follow the law of conservation of

So how did Nakamoto solve the double-spending problem when there is no trusted central authority? By relying on the general honesty of crowds, or at least on their desire to not miss out by being dishonest.

If everyone participating in the Bitcoin distributed decentralized ledger can see what is going on, they can reject double-spending attempts, and furthermore, if there is a reward for adding transactions to the system then:

- Absolutely anyone with enough computing resources, a network connection, and a little bit of computing knowledge can have a shot at packaging transactions into the next blockchain blocks, and then:
- Everyone participating can check that the transactions in the blocks obey the rules of the blockchain system, and if they don't they can reject the block.

It is a bit like a chess league – if you want to play in the league, you have to obey the rules. If you get caught cheating, your game result won't be recorded, and you may even get barred from playing again. More on the intricacies of this can be found in the chapter "Knives, Forks, and Spoons" on page 217.

Sybil attacks

"Sybil" was the pseudonym given to a patient with multiple personality disorder (or dissociative identity disorder as it is now known), in which the patient exhibited sixteen different personalities[24]. In computing terminology it is now used to describe attacks on peer-to-peer networks in which the attacker creates many pseudonymous accounts or identities on the network in order to attempt to subvert the system. For example, by creating lots of

---

mass, but for all practical purposes in everyday life it holds, especially when you are out shopping. Unless you do your shopping extremely quickly, on very dense planets, or in remarkably small shops, which seems unlikely.

identities in a reputation system such as an online store or a social media site you can leave lots of likes and positive reviews for something that is actually worthless.

Sybil attacks can be overcome by ensuring that everyone has a clear, defined and verified single identity on the system – it is a well-known problem encountered in areas such as ensuring "one person one vote" in a democratic political system, or in banking through "know your customer" protocols. The downside of the traditional solutions provided by these is the loss of anonymity.

All your database are belong to us

In mathematics, there are theorems with grandiose titles like "the fundamental theorem of algebra" or "the fundamental theorem of arithmetic". Both express mathematical concepts that may initially seem incomprehensible, but with a bit of thought, anyone can understand them, at which point they seem blindingly obvious. For example, the fundamental theorem of arithmetic says that every number can only be represented in one single way as the product of a set of prime numbers. It is also known as the "unique factorization theorem" for this reason. So, for example, take the number 221, which is equal to 13 times 17 (check it on your calculator). Thirteen and seventeen are prime numbers. The fundamental theorem of arithmetic ensures that 221 cannot also be the product of some other prime numbers. There is one and only one way to factorize any given number – or in other words, while 6 × 8 (which equals 48) and 7 × 7 (which equals 49) are very close, they are not the same.

In the world of databases the "fundamental theorem of databases" is called the CAP theorem. It was proposed by Eric Brewer and subsequently proved by Seth Gilbert and Nancy Lynch[25]. The CAP theorem asserts that in any distributed data store – so that includes not just databases, but file systems, web servers, and blockchains – only two out of three guarantees can be provided regarding consistency, availability, and partition tolerance.

Hang on, regarding what, what, and what?

Well, imagine the distributed data store is a group of experts on a particular topic, and they regularly call each other on the phone to ensure that they all have the most up-to-date knowledge on the subject. In that case:

Consistency is two different people asking the same question to two different experts, and getting the same answer (eventually).

Availability is the situation where, if you ask a question, you will get an answer fairly quickly.

Partition tolerance means that if for some reason a sub-group of the experts go "off the grid" on a retreat or something, when they get back they quickly catch up with the remainder of the group. Similarly, if one of the experts turns to the dark side and starts lying about things, that expert is quickly expelled by the rest of the group.

In commercial systems on the Internet, partition tolerance can never be fully guaranteed. Trans-Atlantic cables can snap, routers can crash, and distributed denial of service attacks can isolate subnets from the main Internet. This limits the choice to either consistency or availability. As availability has the most significant impact on revenue, the system design of distributed data stores for businesses usually reduces to a choice between different eventual consistency recovery strategies.

Seen in this light, although blockchain is a strong eventual consistency recovery scheme with reconciliation through a consensus protocol, it is an inefficient and expensive method for achieving such consistency.

However, when a fourth overlooked guarantee is added to the CAP mix — namely the question of trust — blockchain comes into its own. So let's consider an extended version of the CAP theorem: CAPT, which asks, "to what level can you guarantee consistency, availability, partition tolerance, and *trust*?"

Not my CAP of T

Historically, distributed data stores have been owned and operated by a single entity such as a corporation, often acting as a middleman in transacting between different external parties. The question is then reduced to a binary choice — either you trust the entity and therefore submit transactions to and retrieve data from their system, or you do not trust them and select another service provider, "roll your own" solution, or abstain completely.

A result has been that the issue of trust does not figure in Brewer's CAP theorem. The theorem has been refined over the years to consider consistency and availability as lying on a continuous spectrum, but apart from this, it has remained largely unchanged. Partitions in traditional database network architecture are seen as very unusual events. In a blockchain, the occurrence of partitions, accidental or malicious, is significantly more likely. Blockchain attempts to handle a new emerging case in data storage systems whereby parties that are completely untrusted or only partially trusted are participating in the network on an equal footing.

So let us examine how blockchain resolves the fourth guarantee of trust and allows for an estimate of such trust on a spectrum, from completely untrusted or unknown and untraceable participants on the network, right up to a fully trusted network of participants. This will highlight the observation that ultimately the purpose of blockchain is enabling the sharing of data and transmittal of transactions or states between different stakeholders across low-trust or no-trust boundaries, and that this should inform the development of use cases for blockchain.

What is trust?

When you submit your personal data to a third party for storage, dissemination, and retrieval, or delegate your financial transactions to a bank or credit card provider, you are making a *trust decision*.

Yet hacks such as the Ashley-Madison and Equifax data leaks show that in many cases such trust is unfounded. Large databases containing private and personal information are hacked almost on a daily basis. Similarly, the emergence of Bitcoin as an alternative value transmission protocol emerged as a response to perceived malfeasance by the financial sector. And yet the CAP theorem is notably silent on the issue of trust.

This may be due to the development and deployment of public, decentralized, and distributed systems being relatively new, or perhaps the fact that third-party data storage and transaction systems are closed to inspection. Such "security through obscurity" makes a meaningful assessment of the risk associated with trust impossible until it is revealed as unfounded after a breach. As with the initial formulation of the CAP theorem, trust is then a yes/no option.

Either you trust the system completely (Trust = 100%), or you do not (Trust = 0%).

Understanding how an estimate of trust can be derived for a blockchain requires a review of the conditions under which a "single view of the truth" may be lost and subsequently regained, and is one of the recurring topics of the chapters that follow.

On the next page I will finish this chapter by returning to the practical purpose of trust, using a quote from that seminal Bitcoin paper by Nakamoto.

The root problem with conventional currency is all the trust that's required to make it work. The central bank must be trusted not to debase the currency, but the history of fiat currencies is full of breaches of that trust. Banks must be trusted to hold our money and transfer it electronically, but they lend it out in waves of credit bubbles with barely a fraction in reserve. We have to trust them with our privacy, trust them not to let identity thieves drain our accounts.

— Satoshi Nakamoto[11]

Hash Functions

> You don't do what you want to
> But you do the same thing every day
> *Jello Biafra, 1987[f]*

Two chapters ago I said I would explain what a hash-linked list was, and why hash-linked lists, and indeed hashes, are of fundamental importance in the blockchain world. As is usually the case with blockchain, hash-linked lists only offer one part of the solution, which is to provide non-repudiation. The other part is called consensus – either through proof of work or through some other means.

I've just read back over that paragraph, and realized that there are too many terms and concepts packed into too few words. It's the kind of paragraph that makes sense if you already understand the individual concepts and the effect of their combination, but if you don't, then it's gibberish.

So let's back up, forget about computer science and cryptography concepts, and start by looking at something in the familiar social world, namely what non-repudiation is.

That never happened!

When it comes to complicated social interactions, people often go back on their word. A handshake deal turns into an argument after one party fails to deliver to the other, or delivers something that the second party considers insufficient.

That is why society invented contracts – agreements, usually (but not always) drafted in writing, in which all the terms and conditions are laid out, along with costs, deadlines, deliverables, and above all penalties if the contract isn't honored. Contracts are backed by the courts, and hence governments with their ultimate threat of force: either imprisonment or the seizure of assets.

> **repudiation**: *the act of refusing to accept something or someone as true, good, or reasonable.*
>
> *— the Cambridge Dictionary*[26]

So what happens if one party claims that they never signed the contract? Or that the sheaf of papers being waved by the other party has been altered, and the terms currently being presented weren't the terms that were initially agreed on?

This is known as repudiation, and a number of techniques to ensure the opposite, namely non-repudiation, have been used through history to avoid this, the two most obvious being signatures and witnesses.

Signatures do not just include scrawling your name in your own handwriting or style on a piece of paper. In days gone by things called "seals" were used. Devices such as signet rings or chops (symbols carved into jade or soapstone) for making unforgeable marks in wax or with ink, presumably by the individual who had control of the seal. And in these modern days, we have digital signatures, in which the controller of a unique sequence of ones and zeros can use software based on cryptographic algorithms to create yet another sequence of ones and zeros that only the holder of a digital signing key could have produced.

Witnesses are usually people with "skin in the game", either notaries who are effectively paid witnesses, or other professionals such as lawyers, doctors, or priests, who have something to lose from lying about their earlier attestation.

There is, however, a third way. You can put the document out in public, which means that enough people will have a copy for future comparisons, in which case you are using the world as a witness. But what if your document is very large? Or even worse, what if you want to prove at a later date that you had the document in your possession, but it contains confidential information that you can't simply publish on the World Wide Web?

Cryptographic hash functions to the rescue!

Shorter is better

To begin with, you need to understand what a hash function is: an algorithm that takes as its input a data file of any size (so it will work on any kind of data, whether it's a short string of letters and numbers, or a large video file), and outputs a fixed-length number. Furthermore, if you put the same data in at a later date, you get the same output back. Hash functions don't change their mind over time, and there is no true randomness built into them.

The initial use of hash functions was for indexing and then searching for data. An analogy is car number plates. It is much easier to report a car to the police, and for them to subsequently find it if you can give them the number on the plate. Describing the make, model, color, and distinguishing marks such as fluffy dice hanging from the rear-view mirror doesn't really cut it.

In Finland, number plates are typically two or three letters, a dash, and one, two, or three digits.

However, number plates are simply serially assigned, so there is no algorithm used to generate them. The authorities could have used a simple formula based on the vehicle identification number

(VIN), instead. The VIN itself can't be used, because it is 17 characters long, which would make it too small to read if put on a number plate.

A simple example would be to use the first three letters of the VIN and sum each pair of digits of the serial number (modulo 10) to get the last three digits of the plate. So for example, a vehicle with a VIN of SCEDT26T8BD005261 would be fitted with a much shorter number plate that reads SCE-077, as shown in figure 8.

Here you can immediately see one of the problems with hash functions – different inputs can map to the same output. The first three characters of a VIN number represent the "world manufacturer identifier", and the last six digits are the vehicle serial number, so two identical models of the car made in the same factory nine units apart will often end up with the same number plate.

In the computer science world, this is described as a collision, and a good hash function is supposed to be collision-resistant. Two different inputs to the hash function should have an extremely low probability of producing the same output. Our number plate algorithm obviously doesn't satisfy that requirement, so it's not a good hashing function.

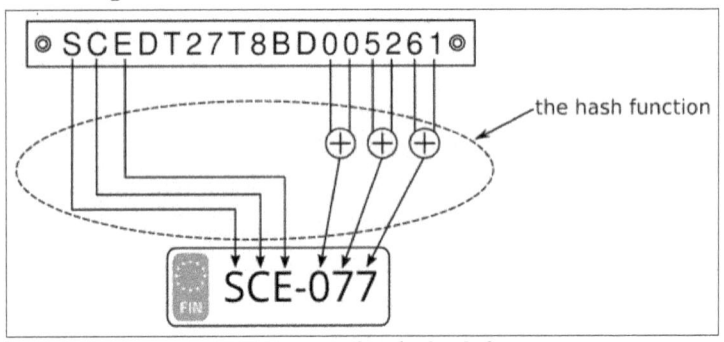

Figure 8: An example of a hash function

The fingerprint of a file

Sometimes a hash of a file is described as a "fingerprint", in that it's often a lot smaller, but it is almost uniquely linked to the file. Almost.

There is a very simple proof that a hash function cannot guarantee uniqueness. Consider a hash function that outputs an eight-digit number for any input. That means that the outputs can range anywhere from 0 to 99,999,999, so there are a total of 100 million possible outputs. However, there have been over 100 million books published[27]. This means that if you fed each book in turn into the hash function and were amazingly lucky in that when processing the first 100 million books there were no two books with the same hash output, it is guaranteed that once you feed in the 100,000,001st book, it has to have the same output as one of the previous books.

However, the cryptographic hash functions that are used to produce fingerprints for files have much bigger outputs. For example, the RIPEMD-160 hash function outputs a 160-bit number, which means there are about 1.5×10^{48} possible outputs. Roughly speaking, that's comparable to the number of atoms that constitute the Earth[28].

Another very popular blockchain cryptographic hash function is called SHA-256, and it has as its output a 256-bit number, of which there are about 1.15×10^{77}. For comparison, the current estimate as to how many particles there are in the entire visible universe is about 10^{80}, so that's one distinct output for every thousand particles we know of (or rather, can estimate the existence of[29]). In any case, they're both numbers that are so big that they make the USA's budget deficit of $3 trillion look like pocket change, even if you count it in cents[30].

Although there may be a lot of 256-bit numbers, any individual number can be represented very simply using a 16 by 16 grid, as in figure 9. When represented as such, it does start to look a bit like a fingerprint, or perhaps four chess boards glued together in a bigger square.

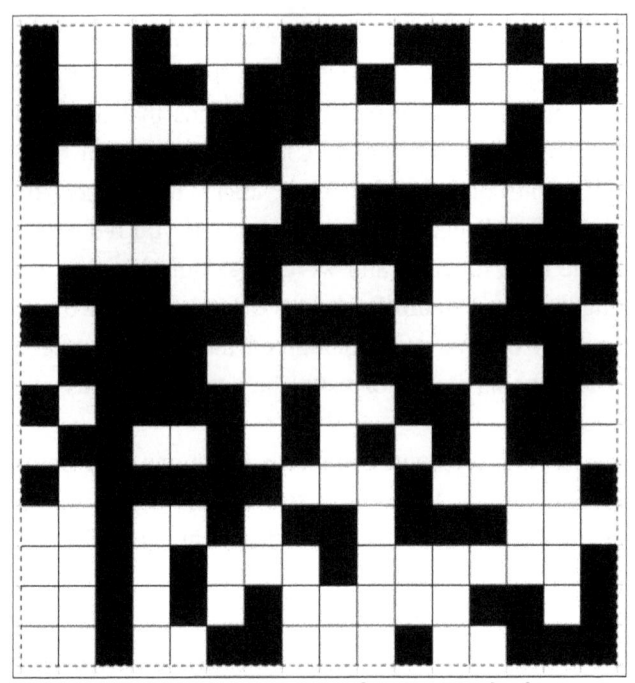

Figure 9: Grid representation of a SHA-256 hash output

Cryptographic hash functions

In the previous section, I subtly switched from talking about "hash functions" to "cryptographic hash functions". To qualify as the latter you need to have a few extra properties. First, let's recap what we have so far:

1. A hash function takes as an input some data of any size (even empty data), and invariably produces an output of a fixed length,

2. Outputs are deterministic, which means that the same input gives the same hash output time after time, even if you perform the hashing again days, weeks, or years later.

3. Collisions (identical hash outputs for two different inputs) are rare.

Cryptographic hash functions also require that:

4. When given a hash output, it is practically impossible to produce an input that when hashed returns that output. Cryptographic hash functions are meant to be irreversible. That's why they are also sometimes known as one-way functions or trapdoor functions.

5. It should be practically impossible to find two different inputs that give the same output (this is kind of a combination of items 3 and 4 on this list, but there is a subtle difference that should become clearer later).

6. Two very similar inputs should, generally speaking, produce very different hash outputs. For a cryptographic hash function to work that way, it has to act in what seems like a random fashion, without actually being random. Instead, cryptographic hash functions should be pseudo-random. See item 2 on this list.

Some papers and textbooks also list a further property, namely that it should be fast and easy to compute the hash output from an input[31]. However, that is not always the case. Fast and easy is a relative term, and for some uses, especially in blockchain, we want the computation of a hash to take a bit of effort. There will be more on that later as well.

Magical elves under toadstools

The ideal cryptographic hash function would be the algorithmic equivalent of a magic elf sitting under a toadstool, with a notebook, a pen, and a coin. We will call him ELF-256.

ELF-256 sits there patiently waiting for someone to pass him a message. On receiving the message, the elf springs into action infinitely quickly (he's a really fast elf):

He checks in his notebook to see if the message is already in there.

- If it is not, he writes it down in his book, and tosses the coin two hundred and fifty-six times, writing down the result after the message for each coin toss: a 1 for heads, and a 0 for tails.

  Then he checks to see if that particular sequence of 1s and 0s has already previously been generated for an earlier message. If it has, he crosses it out and repeats the coin tosses again, and if necessary, again and again until he is sure a new unique number has been generated for the new message.

- If, on the other hand, the message is already in the book, he looks up the number he wrote down after it the previous time he saw it.

  In either case, he then pauses for a fixed duration of time – perhaps a microsecond – and then reads back the list of ones and zeros that are jotted down in his book to the person who handed him the original message.

Oh, and finally, ELF-256 jealously guards his notebook with magic, so no one else can see what is written on the pages.

Why is ELF-256 a perfect cryptographic hash function? We can backtrack through our list of properties and see exactly why:

1. The elf always reads out exactly 256 digits, regardless of the length of the message passed to him.

2. If the same message is passed to the elf sometime later, he will read out the same number that he generated the first time he saw the message.

3. The elf never uses the same output number twice, so there can never be any collisions. Well – there can be, but only once he has generated 2^{256} outputs, which as I previously demonstrated is an almost unfathomably large number.

4. Imagine you are trying to find a message the elf responds to with a sequence of 256 ones. The chance of the elf tossing that many heads in a row is 1 in 2^{256}. Given that the elf takes one microsecond to respond, the odds are that it will take about two thousand vigintillion years*. For comparison, the universe has only been in existence for about 14 billion years. In short: it's not going to happen.

5. The elf does not reuse output numbers, so two different messages can never have the same output.

6. The outputs are generated randomly, so there is no relation between the original messages and the outputs. As a result, two very similar messages are going to get two very different responses from the elf.

Cryptographers who work on designing cryptographic hash functions are trying to come up with functions that behave as well as ELF-256, but competing with magical elves is a difficult task.

Oh the wonderful things that a hash can do

If you have paid enough attention over the last few pages, you should have a decent enough understanding of how cryptographic hash functions work and be able to appreciate how amazingly useful these things are in all sorts of areas of computing. We have already looked at the fact that you can take a confidential document, put it into a cryptographic hash function like SHA-256, and then make the two hundred and fifty-six bit output number public knowledge. At a later date, you can produce the original document, and anyone can hash it with SHA-256 to check that it is indeed the real deal, and has not been tampered with. If you published the hash output in the notices section of a newspaper, you

---

*   A vigintillion is a 1 followed by 63 zeros.

even have a time-stamped record of when you had the document in your possession.

And the best and most interesting uses, in my opinion, are when you start hashing the output of previous hashes. What that means is that you feed an input into a cryptographic hash function, and then you take the output you get and put it back into the hash function again. And sometimes again and again. In the next four subsections, we will have a closer look at some of those applications.

One time hash pads

Up until a couple of years ago, Finnish banks used "code cards" to allow their customers to securely log in to their online bank accounts. The card would have a list of a hundred different four-digit numbers, and each time you used one, you would cross it off the list, and the next time you logged in you would use the following unmarked number. When you ran out of numbers, the bank would send you another card in the post. Now that they've finally switched to authenticator apps, I've got a bunch of them sitting in the drawer of my desk that I should probably throw away, but I'm waiting until winter to burn them in the fireplace. You never know if they might still work, after all.

Such cards are known as one-time password pads, and they are usually constructed randomly. However, there is another way to make them using the repeated application of cryptographic hash functions.

In figure 10, I show what happens when the message 'the quick red fox jumped over the lazy brown dog' is passed into the SHA-256 hash function, and the output is recorded in the next row of the table. Each row that follows contains a hash of the previous row.

I've entered the numbers in hexadecimal to make sure they fit in the table. As modern humans, we tend to use decimal notation for numbers (our digits are 0 to 9, presumably because we have ten fingers), but note that not too long ago the Romans used letters like I, V, X, C, and M instead. So there's nothing special about the way we choose to write numbers today. Hexadecimal is a way of writing numbers if you were fortunate enough to be born with sixteen fingers (the letters a, b, c, d, e, and f are used to represent the extra digits), and as it happens, computers like to pretend that they have sixteen fingers. But don't worry about it too much. Just think of it as writing numbers in a slightly different way.

Back to the story at hand: each time the output is fed into SHA-256 again, to get another number, and so on for seven more goes. You can keep hashing outputs as long as you like, to make a longer and longer one-time hash pad, depending on how many times you think it will be used.

You can try it for yourself, as there are plenty of online SHA-256 hash generators[32]. One thing to note: your first input is text, but the output is a hexadecimal number, so when you copy/paste it into the input box, you need to select the input type to be hex.

You may be wondering, what is the point of all of this? How does it work? To start with, you need to get the last entry in the table to the entity that you want to authenticate yourself to (and there is more on authentication in the chapter titled "Passwords are the Worst" on page 99). And then, whenever you want to prove to that entity that they are talking to you rather than someone else, you give them the entry in the table just before the one they already have.

the quick red fox jumped over the lazy brown dog
dd77f952e29e4a64c2bf5e27993fd2ebf1b0f378237abd299239bb4454d028b8
355a1ef19cb2e02ca528f60a8d9dfe533cb37e0b52ace3fabf960bd710904fe5
69c3610d92b04e41ef0937b27b06bfbea7e55f7716dd534e354f99041e8fff72
324e14abb32ee21573b5c1bdd7d4dff1d485c0ab030bd2d4c9780d5858c08dda
1c554d67a79a27b12a43d7e3e2b212f468312541cefda684c7678ea819745b24
5470bbf5478dc15bb25cd095bffb09bed25abb20063fc7e914d7e28ab80ac40f
665593ea8363949abcd3208a8470cd35be42f30809fd2ef8254244c585161136

Figure 10: A hash function-generated one-time password pad

So what happens then? Well, they take the password you presented them with, and simply hash it with the SHA-256 function. If the result is the previous password that they already have, then they know it is you. Do you remember cryptographic hash function property number 4? It's pretty much impossible to create an input that, when hashed, gives a specific output. As a result, it's more than reasonable for the bank to believe that the person who gave them the precursor number to the output they previously had is the same person. And that's the point of identifying yourself with a one-time password pad: to prove you are the same person they were previously talking to.

Hash linked lists

Imagine you are the proprietor of a popular newspaper. Every day your presses print out a new issue with the company masthead, the date, and the news of the day.

And then one day you discover that an eccentric billionaire has decided to take one of your earlier editions from two months ago, change one of the stories so it says something completely opposite to what the genuine issue actually said (perhaps it is even libelous), and has printed millions of copies. And not only that, but he then paid an army of highly trained ninjas to break into all the houses of your loyal subscribers in order to replace their cherished copies with the false ones.

That may sound like a far-fetched scenario, but in the online world it is actually not that hard to achieve – printing digital copies costs virtually nothing, and hacking allows a single highly skilled computer ninja to break into many digital accounts. How can you protect yourself against this scenario?

Cryptographic hash functions to the rescue! These functions allow us to produce something called a "hash linked list". If each edition of the newspaper contains a paragraph or notice that includes a hash of contents of the paper published the day before, then the eccentric billionaire has a much more difficult task on his hands. Why is that the case?

Because your newspaper history is now a hash-linked list. If a paper from sixty days ago is altered, then its hash is going to be different. That means that the paper from the next day needs to have the notification containing that hash altered too, which alters the hash of that paper. And so on, and so on, through all the papers right up to today.

Suddenly our eccentric billionaire doesn't just have to make a change to the article that he disliked from two months ago, but he has to change every single newspaper from then on. That's a lot more work, and furthermore, with another application of cryptographic hash functions, namely "proof of work", we can make it even harder for him, to the point where he might as well not bother.

Proof of work

The fact of the matter is that in the scenario presented in the previous section we made it a little bit harder for the eccentric billionaire to subvert our newspaper, but we didn't make it impossible. Instead of simply replacing one issue of the paper, our hash-linked list means that he has to replace sixty issues (or more, if the story that he hated was further back in the past). That's a bigger pain in the neck, but it can still be overcome.

This is where "proof of work" properly enters the story. The concept was first invented by Dwork and Moni in 1993 as a means for combating spam emails[33]. Jakobsson and Juels[14] then coined the term "proof of work" to describe the idea and expanded on it, and Hal Finney adapted it to enable the createn of tokens backed by proof of work[34], the precursor to Bitcoin.

Satoshi Nakamoto's insight was to apply that concept to hash-linked lists in order to make it harder and harder over time to rewrite the past, and to put the whole thing on a peer-to-peer network, thereby allowing anyone to view the data in the list, verify that it is correct, and even assist in ensuring so much work is done when adding more data that no one person can go back and re-write it.

In other words, with a historical record stored in a hash-linked list that is secured by proof of work, the further back in the past the alteration you want to make is, the harder it is to perform the rewrite. You have to redo all the work from the point that you want to change, all the way through to the future.

So how does proof of work actually work in practice? Look back at figure 10 - all those entries below the passphrase "the quick red fox jumped over the lazy dog" are numbers. The fifth number starts with 1, and it's therefore the smallest number on the list. That is what proof of work is aiming at – finding a hash output that is below a target level; one that is small.

Hang on, if I hash the phrase, and I get a big number, then that's it. How am I going to get a better cryptographic hash output? The answer is that you have permission to add some "junk" at the end of the phrase. In cryptography, this is called a nonce, which is short for "number used only once".

Instead of feeding the output of the hash function back into the SHA-256 hash function, as we did in the previous section, let's feed our original sentence in again and again with different endings, as shown in figure 11, until we get an output that starts with 0:

This input's hash:	Starts with:
the quick red fox jumped over the lazy brown dog 0	3eec2267...
the quick red fox jumped over the lazy brown dog 1	30a16983...
the quick red fox jumped over the lazy brown dog 2	8e2cf376...
the quick red fox jumped over the lazy brown dog 3	12e08101...
the quick red fox jumped over the lazy brown dog 4	729107f6...
the quick red fox jumped over the lazy brown dog 5	297e5ae2...
the quick red fox jumped over the lazy brown dog 6	9e24b096...
the quick red fox jumped over the lazy brown dog 7	3f938d83...
the quick red fox jumped over the lazy brown dog 8	0ca85b7d...

Figure 11: SHA-256 hashing of a phrase with an added nonce

That didn't take long – only nine tries. Because the SHA-256 cryptographic hash function acts as a random number generator, on any individual attempt the odds are 1 in 16 that we will get an initial digit of 0 (remember, in hexadecimal, there are sixteen possible digits). That means that we have a 50% chance of finding a suitable nonce to go with the sentence within eleven goes. Of course, we could be unlucky and have to try hundreds of times, or we could be lucky and find a suitable nonce in one go.

What if we are looking for an output that starts with two zeros? The odds for an individual attempt are $1/16 \times 1/16$, or $1/256$. To have better than even odds of finding the suitable nonce we are going to need to try 178 different nonces, so it's probably going to take more work. And if we want to find an output with eight leading zeros, well for any individual attempt we have a chance of less than one in four billion that we will luck out and find it. That means to have a better than 50% chance of finding a suitable nonce, we are going to have to try hashing over three billion times.

In other words, the smaller the hash output is required to be, the more work needs to be done to find it. If your computer can perform a SHA-256 hash in 1 microsecond, and I refuse to read an email you send me if it doesn't hash to a number with eight leading zeros, on average it is going to take you about 50 minutes to find a suitable nonce to add to your message that satisfies that requirement. And it only takes me 1 microsecond to check that you have done the work.

And that is how proof of work could be used to prevent spam. Similarly, returning to our newspaper example, an individual issue can be made harder to forge by requiring that a nonce is added to the last page, such that the full contents of the newspaper, when hashed with SHA-256, produce an output with eight leading zeros. Now our eccentric billionaire would have to do fifty hours extra hashing work if he wanted to change an issue that came out sixty days ago. But the downside is that the newspaper office is delayed by about an hour each day when issuing the next paper because they have to do the extra work too. Fortunately, they get to do it day by day, rather than in one big go.

Merkle trees

We've looked at repeatedly hashing a passphrase to generate a one-time password pad, hash linking lists of blocks of data by including a hash of the previous block in the next block, and making people (or rather their computers) prove that they have done some work by challenging them to add some extra data to their messages, which causes them to hash to a low number output. What else can be done with cryptographic hash functions? I will start with an analogy:

Imagine a fictional country, where all the residents are totally obsessed with the law, and the laws are passed by the parliament or that arise from case history out of court decisions are gathered up and bound in special books.

The funny thing is that the contents of those books then become the absolute law of the country, which means that if somebody can tamper with one of them and add a rule that says that "people named Gary are allowed to conduct bank heists with impunity", then anyone called Gary is allowed to rob banks without fear of prosecution. Criminals could tamper with the laws in order to get away with their crimes!

The residents have come up with a very clever scheme to protect these books from such tampering without it requiring an immense amount of effort. The first thing is that they have an amazing machine that you can feed the text of a book into and it produces something similar to an ISBN number as an output that you can stick on the book, but the ISBN number that is produced is unique to each different form of text. It's a cryptographic hash function machine. If you take a book and you change one letter and then put it into this machine, you get a completely different ISBN code out.

The second thing about it is that you can't engineer a book to give a specific ISBN code - they're almost random in that respect. Again, evidence that the machine is a cryptographic hash function.

What the inhabitants of this country could do is to put all of the books in a library, and then gather all the texts from all the books, feed them into the machine, and make one single code for the whole library. That would ensure that in the future if tampering was suspected, they could repeat the whole arduous process, and if the second code matched the first one, they'd know that all the books were intact and no one had messed about with them.

But this is terribly inefficient – it means that every time you suspect a single letter or word in one book has been changed, you then have to go and collect all the books in the whole library from all the different rooms in order to ensure everything is okay.

Instead, they have taken the following approach:

- They group books into pairs. Each book is run through the machine and gets its own code, which is stuck on the back of the book, and then the two books are put on a shelf.

- The pair of codes off the back of the two books are concatenated (that means written one after the other) and that new concatenated code is fed into the machine to get yet another code. The shelf is labeled with that code.

- Each bookcase has two shelves. They repeat the process with the codes on those shelves: they take a copy of the codes of the front of the shelves, concatenate them, and put them in the machine to get a new code, which they stick on the bookcase.

- They have two bookcases in each room. Again, the same process is conducted with the codes on the bookcases, in order to get a label for the room's door.

- And there are two rooms on each floor of the law library so in order to label the floor, they use the codes from the two doors and then finally they put a label on the front of the law library that is the codes from the two floors concatenated and run through the machine.

I'm sure you understand what the process is by now. but you may be wondering, "Why are they doing this?"

If there's a court case, and it requires the laws from book number three, the court officials don't have to go and gather up all the other books to check that just the relevant book has not been changed. They take book number three and check that its code, or hash, matches. That means running one book through the machine, and verifying that the output matches the sticker on the back of the book. Now somebody could have gone in and changed book number 3, then run it through the machine and put a new code on it. But what the court officials can now do is look at the number on the other book next to it, check that's okay, and that together they hash to the shelf label.

Of course, somebody could have changed the shelf label as well, but then the court officials take the shelf label below and they concatenate and check again, and then they check that the two bookcase labels give the room number and that the two room numbers on the floor give the floor number and finally that the two floor numbers give the number on the front of the law library. It still sounds like a lot of work, so let's put it in a list:

1. Check that book codes hash to shelf code,
2. Check shelf codes hash to bookcase code,
3. Check bookcase codes hash to room code,
4. Check room codes hash to floor codes,
5. Check floor codes hash to library code, and
6. Check library code hasn't changed.

That's a total of six basic operations instead of collecting all 32 books (did you work out how many books a library of this type can hold?) in order to ensure that the law in one book is still correct.

There is one final piece, namely ensuring that the code on the front of the library is correct, but as it is displayed out in public on the street (and perhaps they have security cameras pointed at it too), the chances of someone called Gary making all those changes and then getting up on a ladder in broad daylight without being seen are slim indeed.

What I have described is called a Merkle tree (because it was invented and patented by Ralph Merkle[35]), and it should be pretty obvious that in blockchain systems such as Bitcoin the books correspond to transactions. The code on the front of the library, which in cryptographic terms is called the *root* of the Merkle tree, is stored in the block header to ensure it cannot be tampered with, making the library the equivalent of a blockchain block.

These days it is a very common practice to use Merkle trees to allow people to verify a snippet or chunk of data has remained intact and unaltered, but without having to download lots and lots of other irrelevant transactions. You only have to check a single branch of the Merkle tree, rather than the whole tree. As a result, Merkle trees are used in such places as the peer-to-peer file-sharing system BitTorrent, the anonymous communication network Tor, the distributed version control system for software development called Git, and of course: blockchains.

Part One on Identity: Who Are You?

> Why don't you all f-fade away
> Don't try to dig what we all s-s-say
> *Peter Townshend, 1965[h]*

Given the title of this chapter, I bet you probably thought I was going to write about the mysterious founder of Bitcoin, Satoshi Nakamoto. Entertaining though the anonymity of the founding father (or mother, or parents) of Bitcoin is, it is not going to be the topic. Instead, this chapter examines the far more important question of identity and privacy on blockchains – how various chains implement it, what cryptographic tools we have to help us, and in particular, what the implications of these tool-sets are in relation to the concept of "self-sovereign", "self-managed", or as I prefer to call it, "self-owned" identity.

As I have mentioned before "ownership" is possibly *the* core tenet of blockchain, and so identity is supremely important. Although you need to know *what* is owned, you equally need to know *who* owns it. Ownership needs something to be owned and someone to own it, just as a song needs a performing band and an audience. If there is no kind of reliable identity scheme or system, in which each individual controls their own identity, then the whole point of blockchain is lost.

And identity does not need to be a sophisticated web of credentials issued by authoritative institutions like government departments, universities or banks. Bitcoin gets by perfectly well with 26-35 alphanumeric characters that anyone with the right software running on their computer can create, and I've met people whose names, when combined to their titles and letters representing their educational qualifications reach that kind of length.

Unfortunately, despite the fact that each and every one of us has a unique identity regardless of how mundane and boring or flamboyant and notable we are, identity is and remains a complicated many-faceted thing.

The problem of identity

When I started as an undergraduate at Cambridge, we were all given our own small slot in the mailroom for our post – a personal pigeonhole. And one of the first things that was posted in it was a leaflet from the Cambridge University Student Union that contained our student union card.

As it happens, the rest of the leaflet consisted of various adverts for bookstores, clothing stores, and restaurants. As a result, most students simply threw it in the large waste paper bin at the end of the corridor.

I am now going to confess to a minor misdemeanor, without too much trepidation as it was thirty years ago, no one got hurt, and surely there's a statute of limitations on undergraduate tomfoolery?

I wasn't one of the students who failed to recognize the significance of what we received in our pigeonhole on that first day and scavenged five more of the leaflets from the bin. As a result, I had six student IDs. I used my first one properly, carefully writing my name and college in the required spaces and sealing it with the sticky-back plastic coat that it came with. The remaining IDs I filled in with fake names, and in the college section, I wrote in the names of other colleges that looked like they might be interesting to visit.

They stood me in very good stead – each college had its own cheap and cheerful bar, but you either had to be a member or a guest or very brazen and confident, in order to get served. With the IDs, I managed to become an accepted regular at several of them. There are still people out there who genuinely think I was a member of King's College (that's the college that the economist George Maynard Keynes was at – the chap who came up with what we now call Keynesian economics).

Scoring a few cheap beers here and there and making some new friends was all very well, but I could have done far worse things. You see, simply with my proper student union card and my first-year student grant top-up from my parents (about six hundred pounds in crisp twenty pound notes), I was able to open a bank account with a major high-street bank.

Furthermore, with the same ID and a single bank statement printed out and handed to me at the branch (I didn't even need to have it sent to my pigeonhole at college) I was subsequently able to purchase a British Visitor's Passport (BVP) at the local Post Office a few months later, for the princely sum of ten pounds. The BVP[36] was an official British government identification document that you could use to travel to most European countries at the time. It was a yellow-colored piece of cardboard, folded in three, with an officially stamped picture, a unique identity number, and your details and distinguishing marks entered on the last page.

It was only years later (and well after BVPs were abolished in 1996) that I realized that I could very easily have opened other bank accounts under false names with the other student union cards, and subsequently obtained false valid passports. Simply because of poor verification procedures and lax distribution methods I could have had five fake identities, each with its own bank account and passport. Imagine the fun I could have had traveling around Europe staying in fancy hotels and dining at fine restaurants, paying with credit cards backed up by official British government documentation, that I never intended to pay off!

This is one of the reasons most passports have moved on in terms of sophistication and procedural checks, are now issued by central offices, take weeks to be completed, and contain biometric data stored on chips embedded inside them, although even these supposedly advanced identification documents have weaknesses and flaws[37].

Similarly, banks have had to tighten up their customer acceptance protocols in the light of increasing Anti-Money Laundering and Know Your Customer requirements.

Pseudonymity

Back in the late nineties, I worked for a Cambridge software company as a technical writer, producing the user manuals and reference documentation for the programming language compilers and interpreters the company produced. In the room next door, a different group was working on an entirely different product – a database that allowed the British police force to investigate crimes.

One of the problems faced by law enforcement in the United Kingdom back in the late 90s was that pesky legislation meant that they could not just force their way into houses or listen in on telephone conversations. For the latter, a warrant signed by the Home Secretary (the quaint British title for the Minister of Internal Affairs) was required. However, they were allowed to track which numbers called which other numbers, when, and how long the conversations lasted.

Remember that this was before the term "data mining" was in common usage. The police quickly realized how powerful the approach was though.

If you have evidence that person A is a member of a criminal gang, you can go and arrest them. Or … you can start gathering data and build a network of phone numbers that person A calls. Perhaps they call their gang boss, person B, every Friday to discuss how business has gone, and persons C, D, and E regularly during the week to check that their enforcers and heavies are doing their jobs properly. After a few weeks or a month, you have drawn up a network diagram of times and communications, which can be interpreted to determine the flow of information and connections between the members of the gang, without needing to know anything about the content of the conversations.

And then you can swoop in, round up the whole gang, and arrest them.

A similar kind of data mining is possible with Bitcoin. The addresses may be pseudonymous, but every single transaction is visible on the blockchain. As a result, there are a number of different techniques that can be used to forensically investigate the flow of bitcoins around the system, and we can make some pretty good guesses about who transacted with whom.

For example, all the early blocks are owned by Nakamoto, as he/she/they were the only one mining at that point[38]. As a result, if Nakamoto every becomes active again and starts selling some of those early bitcoins, the world will know. I personally know that there are servers out there running software that is monitoring the Bitcoin blockchain for precisely this kind of activity, as well as other "addresses of interest".

A second approach is to build up a database of addresses published on the web. Some people have "tipping jars" on their website, where you can leave them a small donation if you like one of their articles. If these tips are regularly moved to new Bitcoin addresses, we can start building up a picture of which addresses the person controls. We can, in effect get an understanding of all the addresses in their Bitcoin wallet.

Similarly, governments can put legal pressure on Bitcoin exchanges (in fact they are required to in order to ensure taxes are collected properly) to provide information on the identities of clients using the exchange, especially if those clients convert their crypto holdings to fiat currency. Again, government investigators can then track the history of transactions leading to the address that made the conversion and possibly link the exchange client to an unsavory past.

A third sneaky technique is called "dusting". Criminals send small amounts of bitcoin – mere satoshis* – to a lot of different addresses they've scraped off the web. Imagine that one of these addresses belongs to someone who has a second address in their wallet that holds hundreds of bitcoins. If they make a purchase, there is a possibility that these satoshis will get sucked into the transaction together with a few bitcoin from the wealthy address. Now the criminals know the identity of the holder of the very valuable Bitcoin address and can start a phishing campaign or even use extortion in order to steal the larger sum.

As you can see, the anonymity offered by Bitcoin is very weak when you start to dig deeper.

The right to privacy

Hang on – isn't anonymity something that criminals want? And by offering an anonymous monetary system, aren't we helping them?

Well, yes. The combination of, for example, Bitcoin and privacy-protecting systems such as the Tor browser enables the possibility of the "dark web" to engage in financial transactions, by buying and selling illegal goods or even paying for illegal activities such as intimidation or assassinations. It does make life difficult for law enforcement agencies.

On the flip side, privacy-protecting systems can also be a force for good. Dissident journalists trying to expose corrupt politicians, gay people living under a regime that considers their sexuality a crime, or even just wealthy people hoping to avoid becoming kidnapping targets all benefit from privacy. Presumably, this is why the United Nations recognizes the right to privacy as a fundamental human right in its Universal Declaration of Human Rights[40].

---

*   A reminder: the "satoshi" is the smallest unit of accounting on the Bitcoin blockchain - there are 100 million satoshis in 1 bitcoin.

But enough about politics and philosophy. This is a book about blockchain, not human rights.

Tainted coins

There is a term in economics: "fungibility". No, it has nothing to do with mushrooms. Instead, something is described as *fungible* if one unit and the next are essentially interchangeable. All goods fall somewhere on the fungibility spectrum.

At one end we have things such as famous pieces of art, which are totally non-fungible. A Picasso painting cannot be easily and simply be swapped out for another.

At the other end, we have things like pure gold. One kilo of pure gold is very much like the next – if you deposited a one-kilo ingot at a vault, and later came to collect it, you probably would not even notice if they gave you a different identically shaped pure gold ingot unless you'd made some kind of mark or scratch on the original one. And even so, you wouldn't care – 30.57×10^{21} atoms of gold is what you want back, and one atom of gold is very much like the next.

Near the high end of fungibility are banknotes. Generally speaking, a specific one hundred dollar bill is very much like every other one (some may be more worn out than others, but they still all serve the same purpose). But there is one big thing about the Benjamins - they come with serial numbers. As a result, if you receive banknotes that were previously registered as stolen there is the possibility that they could be confiscated by the authorities. So banknotes are not entirely fungible.

And so there is something that many see as a significant problem with Bitcoin, namely that the coins are not fully fungible. Each satoshi is created as part of a block reward, and its subsequent journey from transaction to transaction can often (but not always) be accurately traced on the blockchain, as the record of transactions is totally transparent.

As a result, if a coin was once in an address known to be under the control of a criminal, for example in the account of the dark web trading site Silk Road, and then subsequently transferred to be under the control of your personal Bitcoin address, you might find yourself in a situation in the future where a cryptocurrency exchange or even an online store might refuse to accept your coins because they are "tainted". Or rather, they may accept them, and then not send you the fiat currency or goods that you were looking to exchange them for.

Similarly, coins that are known to have been stolen may, in the future, be tracked, and no longer accepted by law-abiding organizations or citizens.

And so Bitcoin is not fully fungible – the history of various coins means that they may not have the same value to everyone. They are not fully interchangeable.

Mixing

One method for getting around the lower than desired fungibility of bitcoins is the invention of mixing services. You send your tainted coins to such a service with one transaction, and over time, the mixing service combines them with pure clean coins (for example freshly mined ones) through a series of small transactions, and then sends you back your original amount minus a small fee. The returned coins are obtained from a mix of tainted coin transactions and clean transactions to a level where the taint is low enough that other parties will accept them again.

This is a bit like taking stolen banknotes and mixing them with clean cash, in the hope that a bundle of notes that you hand over at the store won't fully be checked and will be accepted, or that if a few stolen banknotes are detected, you won't be identified as the person who committed the bank heist in the first place.

There are a few problems with these kinds of mixing services. The main one is that you are sending your coins to a third party and trusting them to return them to you eventually. The mixing service may want to maintain its reputation and will therefore offer a reliable service, or it may be looking to cash out at some point and abscond with the coins sent to it. If you happen to send your coins at that point, you have lost them.

Secondly, although your returned mixed coins may look less dirty to the outside world, the mixing service could be keeping records as to which coins they mixed, who they came from, and later reveal this information to the world (or blackmail you with a threat of doing so).

Of course, the Bitcoin world being what it is, proposals are already out there for systems that can perform mixing in a decentralized manner. For example, Gregory Maxwell's CoinJoin system[41].

In a CoinJoin transaction, multiple parties that each want to submit a transaction to the system, join together to provide the inputs to a single transaction with multiple outputs. This creates the illusion that one single entity is performing the transaction, and that in turn confuses chain analysis and provides more privacy. In simpler terms, it is like a group of people all throwing some cash into a hat, mixing it about, and then everyone taking their share back out again, with digital signing ensuring that no one can take more than their fair share.

The CoinJoin system works because the single transaction (the throwing of cash into the hat) only becomes valid when everyone has independently signed and submitted their input transactions, and that is done after the output transactions (the taking of cash from the hat) are revealed – so if even one party isn't happy with the generated unsigned transaction, they refuse to sign, and the whole thing becomes invalid. This is what provides all the parties with secure knowledge that they are going to get their cash back; you can verify cryptographically that you are going to be able to withdraw the right cash amount before you throw your cash into the hat.

Another approach is to use a more modern coin than Bitcoin – one that has privacy build into it through the use of several advances in cryptographic techniques. After all, that's the driving force behind cryptography – keeping things secret. And so, in the next few sections, we are going to look at the techniques that these privacy coins use to keep everything secret: not just who is transacting with whom, but even how much they are transferring.

It sounds bizarre and counter-intuitive, but cryptography allows for public ledgers keeping track of who owns how much, without ever revealing who is who, and how much they have.

Ring signatures

A perennially popular method for maintaining anonymity is to hide in a group. Blending in to the crowd has been a way of staying hidden since the size of human gatherings grew beyond a few hundred.

Anyone with two or more children and certainly all school teachers out there will be very familiar with this technique: one of the kids breaks a window, but none of them admit to it. Now you're faced with a problem. Either you:

a) punish someone at random (normally the usual trouble maker), or

b) you punish all of the group, or

c) you punish no one.

None of these approaches is even near to being ideal. Often, in order to protect the innocent, the guilty get away with their crime. At least, that's how it works in my household, much to my annoyance.

A similar approach is used in some truly anonymous blockchains, for example Monero, using something called "ring signatures", invented by Rivest, Shamir, and Tauman in 2001[42]. Here is an example, using an analogy, of how ring signatures work.

In this analogy of ring signatures we have people (who are the equivalent of public keys) and we have some blackmail information on one of those people (that's the equivalent of having the private key to one of the public keys).

Let's say there are six people, and you have no control over five of them whatsoever, but the sixth person will do anything that you tell them to do, because of the leverage you have over them.

ALICE	banana	orange
BOB	apple	banana
CHARLES	pineapple	apple
DEIRDRE	pear	pineapple
ELIZA	grapes	pear
FREDDY	orange	grapes

Figure 12: People and their fruit selections

The aim is to prove that you have this leverage, without revealing which of the six people it is. That's the anonymity part. In cryptocurrency this anonymity is used to reliably authorize a transaction without revealing the specific address from which the transaction is issued – effectively by hiding in the crowd.

Back to our six people, who are now going to play a game of "I went to market", where each person names two items of fruit. The first person lists two fruits that they would buy at the market. And the remaining five participants take the list of two fruits from their predecessor, and swap out one for a new random fruit that they independently select.

So, the game starts with the first person picking two fruits. Perhaps they say, "I went to market and I bought a banana and an orange."

The next person says, "I went to market and bought an apple and a banana."

And the third person says, "I went to market and bought a pineapple and an apple."

As you can see, in each case they drop one of the fruits, move the remaining one to the second position, and name a new fruit in the first position.

So it goes, until we get to the sixth person. Let's say the fifth person said, "I went to market and bought grapes and a pear." Now the sixth person is the one who will do as we say, so we instruct him or her to swap out pear for orange. He therefore says, "I went to market and bought an orange and some grapes."

When you now look at the chain of statements, they form a loop. Anyone looking in from the outside cannot tell where the loop started and ended (especially if you reorganize the list of choices to start with a random person). That's the "ring" part of "ring signatures". Whereas the lists of fruits in each statement correspond to the "signatures".

There are only about two thousand different types of fruit in the real world (and about two hundred common ones), which means that there is a small but real chance the loop could complete accidentally, but in the cryptographic world the fruits correspond to random numbers, and there are trillions and trillions of those to choose from. Therefore the only way the loop could have been completed is on purpose, and by one of the participants in the loop being under our control.

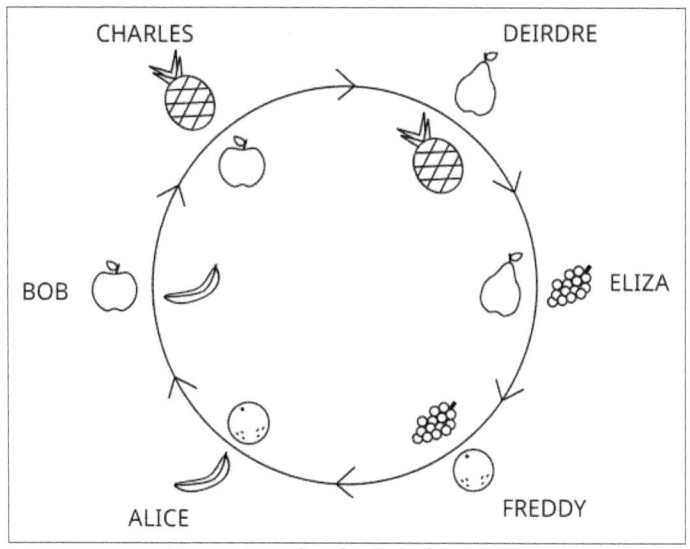

Figure 13: The closing of the loop

And that is how ring signatures work. Simple, but clever.

The hunting of the zk-snark

So, the question remains as to how a public ledger can record transactions and track balances without actually publishing those balances for all to see.

The answer, for the moment, appears to be *zero knowledge proofs*. With a zero knowledge proof you can show that you know something, or you can compare two things, without revealing the underlying data.

Imagine, for example, that two millionaires want to find out which of them has more money, without revealing their actual wealth. A centralized solution would involve both of them going to a trusted third party (maybe an attorney or a notary), and individually telling him their net worth. The third party can then announce to them both which is the richer, without revealing the actual sums.

But of course in the wonderful decentralized world of blockchain, that kind of solution won't be accepted. So here is how they can do it without any outside help:

Firstly, let's assume that they both agree that they're interested in the figure to the nearest million, rounded down. And they've admitted that they're not billionaires. So, they purchase 1000 boxes with locks and keys. Each key only unlocks one box, but they all look the same, and furthermore, each box has a slot in the top that allows a note to be slid in.

They label the first box "less than 1 million", the next one "less than 2 million" and so on, right up to "less than 1000 million".

The first millionaire takes the key to the box that accurately describes his balance. For example, let's say he has 15.5 million. So he takes the key to box 16, because he has less than 16 million, but more than 15 million. He gives the other 999 keys to the second millionaire.

The second millionaire counts all the keys, to check that no funny business is going on, and then throws them into a volcano (they're millionaires – so they can do expensive dramatic things if they feel like it).

The second millionaire then fills in one thousand sheets of paper. Let's assume she has 21.8 million. So on the first 20 sheets, she writes "more than this" and posts them into boxes 1 to 20. On the next sheet she writes ""this much" and puts it in box 21. And on the final 979 sheets she writes "less than this" and puts them into boxes 22 to 1000.

The first millionaire now takes his key, and privately unlocks box 16. In it, he finds a bit of paper saying "more than this". He now knows that the second millionaire is wealthier than he is, but has no idea whether she is a few million richer, or a few hundred million richer.

Similarly, if the bargain is that he shows her the paper, then she knows that she's richer than him, but not by how much[*].

---

[*] The analogy does have one flaw: what if the first millionaire takes the wrong key on purpose?

And that is an analogy of how a zero knowledge proof works – establishing comparisons or revealing the presence and nature or bounds of information without publicizing the underlying knowledge.

With a zero knowledge proof, one person can to prove to another person that a statement is true, without revealing any underlying information other than the fact that the statement true.

So what is up with the snarks? The term "zk-snark" stands for "zero knowledge succinct non-interactive argument of knowledge". The term "knowledge" appears twice in the acronym, something I find both ugly and amusing for some reason. Let us break down the terms:

zero knowledge: we have covered that already – you don't have to reveal the underlying information.

succinct: the assertion (e.g. - my balance is good for this) can be communicated and verified quickly, using only a small amount of data.

non-interactive: the communication doesn't involve a lot of to-and-fro sending of messages to exchange data.

argument: this term is used instead of proof, because zk-snarks do not actually use formal axiomatic proofs, relying instead on probabilistic "proofs", with the probability of them being false set so low that for all intents and purposes they are as good as proofs, with the added bonus that arguments are far quicker to compute and verify than true formal proofs.

(of) knowledge: there is real underlying information. In the case of a blockchain instantiating tokens or a cryptocurrency, it could be a suitable positive balance of the tokens or cryptocurrency, or strong evidence that a particular transaction has taken place.

Summary

Put all the pieces above together, and you have the possibility of a public distributed decentralized ledger whose integrity and veracity can be verified by anyone, and yet the identities of the people using it are concealed, as are the balances that they hold, and the transactions that they have engaged in. I don't know about you, but I find this a truly remarkable creation.

It probably does not come as a surprise that the Inland Revenue Service of the United States of America does not share my admiration for the technical ingenuity of privacy coins, and has even offered a bounty of $625,000 to anyone who can crack the anonymity of cryptocurrencies such as Monero[43]. That seems like a low-ball figure to me. I'm sure there are ways of making a lot more money from breaking privacy coins than accepting the bounty offered.

Passwords are the Worst

> Don't tell anyone or you'll be just another regret
> Rick Wheeler and Tyson Ritter, 2005[i]

One of the problems when talking about blockchain is describing how the validity of a submitted transaction is established. Simply put, there are generally only two requirements for a blockchain token transaction: a suitable balance of tokens exists, and the transaction is correctly digitally signed by an authorized person or entity. If both are met, the transaction should eventually be adopted into the blockchain record, and the change in balance recorded. The same goes for a blockchain data transaction, for example the submission of a smart contract, which must also be constructed correctly according to the blockchain protocols, and be signed by someone who has the authority to submit the transaction in the first place.

In one sense this is the same as an ordinary bank transaction, in that the bank ensures that you are actually the person who holds control over the account, and that there are enough funds in the account to cover the transaction or standing order being submitted (and of course there can't be any other transactions pending that would push the current balance below the amount you are looking to transfer, which is something that blockchains happen to check automatically).

In this chapter, we will be looking at identity, identification, ID, and authorization from a technical viewpoint. These are clearly extremely important in the financial world, but the manner in which determining authorization and validity takes place on a blockchain does not fit the usual patterns and procedures that we are used to from our everyday financial experiences.

For example, on a blockchain you can quite happily send all your digital coins to an address that you just made up on the spot and that nobody actually controls, or as is more usual, because you made a typo when entering the receiving address. In that case, the coins are lost forever. In everyday banking, if it turns out that the transferee bank account doesn't exist, or if you've entered the bank account number of one person and the name of another, then the transaction is stopped in its tracks. Similarly, if you try to transfer large quantities of money to a suspicious account, anti-money laundering procedures will probably kick in, the transfer may be frozen or canceled, and a criminal investigation may even begin.

Almost all forms of identification in our current computer networks, and indeed in most of the real world are based on the same client/server model. You have some client software, out there on the Internet is a server, and you have to authenticate yourself to that server in order to use the services it provides. It's a world where one party requires something, and the other one provides it, and therefore there is an imbalance in the roles and powers of each party. Generally speaking, they reside with the company running the servers.

This has built a strong model in the minds of not just ordinary users of such systems, but even technically trained computer software engineers. And when people hold such a model (often subconsciously) in their minds, everything is seen through a lens of preconceptions and assumptions.

On open public blockchains there are no user accounts in the traditional sense, with associated passwords or other managed authentication systems. Everything is based on a peer-to-peer network: there are no clients and servers. Your identity on the blockchain is managed by no one else but you, as there is no central authority and no user database managed by that authority. Even private permissioned blockchains, generally speaking, use a version of the identity system implemented by the first blockchain, namely Bitcoin. The significance of this difference between centralized and decentralized systems is sadly under-appreciated.

In order to help you become someone who appreciates that difference, I am going to provide a whirlwind tour of traditional identity and authentication technology by starting with a short story, followed by an analysis of some of the problems I perceive within traditional identity and access management systems, and then finally returning back to blockchain in order to emphasize how dissimilar it is.

On a train

Once upon a time, a long time ago, back in the early nineties when the world was a simpler place and it rained a lot more, I was traveling on a train from Cambridge to Edinburgh (with one change at Peterborough). I found myself devoid of anything to do. I had failed to bring a book, I didn't have any spare cash to buy one at the station, and tablets and smartphones were still science fiction. But I did have pen and paper.

So I thought of something amusing to keep me busy – why not invent and memorize passwords? For the first few hours I played the following game:

1. Look out the window,
2. Close your eyes,
3. Count to ten,
4. Open your eyes,

5. Write down the first number or letter you see,

6. Repeat 240 times.

There are a surprising number of fields with very little text visible out of train windows in Britain, especially in Lincolnshire, so sometimes I cheated and wrote down several letters and numbers if I saw a car number plate. However, as a result, I had a list of thirty lines, with each line containing an eight-character mix of letters and numbers.

For the remaining five or six hours, I worked hard to memorize those random eight-character passwords. Yes, it was boring and tedious, but no more tedious than sitting for seven hours with nothing to do.

Then I had another journey from Edinburgh to Ayr, which gave me a further three hours to check that I really had remembered all those codes. By the time I arrived in the lowlands of Scotland, I was pretty sure I had them all memorized. But I wanted to be absolutely certain they were burned into my brain forever.

On the journey back I occasionally double-checked that I really knew them, character for character. And then I tore up the notebook page into tiny pieces and flushed them down the toilet. Those thirty passwords stood me in good stead from 1992 until 2016 when I finally ran out of them. I was very careful to only use these precious memorized codes for significant sites – online banking, work logins, and websites that I actually cared about. This effort taught me two major things:

Firstly, having a system that insists people change their password every month, or every half year, is totally and absolutely pointless. If the password is secure then why change it? If your users are picking weak passwords to start with, do you really think making them change it is going to get them to pick a stronger one? And regardless of whether they have a strong or weak base password, the result of asking them to regularly update it means that they are probably going to come up with a scheme that reuses their password and changes a few characters at the beginning or the end. For example, the current date or a simple counter, as long as it satisfies the password strength analyzer.

And secondly, a password data breach is a hideous crime of negligence on the part of any data-holding company. Any organization that, at the very least, fails to hash their users' passwords with the best available cryptographic hash functions and using a random salt, should require each and every one of the company's board members and C-level executives to donate a kidney or half their liver to people on the national organ donor list.

Shame on you, LinkedIn (2016), Adobe (2013), Dropbox (2012), last.fm (2012), and MySpace (2008) for failing to secure your user data! You wiped out 12.5% of my effort on that train trip through your negligence. And my loss of preciously stored passwords pales into insignificance when you look at the damage caused to many people by having their accounts compromised – the hard-earned money lost, identities stolen, legal troubles caused, and anxieties raised.

Perhaps if every CEO of every tech company had to spend a day memorizing passwords only to have them published on the Internet the next day, they'd spend more time ensuring their company secured their systems.

Or perhaps not. Let's go with the organ-donor approach instead, and move on to a real analysis of what passwords are all about.

Connecting to a server

In the computer security world, there is this idea that the methods you use to gain access to a server can be lumped into three categories:

1. Something you know,
2. Something you have, and
3. Something you are.

I have never felt comfortable about this. To me, they have always looked like the same thing. But to start with, I am going to provide the classical description of these three access methods, then I am going to tear the classical description apart, and finally, I am going to focus our attention on what really matters.

Something you know

This one is simple – something you know is a password that you carry around in your head (or if you're a middle manager, on a post-it note stuck to your monitor). A pin code for your debit card is a password. So is your mother's maiden name, or the name of your first pet followed by the numbers 123.

You know what a password is. You probably type one in every time you log on to your laptop.

When you enter your password, your client software converts it into a message of ones and zeros that are sent over the network to the server that you are trying to log into, and the server verifies that the message is the correct one to allow you access.

Something you have

If you use Google Authenticator, get access codes texted to you, or you have a dongle or key card that you stick in a slot in the side of your computer, then that's something you have. The key to your front door is also something you have (if you're all fancy and technologically advanced and have a keypad that requires a number code to let you into your house, well, then that's something you know.)

The data from the authenticator, key card, or whatever thing you have is converted into a message of ones and zeros that are sent over the network to the server that you are trying to log into, and the server verifies that the message is the correct one to allow you access.

Something you are

Biometrics uses the properties of your body to generate a password in a repeatable manner. Your fingerprint, iris, the sound of your voice, your DNA, or even the echoes formed by beeping a chirp into your ear canal and listening for the characteristics of that echo are all effectively unique per person. An algorithm converts the physical measurements that a biometric reader (often just a camera) generates into a message of ones and zeros that are sent over the network to the server you are trying to log in to, and the server verifies that the message is the correct one to allow you access.

The problem with categories

The first problem should be clear by now – after all, I repeated it three times at the end of the previous three sections: each authentication method involves the same process. Typing in a password, holding a card against a card reader, or pressing your thumb against a fingerprint reader may feel like different processes to you, but under the hood, the same events are taking place.

As for the second problem – here are some things to think about:

- Is that post-it note on your manager's screen something he knows or something he has?

- if you have an RFID chip containing an authenticator program embedded in your arm, is that something you own, or something you are?

- If you are using your thumbprint to unlock your car, but some carjackers cut it off, is it now no longer something you are, but rather something the thieves have?

- Is a passphrase in your memory really something you know, or something you have in your mind, or a part of what you are?

A thing you have, such as a dongle or security card, is really just a crutch for poor memory. Having a debit card at an ATM, as far as the software and network behind the cash machine infrastructure are concerned, could be replaced with people memorizing the data on the magnetic strip or in the chip and typing it in manually.

Similarly for a thing that you are – if the fingerprint scanner also had a keyboard that allowed you to manually enter the data that the scanner reads and generates, and you had the ability to memorize the data that your fingerprint produces and then type it in, it would look the same to the system, but it would be something you know rather than something you are.

Multifactor authentication

This leads to the problem I have with multifactor authentication, which is becoming more and more commonly adopted in the computing world as a standard for secure authentication. Multifactor authentication requires the use of at least two different methods from the list of three just discussed. For example, a password, a fingerprint, and an authenticator code would count as multifactor authentication.

However, you may have created a user account with a username and a password, and then enrolled your fingerprint biometric data to have it attached to your user account, and received a card with your identity number on it, but even though you are presenting something you know, something you are, and something you have to the server, at the point that you log in it is, once again, just messages being sent to the server.

One level deeper there are some differences, which can give us some insight into what multifactor authentication, or indeed any form of authentication should really be considering.

The lines of communication

The question is not about having/being/knowing. Instead, it is about the channel of communication that is used to authenticate the user, what passes over that channel, and how the interactions using the data from the communication unfold over time.

Creating a password when setting up an account, and enrolling biometric data for future authentication, are using the same channel – TCP/IP over the Internet. Once the password or the data derived from the fingerprint are on the server, it is the same kind of message. As far as the server you are connecting to is concerned, a string of data derived from a fingerprint on a user's finger or from a password retrieved from a user's mind are pretty much the same. The difference is in the convenience to the user and the length of the "password" that is created.

A code-card list posted to you by your bank is different, as it travels through the mail, rather than over the Internet. Similarly, authentication codes texted to you use a different channel of communication. Note that neither of these channels is completely secure though, as mail can be intercepted and copied, and phone identities can be cloned or spoofed.

An authenticator application is also different, even though the enrollment is done over the same channel because it is performed at a different time. Authenticators are pseudo-random number generators with synchronized clocks. If both your authenticator and the server have the same "seed", then they generate the same random number at the same time. Ensuring the seed is shared is done once, usually over your Internet connection while you are logged in by using your password, but it could equally be set up through the post or by phone.

But there is so much more that can be done with communication channels and the swapping of secret data than just a spy-movie style exchange – you know, the kind where two people sit next to each other and spout odd-sounding sentences about daffodils in Moscow in the spring in order to confirm that they are communicating with the right person. And what's more, with cryptography you can take the same TCP/IP Internet channel and turn it into something different, and more secure. You don't have to use a burner phone or set up a clandestine meeting in a park to set up a secure channel on the Internet. It can be done right out in the open, in public.

Keeping passwords secret

The simplest method for setting up an account would be to submit a new username and password, in plaintext, over the internet, where it is stored on the server. This is a total disaster – it is like having a loud conversation across a crowded room, where the two parties are shouting all sorts of confidential information about each other that everyone else can hear. The password can be overheard and copied during the shouting match, and then used later by someone else. Similarly, if the password is stored "as is" on the server, and the server is later compromised, a hacker can simply read the secret information straight from the password file. Because users often re-use the same password in different places, the hacker can then go off and try using it on other services.

The next step up in security is to ensure that the communication channel is encrypted before the password for the account is selected, and to ensure that the selected password is stored on the server in such a way that anyone getting hold of the password file (either through hacking or from an inside job) won't be able to derive the password from the password file.

How can I exchange a secret message with you across a crowded room, without anyone else in the room but you knowing what it is? The answer is something called a Diffie-Hellman key exchange[44]. Here's an analogy that explains how it works:

Imagine that we are sitting at opposite ends of a classroom, and I want to send you a note that I've written on a piece of paper. Normally you just pass the note to the person next to you, and they hand it on until it reaches its destination. The problem with that is that all the other pupils in the class can take a peek at it while it travels from desk to desk, and if the teacher intercepts it, I will be in serious trouble.

Instead, I put the note in a little box, which I lock with a padlock that only I have the key for, and I hand the box onward. When it arrives at your desk, obviously you can't open it, but neither could anyone else in the room handing it on. You now put a second lock on the box, to which only you have the key, and pass the box back through the chain of other classmates, to me.

Now I remove my padlock using my key and pass the box back again. When it arrives at your desk for the second time, the only lock on the box is yours: the one you have the key for. You unlock it, take out the note, and have a good laugh at the caustic observation I wrote on it about the ineptitude of our current teacher.

If you want an example of a practical way to do this without boxes and locks, it can be achieved with a simple encryption scheme. The message I want to send is "TEACHER IS BORING". I pick a random number between 1 and 26 – let's say it's 3. Then I bump the letters in the message up the alphabet by that amount. So T becomes W, E becomes H, and so on. This is called a Caesar cipher because Julius Caesar used it in his private correspondence.

The encrypted message is now "WHDFKHU LV ERULQJ", and I send that message over to you.

You can't read that message, and it's going to take a bit of time to crack it with pen and paper. Instead, you now pick a random number as well and perform the same kind of encryption. Let's say you pick 7. You are going to have to loop around the alphabet with W because bumping that letter up by seven letters goes through X, Y, Z, A, B, C, and ends up at D. This process means your new message is "DOKMROB SC LYBSXQ". You send that back to me.

When I get your encrypted version of my encrypted message, I can reverse what I did, by bumping all the letters down by my original secret number, which was 3. The new message becomes "ALHJOLY PZ IVYPUN", which I send back to you.

Finally, you bump the letters of that message down by seven and have now got my original unencrypted message in front of you.

However, at no point was that plaintext message visible to all the students between you and me as they passed our notes back and forth.

The process works because bumping letters up and down the alphabet is what is called "commutative" in the world of mathematics. Moving three and then seven letters up the alphabet, and then three followed by seven down takes you back to the original letter. There are other commutative processes that you will be very familiar with, such as addition, and multiplication. For example, three apples plus seven apples are the same as seven apples plus three apples.

Having covered how two parties, such as a client web browser, and a web server, can set up a secure communication channel over the public Internet, we now turn to look at how the server can improve security by storing the login password that has been agreed on, over the secure channel, using cryptographic hashes.

We looked at cryptographic hashes before, but it is worth having a recap because they play such a varied and important role in blockchain: a cryptographic hash function takes an input (such as your password), and mixes it about to produce a fixed-length output of gobbledygook that:

1. cannot be predicted in advance, that is, it can only be produced by using the cryptographic hash function's algorithm and applying it to the password, and

2. it takes some effort to apply, so you can't do billions of them in a reasonable time, and

3. you get the same output each time you provide the same input.

The idea behind storing passwords securely is to not actually store them at all. Sounds odd, doesn't it? Instead, a hash of the password is stored. Here's an analogy:

Imagine that your password is a number of different quantities of ingredients selected from a very long list of possible fruits and vegetables. Perhaps your selection is an apple, three carrots, a hundred grams of grapes, and a tablespoon of shredded coconut. You have agreed on this over a secure channel, as just described, with a chef running a members-only cooking club. Now, the chef could write down that recipe, and demand that you produce the ingredients every time you want to go into her kitchen. However, if someone broke into the chef's room and took a copy of the list, they would be able to impersonate you by producing the same list.

Instead, the chef doesn't keep a list of the ingredients but rather, she makes a "log-in smoothie". When you agree on your password, she takes the ingredients and puts them in a blender, and then keeps the resulting drink in a bottle with your name on it.

The next time you turn up with your bag of ingredients, the chef takes them and makes a smoothie with them, and then takes a sip of the resulting broth and a sip of the smoothie she has stored, and only lets you in if they taste the same (we do have to pretend that these concoctions do not spoil and that the chef has an excellent sense of taste).

If someone manages to break into the chef's room, all they can do is steal a sample of the smoothie, and then spend weeks and weeks in their kitchen trying to recreate it through trial and error.

Your list of ingredients is the equivalent of a password, and the blender is the equivalent of a hash function. It is even a one-way process: you cannot take a smoothie and convert it back into the raw materials used to make it.

The second thing that has to be done to this password hashing procedure is adding a nonce (remember those from the chapter "Hash Functions" earlier in the book?). It needs to be added to the password before hashing it. In this context, the nonce is called a "salt", and prevents attackers from creating things colorfully called "rainbow tables". By taking the time to run the hash function over all words in the English dictionary (and other languages), an attacker can build up a list of commonly used passwords and their corresponding hashes at their leisure, and then use the resulting list to quickly lookup which hashes correspond to which passwords.

But by adding a random different string to each password, and storing that string (namely the salt) next to the hash of the password plus salt, when the client submits the password, the server can attach the salt to it, hash it, and compare the results.

To extend our smoothie analogy: a determined attacker could spend all their spare time making as many different common smoothies as they can, effectively building up a library of smoothies, and then when they manage to steal one chef's samples, they can quickly perform a comparison to reverse-engineer the recipes.

However, if each and every chef has their own blend of special spices that they add to each smoothie in their collection, then the thief cannot prepare their own library in advance. The general approach no longer works, and the effort put into cracking the recipes of one chef no longer transfer to all the others.

In cryptography adding random flavors and spices to a password before hashing it is, appropriately enough, called "salting".

But that is enough about the practicalities of dealing with authentication and passwords – it's making me hungry. I have only scratched the surface of what can be done in this space, and perhaps the complexity of what I have presented gives you an idea as to why data breaches are so common.

Make mine a double

The previous section described how our current familiar user account systems work. Everything from your online bank, to your social media accounts, to your online shopping accounts, will have systems at the back end that work the way I described.

Blockchain, as usual, likes to be slightly different.

Blockchain addresses

There is one huge discrepancy between traditional username and password accounts managed by a central authority and blockchain accounts. In the centralized world, an account is created on the centralized database, and then a password is associated with it afterward. That means that if the password is compromised or forgotten, an administrator can change it for a new one. Often this process is automated: you click on the "forgot your password?" link, or go to the "manage my account" page, and select a new password. Behind the scenes, your new password is salted and hashed, and the old hash is replaced with the new one.

On a blockchain it is different. The account "name" (for example a Bitcoin address or an Ethereum address) is *derived* from the password, and the password is actually the private key. The two are inextricably bound. This means that if the password for an address is compromised, you have to transfer out any token balances you have as quickly as possible to a new address. And if you lose your password, you have lost any balances associated with that particular address. Looking after your private keys is therefore of paramount importance in the blockchain world.

A second difference is that with a user account you authenticate once, which provides you with a user session, and then you can keep using the services provided without further authentication until the session expires. In some cases, this may be for a few minutes or hours, and in other cases, it might be for as long as your browser or client software is open and running.

With a blockchain, every transaction you submit that adds data, for example by deploying a smart contract or transferring cryptocurrency, has to be digitally signed. In effect, you are required to authenticate each and every single transaction.

An analogy is that a traditional website, be it a banking site or some other service, is like a nightclub – you identify yourself when you go in, and after that, you don't need to show your identification every time you want to buy a drink. Whereas a blockchain is like a bar – you need to show your ID every time.

This gets unwieldy after a while, and so a new software application arose fairly quickly to simplify the process. The first Bitcoin Core release already contained the fundamentals of a basic blockchain wallet, and wallet software has been improved upon ever since.

What's in your wallet

One of the key* elements of blockchains as far as users are concerned is the "wallet software", namely the application that allows them to submit transactions, and to see what their current status or balance on the blockchain is.

Unfortunately, the word "wallet" was a rather poor choice, because it gives the impression that the tokens and coins that you own on a blockchain are somehow in your possession in that software wallet, in the same way that you physically hold cash in your real wallet. A blockchain wallet is more like the equivalent of a conventional wallet that only contains debit cards. And it contains a lot of them. Just as a debit card and the PIN that goes with it allows you to unlock and spend the money that is on your bank balance, and hence stored in a database in a bank far away from your wallet and card, so a blockchain wallet contains the private keys to your blockchain addresses, and again, the status of your digital assets that they can unlock and spend are stored in the blockchain peer-to-peer network, and not in your wallet.

I have to digress because this is quite a significant point, but it doesn't really fit into any of the chapters that precede or follow this one. Governments have put all sorts of regulations in place at their borders to stop people wandering in or out of their countries with suitcases full of gold or dollar bills. However, open permissionless blockchain assets such as Bitcoin are out there floating in a decentralized distributed cloud of nodes spread all over the world, and transactions sent to that network are censorship-resistant. This has a significant consequence – anyone with cryptocurrency or other digital assets can cross borders with nothing more than the private key on a printout in their back pocket, or even in an email they sent themselves weeks earlier, and still access them on the other side of

---

*   Pardon the pun.

the border. That means that you can smuggle the equivalent of millions or even billions of US dollars in value far easier than ever before, provided there is someone on the other side happy to make the exchange from cryptocurrency to the local currency.

Back to wallets though: at the heart of wallet software lies what is essentially a password manager, with the passwords being the private keys of your addresses. The neat thing about an open permissionless blockchain is that you can create new addresses in an instant and at will: as many as you like, with only the speed of your computer being the limiting factor. Compare that to the effort required to set up a bank account! In a permissioned blockchain you generally (but not always) require an authority to approve new addresses, so they are often more like traditional banks in that respect. However, in a decent blockchain, even if it is permissioned, once the address has been approved, you should have far more freedom to act than in a normal centralized system.

So how does a wallet generate such an address? Different blockchains use different mechanisms, but the underlying principle is generally the same, and it starts with picking a random secret number, which is the private key for the address. That's the number you are repeatedly reminded must be kept completely private, because anyone who gets hold of it can do what they like with the balance it controls. So the first step in creating a new address on a blockchain is typically no more complicated than getting your computer to toss a coin 256 times, and computers can do that kind of thing very quickly.

The second step is to derive your public account address. This is a bit more complicated, and to understand how it works you need to know what hashing is (which you do, because you read the chapter on Hash Functions), and also what asymmetric key cryptography is all about. Fortunately, that is the topic of the next section.

One-way tickets

When we looked at the Caesar cipher earlier, you may have noticed that the same number was used to encode and decode a message. Bump all the letters three steps up the alphabet to encode, and bump the letters three down to decode. In a sense, the private key for encrypting and decrypting is 3. This makes the Caesar cipher something that is called a symmetric encryption scheme because the same key (in this case, the number three) is used to both encode and decode messages.

What if it was possible to have an encryption system in which the key to encrypt a message was different from the key required to decrypt it? I have no idea if this was the thought that went through the minds of the inventors of asymmetric key cryptography[*], but as an inventor I would like to think that it was that kind of thinking that triggered the search and then discovery of what is now called asymmetric key cryptography, or public-key cryptography.

I think this chapter has already been a bit too technical, so I won't cover the underlying principles that make asymmetric key cryptography work. Instead, it is best to consider what its functions are:

- there is a private key, and a public key derived from the private key in a somewhat similar manner as using a hash function, such that the public key cannot be reverse-engineered to determine the private key;

- the private key must be kept private, and the public key can be shared with other people, or even on a blockchain, hence the name;

---

[*] It was initially thought that Whitfield Diffie, Martin E. Hellman, and Ralph Merkle were the inventors of public-key cryptography in 1976, but on the unsealing of a GCHQ (the United Kingdom's Government Communications Headquarters) secret report it was revealed that James H. Ellis preempted them in 1970.

- anything encrypted with the private key can only be decrypted with the public key, which means that the private key can be used to "sign" something by attaching a signature to the something;
- a signature is simply a copy of the transaction or document, or more usually, a hash of the transaction or document being signed, encrypted with the private key;
- the signature can then be verified by decrypting it with the public key, and checking that the decryption produces the hash of the transaction or document that was signed;
- in the case of a transaction, if the signature is valid, and the transaction concerns a balance registered on the blockchain as belonging to the public key, that means the controller of that public key (that is, the holder of the private key) has authorized the transaction correctly, and the blockchain nodes will consider it valid.

So what is the analogy for all of the above, I hear you ask? I haven't come up with a good one personally, but there is an excellent one by Panayotis Vryonis at his blog, in an entry called "Public-key cryptography for non-geeks"[47]. In it, Panayotis presents a lock-box with an unusual lock mechanism, in which a physical implementation of a private key only turns clockwise in the lock, and the public key only turns anti-clockwise. The lock has three settings: locked at 9 o'clock, unlocked at 12 o'clock, and locked at 3 o'clock. This means that a person with one of the many copies of the public key distributed about can open the box, put in a message, and then lock the box by turning the key from 12 o'clock to 9 o'clock. Now only the single person with the private key can unlock the box and read the message. Similarly, the person with the private key can put their mark on a document, place it in the box, and turn the lock from 12 o'clock to 3 o'clock. Anyone can later verify that the document was marked by the person with the private key by unlocking the box back to 12 o'clock and looking at the document because only the private key holder could have locked the box in that manner.

What could go wrong?

Losing your private key to a blockchain address is like losing a bundle of cash out of your back pocket. Worse than that, actually – the bundle of cash promptly falls into a fire and combusts.

As I keep repeating, it is therefore vitally important to look after your keys. Good blockchain wallets use a mnemonic sentence, called a seed phrase, to generate all your addresses from one source. As a result, the seed phrase has to be totally random when generated to ensure that no one else can guess it.

Some people write out the list and then store it in one, or even several bank deposit boxes. Splitting it up into several pieces, making several copies, and then storing them with different trusted people is another approach.

I've seen products offered where you use a template to punch dents into a metal plate matching your private key or master key, and then store the plate in your attic, or bury it under the oak tree in your garden. These elaborate schemes are used because if something valuable is attached to the Internet, at some point it is going to get hacked.

An example of not thinking through security comes from the early days of Bitcoin, when the wallet software was not amazingly well thought out – the private keys were written in plain text to a file on your hard drive called `wallet.dat`. Anyone with access to your computer could copy and download the private key file, and then withdraw all the balances. For a while there, was even a thriving underground market in trojans and malware deployed to seek out the unprotected files and send them back to criminals, who would then drain the balance of the addresses derived from the secret key[45]. And this was when a single bitcoin was only worth about 10$ on the open market. Imagine the efforts criminal hackers are expending nowadays to obtain your private keys!

Fortunately, later the Bitcoin Core developers added functionality to encrypt and protect the `wallet.dat` file, but it was nearly twenty months after the software was first released[46].

In any case, the wallet part of Bitcoin Core is really an afterthought, as the main purpose of the software is to function as a node on the peer-to-peer network. For decent wallet software, you need an application whose sole purpose is to function as a glorified password manager with an understandable user interface. If you are looking for a cryptocurrency wallet, you will have to do your own research, as I don't want to be held responsible for directing you to something that later gets hacked.

Sorry about that! But let's stop worrying about hackers and think a bit more about who we are, which is the topic of the next chapter.

Part Two on Identity: Self-Sovereignty

> Identity is the crisis, can't you see?
> *Poly Styrene, 1978[¹]*

Two chapters ago I talked about identification, and then a lot about hiding who you are from the world: the mechanisms that some blockchains provide to ensure anonymity for both your identity and for your actions. Unfortunately, privacy is one of those things that is both incredibly important, and not appreciated by most people until they find themselves in a situation where they really need it. At which point it is too late.

In this chapter I am going to look more at the opposite side of the coin – for most of us, for most of our lives, we have to repeatedly prove that we are the person we claim to be. Traveling across borders, claiming benefits from the state that we are entitled to under the law, withdrawing money from the bank, picking up medicine from a pharmacy, or even buying a beer in a bar usually require some kind of identification. And we rely exclusively on third-parties to provide us with the mechanisms to do so.

Blockchain may well be the key to changing that, and in the field, this is known as "self-sovereign identity".

But to begin with, let's start off by examining what identity actually is at a fundamental philosophical level. Identity is something that pretty much everyone who is or once was a teenager has agonized about for endless hours, and yet it is also a topic that has fascinated and perplexed philosophers throughout the ages.

In my experience, one of the few benefits of getting older is that you find yourself spending less and less time lying awake in your bed wondering, "Why am I me and not someone else?", because instead you spend more and more time wondering, "Why does my back hurt so damned much, and why can't I read the ingredients label on this packet of noodles?"

Clearly, a topic that both philosophers and teenagers obsess over is not going to be a simple one that a handful of computer programmers are going to be able to solve in a few lines of code, but it is fun to examine. So let's skim across the surface before diving in.

The ship of Theseus

In philosophy, the problem of determining whether something still remains as it is over time is known as the metaphysics of identity, and the earliest and most famous example of the paradox of identity is known as the ship of Theseus.

> *The ship wherein Theseus and the youth of Athens returned had thirty oars, and was preserved by the Athenians down even to the time of Demetrius Phalereus, for they took away the old planks as they decayed, putting in new and stronger timber in their place, insomuch that this ship became a standing example among the philosophers, for the*

> *logical question of things that grow; one side holding that the ship remained the same, and the other contending that it was not the same.*
>
> — *Plutarch*[48]

The paradox is also known as the grandfather's axe problem: I inherited my grandfather's axe – he used it all his life, replacing the head three times, and the shaft ten times. Question: is it still the same axe he had as a young man?

When you apply the concept of identity to a person you add an extra level of complication, because not only are you faced with the physical presence of a person, changing over time as they age, but the *mind* needs to be considered too. After all, you are still the same person after a radical badly judged haircut or worse, a tragic accident involving the loss of an extremity, aren't you? Yet these kinds of events can subtly or even dramatically change who you are, or rather who you or others perceive yourself to be. And when it comes to issues of the mind regarding the integrity of personal identity ... well, then we enter a whole new arena of difficulties, both intellectually and emotionally.

For example, a body hosting a mind that woke up every day with no memory of the days before might have the same physical identity, but would it have anything that we would label as a solid, complete, and reliable identity? Self-identity is the total sum of our experiences over time[49], and our awareness of the majority of the parts of this sum, especially those judged important, and some kind of integration of those experiences into a continuity is essential. However, what constitutes "the majority of the parts" in this case? How do we assess the relative importance of them?

But I think that is enough rapid metaphysics to illustrate that identity is not a simple or trivial concept. As far as the state, the law, and indeed the people and companies you transact with are concerned, as long as you appear sound of mind and body, and are indeed physically the person they think they are transacting with, then Theseus's ship isn't really a problem. As long as a second ship doesn't come along claiming more right to the identity of being the boat piloted by the ancient Greek, everything should be fine.

The network of our identity

When it comes to identity, in the real world we are more concerned about what the ability to confirm your identity can actually give you in a real practical sense (the right to buy a six-pack of beer, drive a car, or vote in a national election), then any answers to metaphysical questions about the meaning of identity can provide.

Having an officially recognized identity is something that most of us take for granted, but as any refugee or asylum seeker who has had to leave everything behind to flee to a new country can tell you: not being "in the system" is a living nightmare[50].

But for the rest of us the formal system is thorough – starting with the signing of a birth certificate or entry into a population register, receiving an identity code, and then expanding ever outward with school records, a driving license, passport, bank accounts, credit history, further educational credentials, an employment record, stacks of utility bills, and so on and so forth. Each of these is a further attestation as to your official identity, but they all have one thing in common: they are issued by a central authority that you have no control over.

On the other hand, we also build up a social identity, namely a network consisting of friends and neighbors, your general practitioner or doctor, teachers, work colleagues, and perhaps even your local priest or pastor if you're that kind of person. All of whom provide a different kind of evidence (or even understanding) of your personal selfness. This identity network is decentralized.

Finally, we have our virtual identity – things such as email accounts, social media accounts, our profiles on bulletin boards or groups, and the networking and conferencing software that we log in to. Once again, these are centralized, and the various corporate entities running the services offered make fortunes selling information about our preferences to advertising agencies, and pass on all sorts of details about us to government authorities.

That is a lot of identity "stuff" to keep track of, and it also means that there are lots of front lines where a determined hacker in any of the three spaces can try to subvert or steal your identity.

In practice, most of us are only safe because we are uninteresting and there are so many of us. Miscreants wanting to mess up the system tend to go after the big names, famous people, and the wealthy, and even if they target an ordinary everyday victim, the odds are that it won't be you or me. But the fact remains that the credentials that form the basis of our official identities are in the hands of other people, and we blindly rely on them to ensure the data that makes up that identity is kept safe and secure. As the previous chapter showed, these centralized guardians have a poor track record in doing so, not just for basic data about us such as our names, email addresses, and so on, but even the most important thing, namely the passwords used to keep the data thieves out. If we can't rely on central authorities to safeguard the "keys to the kingdom", how can we trust them with our confidential medical data, our financial data, or in fact anything?

Furthermore, it is not just lax security that is a problem. Large tech companies are ever building larger and larger databases recording all sorts of meta-data about us: what we've purchased, what products we've looked at, what websites we visited, and so on and so forth. With this, they can build up an overview of our hobbies and interests, our political persuasion, our beliefs (religious or otherwise), and even some of our deepest and darkest secrets. This data in isolation is not worth much – good luck trying to sell details about yourself. However, in aggregation, it is a gold mine for advertisers, businesses, and political organizations, who use it to target their messages with laser-like precision.

Some definitions

When you start digging into the literature surrounding identity, you will quickly find that it becomes dry, academic, authoritarian, and sometimes even argumentative. I am all for preciseness in definitions, but only when the definitions help in understanding or guiding real practical implementations[51]. Splitting hairs with your grandfather's axe may be entertaining to some, but the rest of us just want to understand enough to get to work. Here are some quick and dirty definitions of terms used in the field of identity:

Identity: who you are,

Claim: a statement about your identity,

Identification: claiming that you are who you are,

Verification: a one-off process using extra credentials and attestations to thoroughly check that you are who you are,

Credential: a collection of claims about your identity, issued by an authority,

ID: a credential you are given after the verification process that you subsequently use to authenticate yourself,

Authentication: using a verified form of ID to prove you are who you are.

The difference between identification and authentication is an especially subtle one. Here's a practical example: I may be working late at night in an office writing some code, and my identity in that context is that I am an employee hired as a software developer. A security guard on patrol walks into the office, and asks me to identify myself, and so I tell him my name and job title. He asks me for proof, so I hand over my employee badge, which is an authentication process. The badge was provided to me by the Human Resources department, who verified that I was who I claimed to be using my government issued passport and my bank account details when I was hired. The badge now functions as a form of ID, and in this case it is something I have. The security guard is convinced that I am allowed to be on the premises, so I can continue working.

There is an article by Christopher Allen that is both superb and remarkably short, which addresses the core issues of practical identity management systems and introduces the key concepts of self-sovereign identity[52]. The paragraphs that follow are really just a summary and commentary.

Centralized identity

To be able to authenticate someone who you have identified, you need to be able to trust the verification process. Traditionally this has been done by relying on central authorities such as governments, the police, and banks to perform a thorough vetting of the person seeking to obtain ID. Passports, driving licenses, and bank account login codes are not just handed out like Universal Life Church ordinations, after all[53].

The traditional identity system is a hierarchy, typically with a government at the top of the pyramid. A utility bill may be used to prove that you live at a certain address, but that bill is only being sent to you because you set up an account with the water or electricity company using your bank account. Your bank allowed you to open that account because you went into a branch office in person with your driving license, which you got from the local police station (in Finland, anyway – in other jurisdictions it may be a different branch of the government that handles that side of things), and they want to see a passport. And so the chain of validation can be traced back to a centralized government, which forms the root authority for the identity system. As Allen puts it, "However, the root still had the core power — they were just creating new, less powerful centralizations beneath them".

Ultimately, we're still living in a kind of feudal system, albeit with less rigid class definitions, and mere "users" are at the bottom of the heap.

Federated identity and delegated authentication

For much of the Internet, having an "absolute identity" is not essential, especially if no financial transactions are taking place. Your Facebook identity does not need to be tied to your Github, StackOverflow, or Twitter identities for these systems to still function and provide you with a service.

An advantage of the "silo" nature of traditional Internet sites is that of privacy. For example, your political comments on a social media site do not have to be inextricably tied to your code contributions for an open source project on another site if you are able to create accounts on both sites using different email addresses.

The downside is that, as a user of the various services that different sites offer, you will end up with many different accounts, for which you personally have to store and protect email addresses, usernames, passwords, and other authentication factors.

In practice, most people are not that concerned about privacy, so they use the same email address and often reuse their password. As discussed in the previous chapter, the result is that if one site is hacked, your accounts on all the other sites are compromised too. Om the other hand, having just one account is a lot more convenient. There are a number of different terms used, and as is usual in the world of identity, they have subtle differences, mostly in terms of what is going on under the hood. From the user's perspective, regardless of whether you are using a federated identity and access management system, a single sign-on solution, or delegated authentication doesn't really matter – the upshot is that you only need to create an account on one system, log in once, and can then wander from site to site, or service to service, clicking on the "Login using Google/Facebook/Twitter/LinkedIn" button (or in some cases seamlessly transferring without even knowing that authentication and authorization are happening).

However, regardless of whether you are using a federated identity or a delegated system, the fact remains that behind it all there is a single central authority that you have selected, which is holding your credentials. If that authority decides to kick you off the system, you have then also lost access to all the other systems that you used the identity service provider for.

Again, as Allen puts it: "It's central authorities all over again. Worse, it's like state-controlled authentication of identity, except with a self-elected 'rogue' state."

Decentralized identity

In the same way that we outsourced our cash holding to centralized authorities known as banks, we have outsourced our identities to governments and technology companies. Blockchain offers the opportunity to not just reclaim our ownership of our wealth, but also ownership of our identities. The term used for this is "self-sovereign identity". I happen to think that it is a poor term, but it is a starting point.

> **sovereign**: *having the highest power or being completely independent.*
>
> — *the Cambridge Dictionary*[54]

The constellation of claims, attestations, and credentials that comprise the practical means for us to assert our identity is never going to be completely independent of other parties. The use of the word "sovereign" therefore seems to be a bit over-reaching.

This is why I prefer to think of SSI as a "self-owned identity", or "self-managed identity", in that its primary purpose is to ensure that there is no single authority that can arbitrarily revoke your access to your credentials, and hence a part of your identity.

I am thinking here, for example, of the dramatic rise in the number of revocations of citizenship the British government has instigated in recent years on the grounds of it being "conducive to the public good" - up from 4 in 2014 to 104 in 2017[55]. Then there are the cases of Facebook users having their accounts suspended for no known valid reason, and therefore losing photographs, connections, and precious memories in the process[56]. Similarly, you can spend years establishing a social presence or brand on LinkedIn or Instagram, building a livelihood and a business around that presence, only to wake up one day and find that through a few keystrokes on the part of an administrator or the actions of an AI, that section of your life is gone.

Censorship of speech and books may be reprehensible. But think about censorship of one's very identity – now that is truly abhorrent.

These truths are not self-evident

In 2016, Allen listed ten principles of self-sovereign identity in what is now recognized as a seminal blog post on the concept of decentralized identity, and those principles are: existence, control, access, transparency, persistence, portability, interoperability, consent, minimalization, and protection. If you are going to provide a long list of things that should be considered, then having ten items in that list is definitely the sweet spot: Moses made sure of that back in the days when tablets were slabs of stone rather than touchscreen computing devices.

The ten principles made quite an impact on the identity community, and two subsequent publications, in particular, are worth considering when examining them: lifeID's "self-sovereign identity bill of rights"[57] that attempts to expand them into calls for action, and Michael Schutte's critique of them[58].

I did warn you that identity quickly gets wrapped up in academic arguments about philosophy and politics, but in the paragraphs that follow I will try my best to examine them in a practical everyday manner. Philosophy and politics are all very well for those who have both the time and the financial support to engage in them, but for the rest of us? We just want to live our own individual lives in a manner that minimizes the effort we have to put in to get through the day, achieve the goals we set for ourselves (either consciously or unconsciously) with as little fuss and bureaucracy as possible.

Fortunately, blockchain offers the possibility of eventually making that dream a reality, but we do have a lot of work and a lot of thinking on our hands before we get there.

1. Existence

Allen starts by stating that "users must have an independent existence", which lifeID extends to the requirement that "individuals must be able to establish their existence as a unified identity online and in the physical world". Schutte calls this out as a false assumption, in that it presents identity as an object rather than a continuous process.

My take on this is that practically speaking, you and I both know that you are you, and I am me. Unless one of us is an aspiring identity thief, we both want to live in a world where those identities are and always will be distinct. Only the correct individual should have access to the "things" that that person has earned – the house they live in, the car they drive, the qualifications they have gained, and the rights that those qualifications afford them. After all, we don't want to be operated on by a "surgeon" who has never held a scalpel, or a "taxi driver" who doesn't even have a driving license.

On a day to day basis we do not care about Heraclitus's observation that our personal identity is like a stream – the same flowing body of water, but different from second to second. We just want to get on with life knowing that we are dealing with the people we think we are. Reflections about our existence can be pondered on when we're old and grey and our kids are looking after themselves (and our grandchildren), or when we are teenagers and have enviable hours and days to spend agonizing about who we are (and possibly reading too much Jean-Paul Sartre if really precocious).

Furthermore, we want the distinction of identity to carry over from the real world into the digital world. It seems to me that anything that puts that distinction in jeopardy is bad, and anything that secures that distinction is good.

2. Control

Allen's second principle is that "users must control their identities". LifeID extends this to state in their bill of rights that "individuals must have the tools to access and control their identities". Schutte makes the point that controlling your identity is all about claims, namely assertions you can make about your identity: what your name is, when you were born, what qualifications you have attained, where you live, and so on.

However, most of these facts about your identity are attested by other parties. How are you going to control what other people say about you? Clearly, you can't. What you can do in a free self-sovereign environment is selectively present what claims were made about you, but this can only be achieved if you are in control of the representation of your identity and all the facts and attestations that accumulate around it.

I am guessing that this is what Allen meant by control, but it is not completely clear from his subsequent words, as he goes on to talk about choosing between celebrity and privacy.

The bigger question is about what baggage concerning your identity should be available to other parties, regardless of your personal preferences. You may want the control to prevent a potential employer from knowing about a prior criminal conviction, to hide a medical condition from an insurer, or your children from a previous marriage from a potential future partner. How much control should you be allowed to exercise over the persona you present to others?

Control is a tricky problem when it comes to trying to quantify it in any practical sense, and I have to confess that I do not have the answers.

3. Access

Allen states that "users must have access to their own data", and lifeID expands on this by explaining that "the platforms and protocols on which self-sovereign identities are built must be open and transparent". One side of this is, I would say, self-evident. If I don't have access to the data surrounding my online identity, and I can't see how the system that is handling it works, or who it is being handed to, and when, then it is not my own data.

Schutte goes on to point out that there is a flip-side, namely that "identity is in the eye of the beholder", and gives examples of personal observations made by one person about a second person that affect the way the second person's identity is perceived. The example given is seeing them slap a child, writing it in a paper notebook, and sharing that observation in private with someone else.

I take this to mean that there is not and can never be a clear-cut system for judging in every single case what data concerning my identity should be owned by me, and what data should not, and furthermore that there are some impracticalities that cannot be overcome.

If someone writes a review of my book in a language I do not speak on a private website I don't even know the existence of, under this "access" principle of self-sovereign identity should I really have the right to easily retrieve that review? Could the right to make such demands even put pressure on other people's freedom of speech?

4. Transparency

"Systems and algorithms must be transparent", says Allen. This is an extension of the previous principle, in that knowing that you will have access to your data means knowing how that data is stored, manipulated, and retrieved. LifeID goes one step further, stating that "users must have the right to participate in the governance of their identity infrastructure". Schutte then raises the point that the sheer quantity of data that this entails, and the amount of technical proficiency required to take advantage of such transparency (and presumably participation in governance) will be overwhelming to most people.

The same problem is seen in democratic systems where "one person, one vote" holds sway. Regardless of whether you are a lifelong researcher of political theory and economics, or totally uninterested in the governing of your nation, you get just one vote. Most of us do not have the time to fully research each and every political issue in depth, so we have systems in which we elect representatives who appeal to us on a broader level, and who are meant to make a career of representing us. The idea is that the system is transparent enough to minimize corruption and profiteering.

So really it is about auditability – the potential for anyone so inclined to examine parts of the system to check for malfeasance.

Personally, I see no problem with requiring that the protocols and source code for self-sovereign system are open source, freely available, and for anyone who wants to, to be able to participate in discussions on how they should be advanced and developed. I use plenty of open-source software that I do not examine. If I have a concern, then I might download the code and look at it, or more likely, check that someone whose opinion I respect has done so for me.

There is only so much time allotted to each of us, but it would be nice to know that the option of auditing the identity system you have to use and being able to influence its direction was there if you felt so inclined.

5. Persistence

When Allen says that "identities must be long-lived", he is addressing one of the most serious problems in the current online identity space (and indeed in the real world). It is not just that a central authority managing your identity can arbitrarily decide to "delete" you, but that companies and even nations are not guaranteed to continue to exist. LifeID specifies that "identities must exist for the life of the identity holder", but in actual fact, there may be a need for them to exist beyond that, for example for the benefits of the individual's descendants. Think here, for example, about royalties or the value of a personal brand built up around an individual.

6. Portability

Anyone who has moved banks, changed accountants, insurance providers, or domain name registrars, will know that such changes involve a lot of bureaucracy. This friction is used as an advantage by companies, as it provides lock-in. Allen states that "information and services about identity must be transportable", which a Google or Facebook account clearly is not.

In a system based on a blockchain every transaction, every interaction, and every credential could take the form of a data structure signed by the relevant party, so in principle, there is no need for such lock-in. It is a digital return to the concepts of degree certificates or letters of introduction.

At its simplest, for example, if a university has a known public key associated with its degree issuing department, and a graduate similarly has a public key, then the university can present the graduate with a digital file stating their subject, grade, date of conference, their name and their public key address, digitally signed with the university private key. If the digital degree certificate is encrypted by the university with the graduate's public key, the presentation can even be made on a public forum such as an open permissionless blockchain, and yet remain confidential. The graduate can then keep a backup copy on their own hard drive, or even print out a paper copy and store it in a filing cabinet (or if they are really odd, frame it and hang it on their wall). In any case, there is now a permanent unforgeable record of the degree on the blockchain.

7. Interoperability

"Identities should be as widely usable as possible", says Allen. Although at first this may appear to be a restatement of principle 6, portability, it takes that concept one step further. Portability covers the possibility of moving your digital identity from one system or platform to another – it is a form of translation. Interoperability, on the other hand, is either ensuring that systems conform to a standard (which is hard), or that portability translations can be performed on-the-fly.

Schutte raises the point that claims made in relation to an identity have context, and that in a cross-platform system there is a risk of a loss of meaning. Some facts about your identity, such as your age, may be reasonably clear-cut: proving on one system that you are over eighteen years old using credentials from another system should not cause too many problems for a decent software developer. However, when you expand the purpose of an identity system to include credit ratings, eligibility to pilot a light aircraft, or to provide evidence of no criminal record, an interconnected web of claims based around facts starts to form, and that web can grow in complexity fairly quickly. Especially if the requirement is to prove the non-existence on one system of a suspected claim on the other system, for example, the revocation of a driving license, or the absence of a criminal record.

Add in claims about reputation, such as professional or character references, and we are in the arena of the subjective, which adds a whole new dimension of complexity and uncertainty. Unless there is a way to construct a decentralized marketplace that uses the wisdom of crowds[59] to determine things such as how many "likes" on a Facebook post equate to one Amazon five-star review.

8. Consent

One of the main benefits of ownership is that you, as the owner, get to decide who is allowed to use your possessions. If you have a car, you can lend out the keys to a friend you trust, but random people off the street can't drive away in it. Obviously, if a self-sovereign identity is to be "owned" in some sense, then the owner should have control over it, and be required to provide consent when identity data and claims related to that identity are shared. Hence Allen presents principle 8, "users must agree to the use of their identity".

This is not going to sit well with the Googles and Facebooks of the world, who make significant profits from selling on the data and patterns of activity that we hand over to them for free in exchange for the services they provide. The intelligence agencies of the world are also presumably not that keen on the idea of encrypted personal data controlled by the subject of that data.

There is one significant problem with the requirement for consent, namely those occasions where an individual is legally required to disclose some information about themselves. Key disclosure laws, under which individuals are required to surrender cryptographic keys to law enforcement agencies, can be very broad and blunt in their application. In the United Kingdom, the Regulation of Investigatory Powers Act 2000 (part III)[60] does not even require a court order or warrant for government agencies to be able to demand that an individual hand over their decryption keys and failure to do so can result in a two-year prison sentence. Governments have long been able to seize physical property under asset forfeiture laws, and with self-sovereign identity, it appears identity forfeiture may become a reality.

9. *Minimalization*

The online representation of an identity will, over time, accumulate a lot of attributes, claims, and transaction histories. If all you are trying to do is buy a bottle of whiskey online, or digitally vote in an election, the party requesting identification does not need to know your exact birth date. A simple confirmation that you are old enough (and in the latter case, are a citizen of the relevant country) is enough. They certainly do not need to know your eye color, your online browsing history, or what you sold on eBay last week.

This is the idea behind minimalization, as defined by Allen: "disclosure of claims must be minimized". For once, Schutte agrees that it is indeed a good one.

However, as usual, there is a problem. As anyone involved in data forensics knows, no matter how careful you are about what you reveal, further information has a habit of leaking out. The analysis of patterns of transactions and times at which they occur can reveal a surprising number of additional facts that you may not want the world to know about. For example, Satoshi Nakamoto went to great lengths to hide their identity, but there are timestamps for code contributions and comments made on bulletin boards that suggest Nakamoto was living in an Eastern Standard Time zone[61].

10. Protection

At last, here we are at the final principle: "the rights of users must be protected". It has been quite a journey, and I can't help wondering why everything has to come in lists of three or ten. In any case, this principle deserves its own quotation, rather than including it in the body of a paragraph, as I did with the previous Allen references:

> *Where there is a conflict between the needs of the identity network and the rights of individual users, then the network should err on the side of preserving the freedoms and rights of the individual over the needs of the network.*
>
> — C. Allen[52]

This principle amuses me because it reminds me of Star Trek II: The Wrath of Khan[62]. Do the needs of the many outweigh the needs of the few or vice versa? It depends on each individual case, and probably on your own political perspective. But I do not read that Allen is proposing that the individual user's rights should *always* supersede those of the network, just that the balance should shift to favor the former over the latter in cases of doubt.

Of course, at the moment the user has no power whatsoever, other than to refuse to play the game in the first place.

But ... why blockchain?

Identity is heavily embedded in the foundations of blockchain. As previously stated, even for just a simple cryptocurrency it is necessary that not only "what" is owned is recorded, but also "who" owns it, and this is done in a secure manner through asymmetric key cryptography. Ownership of a private key means ownership of assets recorded on the ledger against the corresponding key, and such assets can include encrypted data, such as identity data or claims.

However, recording sensitive personal data on a public forum, such as a blockchain carries significant risks, even if the data is encrypted. Firstly, it cannot later be deleted, which goes against article 17 of the European Union's General Data Protection Regulation (GDPR)[63]. Secondly, even though data may start out encrypted, all it takes is one leak of the private key, and there is no longer protection.

It is, therefore, wiser to store personal data in a database, preferably still in an encrypted form. Publishing a hash of the data on the blockchain can then provide evidence that no tampering has taken place.

Similarly, identity transactions can be initiated on a blockchain through a transaction. Again, any personal data in response to the transaction making the request should be transmitted out of band, that is: definitely not on the public blockchain. But the blockchain can be used to set up such a channel of communication though, by sharing the location of the channel and a shared encryption key, all encrypted using the public key of the requester.

Privacy coins show the potential for blockchains to selectively reveal information. Although not exclusive to blockchain, techniques such as ring signatures and zero-knowledge proofs (which were discussed in the first chapter on Identity on page 83) allow challenges about claims and credentials to be met without sacrificing privacy.

An open permissionless blockchain that is open-source provides transparency as to how the system functions, and the opportunity for participation in governance.

Simply put, in principle blockchain ticks all the boxes. In practice? Well, that's another question.

Figure 14: An example of a false claim about the author, who was never arrested for a traffic violation as a young man.

Cryptocurrencies and the User Experience

> Cash them in and buy you all the things you need
> *Patti Smith, 1975[k]*

Cryptocurrencies are the first real successful use case for blockchain, and so it would be remiss of me to not examine them in detail. And so, in this chapter, I look at the problems faced by crypto-enthusiasts and developers in bringing cryptocurrency – this new form of money, or asset, or whatever you want to call it – to the general public.

Tales from the crypto

Bitcoin has been all over the media on many occasions in the last three or four years, so most people have heard of it. Some of them have even read about other cryptocurrencies, or possibly studied the topic of this book: blockchain, the underlying engine that makes cryptocurrencies work.

But for most people, the exposure is fairly limited. Bitcoin, Ether, Tether, Ripple, Bitcoin Cash, Link, Binance coin, Litecoin,

Dot, and Cardano: these are the top ten cryptocurrencies by market capitalization, together valued at about a third of a trillion dollars at the time of writing. That's more than three times the market capitalization of, for example, IBM.

So it's clear that over time they really have become a big deal. There are, however, hundreds more of these cryptocurrencies, and once you start counting the tokens that exist on the Ethereum blockchain and other public blockchains, the number becomes surprisingly huge. I would guess we are currently at many thousands.

No one person can fully understand them all or grasp the purpose (if there actually is one) of each and every one. And yet a dozen years ago *not a single one of them existed*. It certainly looks like some of them are here to stay for the long run, and more and more people are going to have to become familiar with them. They have become part of our financial landscape.

But why are there so many? What are they for?

It is the same story that we have with traditional currencies, with languages (human and programming), and even with religions. Humanity seems to embrace schisms and splits more readily than recombination and reunification.

Cryptocurrencies and blockchain tokens are no different.

The sum of the parts

The internet, peer-to-peer networks, cryptography, and numerous other computer inventions that I have talked about earlier have provided us with the tools to enable decentralized finance – transactions that do not require a bank or a credit card company to allow the exchange to happen, and that can even occur with far more automation than a simple direct debit or standing order.

As blockchain is a synthesis of all the aforementioned inventions, with all these surprising emergent properties, I believe it is set to take a central role in decentralized finance in general through these cryptocurrencies, tokens, and things called smart contracts (which are in effect the next generation of direct debits and standing orders and are discussed more in "Clever Covenants" on page 189).

However, as is always the case with new technology, the current state of cryptocurrencies means that there are plenty of risks for the average user. It is still easy to make mistakes and send vast sums of money to the wrong person, or even into the void. It is hard to make sense of what is actually going on.

For comparison: the first cars that were produced would be impossible to drive by today's motorists. It takes time for new inventions to mature, for flaws to be detected and fixed, for the interface between users and the technology to evolve, and most importantly: for a model to form in the minds of the average person that allows them to deal with the new technology.

In short, the user experience needs to mature. It's all about the audience. So, what is this "user experience", or UX as it's called by practitioners? Well, the clue is in the name:

> **user**: *someone who uses a product, machine, or service*
>
> **experience**: *something that happens to you that affects how you feel*
>
> *— the Cambridge Dictionary*[64]

The level of the experience depends on the skill set of the user. Something that is going to be used by software developers or IT systems administrators will look very different, and probably be a lot more complicated, than something that is going to be used by a trader, investor, or a company executive.

And it has to be even simpler and more reliable if it's for your eccentric bohemian aunt.

Think about the difference between the controls and dials on a motorcycle, and those found in the cockpit of a light aircraft. The former is much simpler than the latter because pilots are navigating in three dimensions, whereas motorcyclists are barely navigating in two.

Although far better than it was only two or three years ago, the cryptocurrency user experience is still terrible. Users are being faced with an aircraft cockpit when it should be more like a motorcycle (or a bicycle).

I have been looking at cryptocurrencies since late 2009, understand how blockchain works and how the mathematics that drives it is used, and yet I still feel like my heart is in my mouth any time I have to conduct a significant cryptocurrency transaction.

Intuitive models

Back to the car analogy: in the picture below you can see a dapper young Henry Ford in the late nineteenth century, sitting on his quadricycle, one of the first cars ever made. Note that the car does not have a steering wheel. Instead, it has a tiller, like a boat.

Figure 15: Ford on his Quadricycle in 1896

Early car makers had to invent the interface from scratch, and so there were many different attempts before we finally settled on the familiar steering wheel, gear stick, and the accelerator, brake, and clutch pedals (in a convenient CBA order).

The tiller lost out because it is counter-intuitive to most people: you pull it to the left to go right. A steering wheel makes more sense: you turn it to the right to go right.

Our children see us driving cars, and play driving games, so by the time they get behind the wheel of a real car they understand the model, which becomes so ingrained that the fact that it is a model is forgotten.

Or to put it another way: I want to go right, so I turn the steering wheel to the right, and the car turns to the right. Now that is simple.

Under the hood

However, hidden away beneath the bodywork of the car there are all sorts of mechanical things: the pinion gear turns clockwise, the rack moves to the left, the tie rods pull or push the steering arms to the left, and the wheels move clockwise around the kingpins.

Did you glaze over at that last sentence? I know I did while writing it. You don't need to know what pinion gears, racks, tie rods, steering arms, and kingpins are to make a car go in the direction you want. The interface hides all this from you, and decades of engineering ensure that (hopefully) things do not go wrong.

For example, the system is designed to ensure the wheels do not turn through ninety degrees, bringing you to a sudden, unexpected and unpleasant stop.

In the world of cryptocurrency, there is no generally understood mental model, and the hidden mechanics that make blockchain work on both a technical and social level still contain not just myriads of undiscovered bugs, but also plenty of interesting valid constructs that are counter-intuitive and can lead to all sorts of misconceptions or even disasters.

In short, you can crash, and have no idea what went wrong.

Familiar numbers

In the picture on the next page there are some numbers. Most, if not all, will be so familiar to you that seeing them will immediately conjure up images in your head. Because you encounter them regularly they are comfortable and not intimidating.

```
3782 8224 6310 0005

|||||||||||||||||||||||||||||
5000157024671

+1-800-273-8255
```

Figure 16: Some familiar numbers

Okay, I confess: I cheated a bit. By not just presenting the numbers, but also using clues that provide extra information as to what they are I primed your understanding. But that is kind of the point that I am trying to make:
- Credit card numbers use a very distinctive font and consist of four groups of four digits.
- Bar-codes have black and white lines above them, as well as the digits below, and they are on everything you buy in the supermarket which makes them very familiar.

- Phone numbers have a certain structure and use particular symbols such as + and - to group the digits.

Unfamiliar numbers

Now have a glance at the next three "numbers", which will probably look unfamiliar:

> 1Q2TWHE3GMdB6BZKafqwxXtWAWgFt5Jvm3
>
> 0C28FCA386C7A227600B2FE50B7CAE11EC86D3BF1FBE471BE89827E19D72AA1D
>
> element side kiss economy supply despair oxygen suggest banner remind strike wood

Figure 17: Some (probably) unfamiliar numbers

To begin with, they don't even look like numbers! They contain letters, but those letters encode the private and public keys of cryptocurrency systems. In computing (and mathematics), letters or even words can be used as numbers.

- The first number is a traditional public Bitcoin address, which is a bit like a bank account number.
- The second is a private key in hexadecimal format (that is, numbers in a format that are used by computers or would be used by people if they had sixteen fingers). Private keys are like PIN codes for your bank card, but they are much longer and therefore much harder to guess.
- And the third is a "seed phrase" for a cryptocurrency wallet program. You can think of that as a "master key" that allows you to generate as many cryptocurrency addresses as you like, each with its own public address and private key. If your software wallet is lost (for example, by dropping your phone into the ocean while photographing whales), the seed phrase can be loaded into a new copy of the wallet software on your new phone, and all your old addresses and their private keys can be recreated.

The failure of analogies

In the previous section, I sneakily slipped in a bunch of analogies, comparing cryptocurrencies to various banking concepts.

> ***analogy****: a comparison between things that have similar features, often used to help explain a principle or idea*
>
> *— the Cambridge Dictionary*[65]

We use analogies all the time. For example, a car is like a horse and cart, but the horse lives inside the cart and doesn't die if you don't feed it for a month. Analogies can be used to anchor the unfamiliar by linking it to the familiar.

The problem is that analogies are never exact, and as someone coming fresh to a new idea, you don't know which parts of the comparison are accurate and which are misleading.

What's in your wallet?

Let's start with "cryptocurrency wallet" – the software running on your desktop or mobile phone that handles your cryptocurrency addresses.

Now, some people may have something approximating the correct image in their minds, namely that the wallet is like that folded leather thing in your pocket, containing all your debit cards. Each card corresponds to a cryptocurrency address, and each card has its own PIN number.

That's sort of correct, but misses one essential point – in the old familiar system your bank or credit card provider is needed for you to be able to spend money. They can arbitrarily veto your transaction, which is not the case with cryptocurrencies.

But other people may look at that analogy, and think simply in terms of cash – a stack of ten, twenty, and hundred dollar bills folded up within the wallet. And that would be wrong. There is something much more subtle going on underneath. For starters, with cash, you don't need to know a password or private key in order to spend it.

And so a cryptocurrency wallet is kind of a combination of the two examples above, and a password manager to boot, and yet it's also something different. Furthermore, the "debit cards" in your cryptocurrency wallet are supposed to be "one use only" – although they don't have to be – with the balance left over credited to a new card spontaneously created within the wallet.

A lot of significant subtleties are missing in the wallet analogy.

Then there are those things described as "paper wallets" – a printout that has the public and private key of a cryptocurrency address on it. Again, wallet is a terrible name, because that piece of paper is more like a bearer bond. Suddenly you have reverted to something more similar to cash than plastic cards in sleeves, and yet the word "wallet" is used for this kind of instrument as well.

As soon as you start digging, the analogy breaks down. It is like the story of the blind men encountering an elephant for the first time, wherein each touches a different part and compares the animal to a snake, tree trunk, wall, rope, and a spear. They are all right in their own context, but wrong in comprehending the whole.

A cryptocurrency wallet is like an elephant – all the parts resemble something familiar, but the combination of those parts is a separate entity in its own right, and focusing just on one part will lead you astray.

The parable of the panicking cryptocurrency owner

A month ago I received a desperate message through LinkedIn from one of my business connections. He was using a "wallet custodian" – a website that purports to hold your bitcoins for you. You log on with a username and password and are presented with web pages that look exactly like a genuine cryptocurrency wallet.

However, the wallet custodian has control over your funds, not you. In that sense, they are more like a traditional bank, although not bound by as much (or indeed any) regulation to protect you.

Remember the saying from the chapter called "Passwords are the Worst"?

"Not your keys? Not your coins!"

What this means is that if you are not the only person to have the private key to your cryptocurrency address in your possession (or if you don't have it at all, but an exchange or wallet site does), then they are not truly under your control. If the website owner wants to abscond with your coins then they can. And good luck getting them back!

The site my connection was using did allow users to download the private keys to the addresses, but he found that they had locked him out and suspended his account, so he couldn't get in to do that. Here are some of his misconceptions. He didn't know that:

- his wallet had multiple Bitcoin addresses,
- each address had its own private key, and
- if you have the private keys you can still access your coins through a different software wallet, without having to use the intermediary of the wallet custodian.

In an ideal world, he shouldn't have to know all of this, but we're not in that ideal world yet.

The engineer and the aristocrat

Back in the early days, say the 1880s or so, the motor car was the preserve of enthusiastic engineers. Somewhat later around the turn of the 20th century, when you didn't have to manufacture parts yourself and cars arrived in complete (if somewhat unreliable) packages, wealthy enthusiasts and aristocrats became involved.

With cryptocurrencies, we are now in the equivalent of cars in the 1930s. The era of mass production is well and truly here, but ... you still need to know how to maintain your vehicle yourself. The airbags, seat belts, and traction controls of the cryptocurrency world should arrive sometime in the not too distant future though.

In the meantime, if you are going to get involved in cryptocurrency and blockchain, you will have to look under the hood and get your hands greasy a bit more than may seem comfortable.

And if you crash, it's guaranteed to be painful.

Model transference

Last week I bought a ride-on mower (i.e. a quadricycle that cuts grass) and to my consternation, I discovered that the controls it had were not like those of a car. Instead of a clutch pedal and a brake, those two functions were wrapped up into one single pedal. How on earth was I supposed to control this machine?

Well, it took me about a minute to work it out. Push the pedal about half-way down, and it works like a clutch to allow you to change gears. Push it all the way down, and it works like a brake. And that's kind of what I do in my car anyway, just with two feet instead of one. Problem solved.

The ingrained model that I had for driving could be transferred quickly from the car to the mower. Within a few minutes I was driving around the garden, cutting the grass, and within half an hour my internal driving model had adapted to comprise the subtle differences of ride-on mowers.

We need similar models and analogies for cryptocurrency software before the non-experts out there in the world can deal quickly and efficiently with the new world that blockchain is opening up.

And looking at the history of other game-changing innovations, I am sure we will get there. But it will take time, and there will be many mistakes and many misconceptions to deal with along the way.

So for now, if you decide to invest in cryptocurrencies: you have to be careful and do your own research. In the future, all those technology and usability experts will have sorted it all out for you, but as of the end of 2020, we are not quite there yet.

The Network Effect

> No reply oh can't you see
> No reply it's ruining me
> *Peter Shelley, 1978[i]*

The author and prolific correspondent P. G. Wodehouse once revealed that he never posted his mail. After sticking a stamp on the letter he claimed he would then toss it out of the window, safe in the knowledge that "someone always picks it up, and it saves me going down four flights of stairs every time I want to mail a letter"[66]. Some people think that Wodehouse was relying on the basic decency of post-war British citizens (and it certainly ties in nicely with the world he created in his novels featuring bumbling aristocrats and sly butlers), but I think there is something deeper going on, and that deeper thing has something to do with networks.

Blockchains run on decentralized peer-to-peer computer networks. Now, if there is one group of people in the world who truly and instinctively understand the power of the network it is salespeople. Oh, and business development people, politicians, and journalists. And Freemasons, the more clued-up alumni of elite schools and universities, and former members of the military. So that's seven groups. There are probably at least seven more that I could list if I felt inclined to look further. To all members of such networks, much of this chapter is going to seem intuitively obvious.

The rest of us are, strangely enough, a bit in the dark about the social power of networks, especially those of us attracted to engineering, science, and mathematics.

We all know from a very early age what those networks are – pretty much everyone has a family, a group of friends, and possibly even work colleagues in their personal network, along with their Facebook, Instagram, and LinkedIn friends. However, many of us don't know what these networks are *about* or spend any time thinking about the underlying significance of what is going on in them. We certainly don't ponder on how we can use those social networks in any kind of productive way. They are just there, and we drift about in them obliviously.

So let me put it bluntly: the fundamental power of a network lies in the fact that you can leverage the skills and resources of that network, and furthermore, you can amplify the power of those skills and resources by tapping remote members, even if you don't know each individual on the network personally.

Engineers do not pay enough attention to social networks, because they don't think about resources enough (those are the things that, if they are lucky enough to have a job, appear as if by magic on request when they ask their employer for them. On the proviso that they are doing a job that is considered of value). It is something I wish I had known about decades ago, and it is a strange discrepancy, because technically speaking, engineers understand the methods of communication that networks function on very well. They just don't understand the value that is carried over those networks.

To put it in clearer terms for software engineers – there is a big difference between going to the developer sitting next to you in the office and asking, "Can you explain polymorphism in the Python programming language to me?", and saying, "Do you know someone who can explain polymorphism in the Python programming language to me?". The former question will probably either get you a "no", or a half-baked explanation that makes no sense unless you're lucky enough to sit down next to someone who really understands the question and the answer in-depth. The latter may actually get you a thirty-minute one-on-one with the company expert on object-oriented programming.

As engineers we are used to determining the focus of a question we have, identifying to the best of our ability within the network we have who can answer that question, and approaching them and only them.

True networkers ask open, exploratory questions. That's why they say things like "Is there anyone you know who needs blockchain consultancy?" rather than "Do you need a blockchain consultant?"

The worst network diagram ever

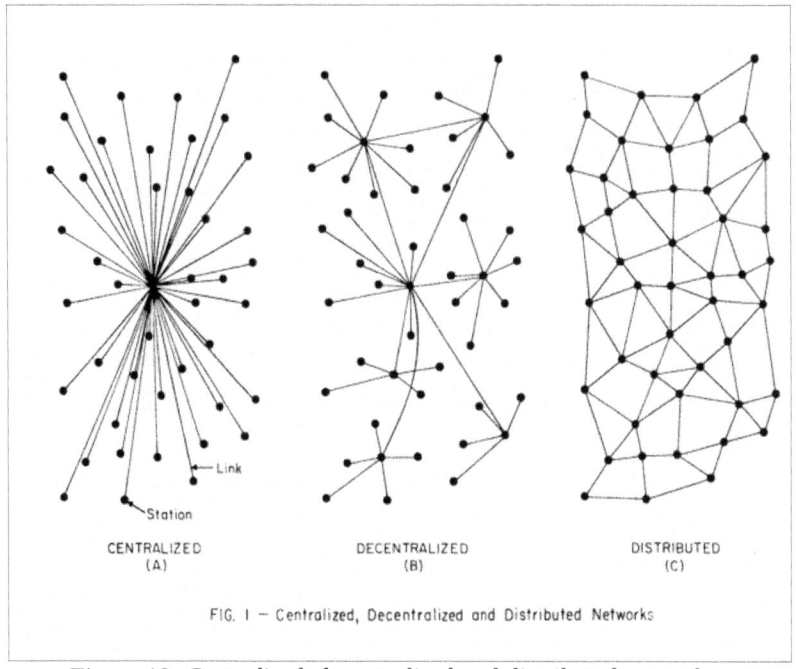

Figure 18: Centralized, decentralized and distributed networks

Back in 1964, Paul Baran drew a simple diagram to explain different kinds of networks[67]. In recent years it has been cropping up in all sorts of blockchain publications, again and again, in order to explain decentralized and distributed networks. As is usually the case, most of the re-posters have not actually bothered to go to the source to find out what the real meaning of the diagram actually is.

It's actually not a bad diagram in and of itself, but back in 1964 the concept of decentralization was still being investigated, and was very different (and even more revolutionary) than it is today. So it is that middle image in figure 18 that causes all the problems.

Looking at Baran's diagram makes me think of that fascinating, colossal, marvelous, and ultimately pointless work by Russell and Whitehead, the *Principia Mathematica*[68], in which two of the greatest mathematicians, logicians, and philosophers attempted to formalize all of logic and mathematics (even "proving" on page 379 that 1+1=2). Hopefully, Baran spent less effort than that on his paper.

What is the core of the problem I have with this diagram? It is the fact that it is mixing up two different concepts in one image – centralization versus decentralization, and distributiveness versus ... erm ... un-distributiveness? Concentratedness? And there is the second problem – most people think the opposite of distributed is centralized.

In a centralized network, there is a "server", which receives requests from "clients" and responds to them. You can imagine this as a guru sitting on a hill, with all the knowledge of the world at her disposal, and disciples approaching the guru, asking questions, and getting answers.

This is how most of the web works – your browser is the client, the webserver is (as its name suggests) the server, and you ask the question and get the answer. The server may occasionally get extra information from a client to pass on to other clients but is ultimately the central authority holding and distributing the "single view of the truth".

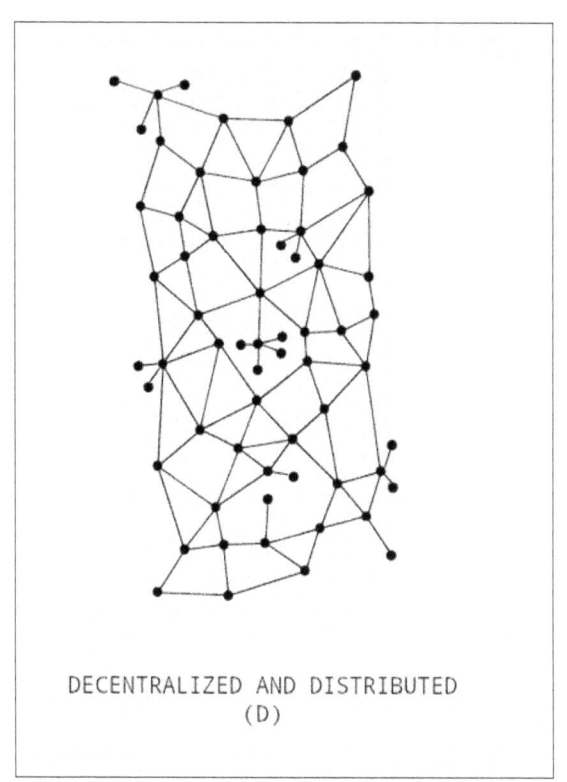

Figure 19: Decentralized distributed network

In a truly distributed system, on the other hand, there are no real clients and servers. Or perhaps a better view is that every node is both a client and a server. Each node in the network can both ask questions and respond with answers.

The key point in a distributed network is that if the node asked doesn't know the answer, it forwards the question onward to other nodes, who then forward it further, and so on, until there is a node that responds, and the answer trickles back to the original questioner.

Similarly, if one node received some external information (for example a submitted transaction, or because it finds a new block), it broadcasts this to its local connections, who broadcast it onward to their connections, and so on, until eventually, every node has the information. In that respect, peer-to-peer node communication is very similar to the way gossip or a common cold spreads around a community. There is even a peer-to-peer communication protocol called Gossip[69], the name of which I suppose reflects that very principle.

In practice, distributed networks have decentralized elements and vice versa, as shown in figure 19.

Blockchains and networks

As stated before, a blockchain runs on top of a peer-to-peer network. If you are going to provide a system that is decentralized in any meaningful sense of the word, that is how it has to be. That doesn't mean that anybody can walk in off the street and join your network – you can have entry requirements – but if there is one entity that is superior to all the others, then it is not an open permissionless blockchain, it is a centralized system.

Permissioned blockchains (the current blockchain structure of choice for companies) face a problem with monotonous regularity – the autocratic node.

I think this is down to the way that our corporate systems have evolved. Companies have taken their playbook from the military, which in turn is based on medieval feudal systems. A command-and-control structure is built into pretty much every formal environment that we are familiar with. We may dress it up in democratic elections or other popularity contests, but from our home lives (in which our parents were autocratic rulers) to school, through to our jobs and the very foundations of the country we live in, there are people who are in roles of authority and who have the power to make decisions that affect us deeply.

The handshake problem

For those not familiar with the Netherlands, here is an interesting cultural fact about the habits of people living there: when you arrive at an adult birthday party, you congratulate everyone present in turn on the birthday of the host, and not just the person whose birthday it actually is. Even the Dutch will readily admit that this is true and that it's the weirdest thing.

So, strange cultural habits aside, the question is: if a party has N people arriving one after the next like the dwarves at Bilbo Baggins's hobbit hole, how many felicitations will there actually be?

There are a number of ways to answer that question, and some of them are more efficient than others. Unfortunately, the efficient ways are not necessarily the easiest to understand or the most illuminating. So let's start with a simple approach:

- The host doesn't congratulate herself.
- The first guest arrives. We have two people, and one congratulation is uttered.
- The second guest arrives and congratulates the first guest and the host. So that's 2, plus the one previously given.
- The third guest arrives, and congratulates the first and second guest, and the host, so that's 3, plus the previous 2 and 1.
- Now we can see a pattern. When the Nth guest arrives, the total becomes $N + (N-1) + \ldots + 3 + 2 + 1$.

That's easy enough to total up. If there are five guests invited, that means there are going to be six people present (don't forget to count the person whose birthday it is). Plug $N = 5$ into the formula we just came up with, and you get $5 + 4 + 3 + 2 + 1 = 15$. That's just about small enough to do in your head by imagining the guests arriving, putting a different face to each one, and counting each congratulation in your head.

But what if it was a really popular birthday with a hundred guests – is there a simpler way?

The first person in recorded history to solve the problem in a more efficient way is also one of the most famous mathematicians in history, and the surprising thing is that a) he was a schoolboy when he did so, and b) that it was as late as 1784. Johann Carl Friedrich Gauss was born in 1777 and died in 1855, and has been described as "the greatest mathematician since antiquity". He was seven when he came up with a simple formula to sum the first N counting numbers in your head.

I think it's easier to demonstrate how Gauss derived his formula visually. Numbers of the form *N + (N – 1) + … + 3 + 2 + 1* are called triangle numbers because – well, look:

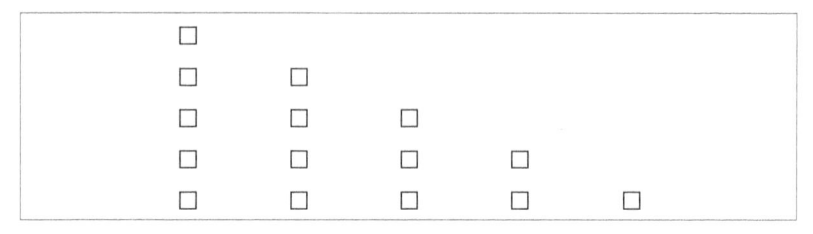

Figure 20: The sum of the first 5 numbers

If we have our triangle number twice, we end up with a diagram like this:

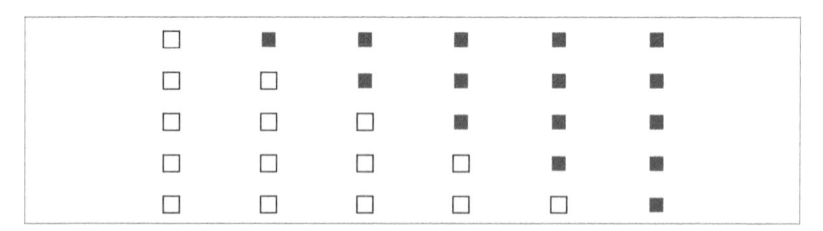

Figure 21: The sum of the first 5 numbers represented twice

I've represented the sum of the first five numbers once with white boxes, and once with black boxes, and so we end up with a rectangle that's 5 boxes high, and 6 boxes wide. So there are 6 × 5 boxes in total.

That shows us that *(5 + 4 + 3 + 2 + 1) × 2 = 5 × 6*. Or rearranging it a bit, *5 + 4 + 3 + 2 + 1 = (5 × 6)/2*.

Generalizing, we see that the sum of the first *N* numbers will be:

$$\frac{(N)(N+1)}{2}$$

So at a Dutch birthday party where a hundred guests have been invited, there will be 100 × 101 / 2 = 5050 birthday congratulations. That's a lot of people saying "Gefeliciteerd!"

At this point, you may have a couple of questions. The first one is probably, "why am I talking about people congratulating each other at a birthday party?"

The answer is because it demonstrates the quadratic growth (a fancy mathematical way of saying at a squared rate) of connections in a network as the number of nodes increase. Party guests are like nodes on a network, and the congratulations uttered are like connections between the nodes. This is variously known as "the network effect", or "Metcalfe's law" – the effect of a network is proportional to the square of the number of connected users of the system[71]. And now you know why it's square, and not exponential.

The second question may well be, "why did you title this section 'the handshake problem'?"

Normally the problem is posed as follows: "A hundred people turn up to a business meeting, and they all shake hands. How many handshakes are there?"

Personally, I find birthdays more fun than business meetings, and in any case, due to Covid-19, many of the business people won't be shaking hands anyway.

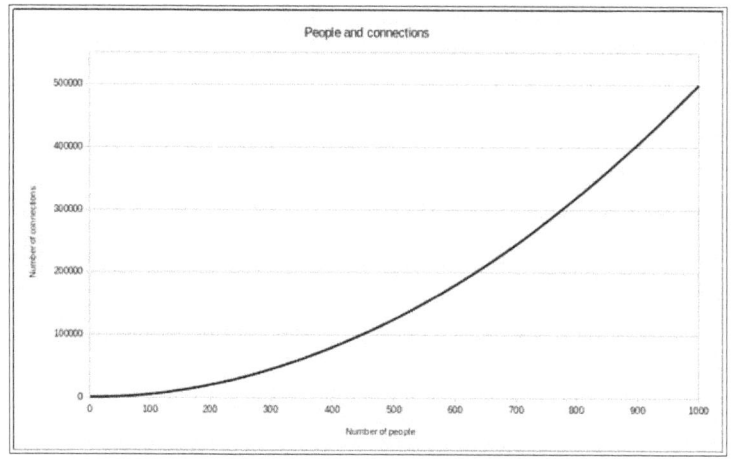

Figure 22: Quadratic growth of network connections

The birthday paradox

Speaking of birthdays, what are the chances that two of the guests will have been born on the same day and month? This question may not appear directly relevant to networks, but it uses some of the same principles I talked about in the previous section, and also helps you understand the worry about "collisions" mentioned in the earlier chapter about cryptographic hash functions (I told you they would keep turning up in unexpected places). There is even a term in cryptography – the birthday attack – which uses precisely this principle.

The thing about the birthday paradox is that it's not really a paradox – rather, it's a problem with a counter-intuitive answer. When the question is asked, our natural response is to rephrase the question into "what is the chance that someone has the same birthday as me". So our gut feeling is that it should be about one in 365, as there are 365 days in most years. We'll forget about leap years to keep things simple.

However, when you have a group of people, you need to compare each person's birth date with every other person's in order to determine if there's a match. So from the previous paragraph, we can calculate how many comparisons there are going to be. Let's say there are 22 people at the party. From our formula, that's:

$$\frac{22 \times 23}{2} = 253$$

Two hundred and fifty-three comparisons are a lot more than the initial gut feeling of twenty-two.

If you want to dig further into the mathematics behind the birthday paradox, there is an excellent Wikipedia page on it[72].

Erdős numbers

I mentioned very early on in the book that I would talk about Erdős numbers[70]. People unfamiliar with mathematics and mathematicians, but familiar with movies may know of them as Bacon numbers, in which the same idea is applied to the actor Kevin Bacon. However, Erdős numbers pre-date Bacon numbers by about a quarter of a century.

To have an Erdős number you have to either be Paul Erdős (who is defined as having an Erdős number of 0), or have co-authored a paper, mathematical or otherwise, with someone who has an Erdős number, in which case your number will be one greater than your co-author. Similarly, to have a Bacon number you either have to be Kevin Bacon (who has a Bacon number of 0), or have acted in a movie with someone who has a Bacon number (in which case your number will be one greater than your co-actor).

For example, I mentioned earlier that I have an Erdős number of six. This is because of the following connections:

6. Keir Finlow-Bates co-authored a paper with

5. Stephen Lerman, who co-authored with

4. Anna Sierpińska, who co-authored with

3. Jan Krempa, who co-authored with

2. Richard Wiegandt, who co-authored with

1. Ervin Fried, who co-authored with

0. Paul Erdős, who has an Erdős number of 0.

The median Erdős number is 5, which correlates well with the common public perception of "six degrees of separation", namely that almost everyone in the world is connected to everyone else by a chain of at most six acquaintances.

What do Erdős numbers teach us? That the value of immediate connections in a network may be more apparent, but that there is a whole world of further connections hiding behind them, sitting there, just waiting to help you.

On Value

> I'm waiting for my man,
> Twenty-six dollars in my hand
> *Lou Reed, 1967[m]*

I want to get one of my personal axioms out in the open at the very start of this chapter:

I believe that "value" is a purely psychological property.

Doesn't sound too controversial, does it? Yet I have had numerous arguments with people on LinkedIn about this very same assumption. They may say that they accept that value, like beauty, is all in the eye of the beholder, but their subsequent actions and statements belie this. The "tell" is always in their use of the word "inherent" or "intrinsic", especially when it occurs before the word "value".

When it comes to value, I think that emotions start to become involved. If someone perceives something as being valuable, they start to feel desire, excitement, and possibly even greed. They become emotionally attached, and over time, start to believe that this value they perceive is some kind of absolute built-in property of the item in question. How could anybody not feel the same way they do?

I see it in my kids all the time. A new toy, game, or gadget appears on their radar, and it becomes all they can think about and talk about for weeks.

Now I'm not going to claim that feeling strong emotions about inanimate objects or immaterial concepts is necessarily a bad thing. Getting all fired up about something can provide you with the drive and determination to explore, understand, and then possibly even improve and enhance (or profit from) whatever it is that has grabbed your attention this week, month or year.

To draw another punk music analogy – it's fine to use your emotions to write songs, but you have to make damned sure you've rehearsed them again and again until you can perform them competently before you get up on stage and start thrashing them out to the crowd.

Elementary, my dear Watson

I have reproduced a carefully selected portion of the periodic table of elements on the next page.

As you will see when you turn it over, elements such as gold (Au), platinum (Pt) and silver (Ag) have an atomic mass, electronic charge valances that they can take, and a known number of protons at their nucleus.

Each and every atom also has a location in space, and velocity (although thanks to the Heisenberg principle we can't work both out accurately at the same time), but as you can see there is no field in the period table for "value".

Value is something that only exists in the minds of people.

What's more, value is not absolute across different human beings – it varies from person to person, over time, and depending on the situation. Water, when you are stuck in a desert dying of thirst, has more value in that circumstance than if you are living next to a freshwater reservoir.

28 +2 **Ni** Nickel 58.693	29 +2,+1 **Cu** Copper 63.546	30 +2 **Zn** Zinc 65.38
46 +4,+2 **Pd** Palladium 106.42	47 +1 **Ag** Silver 107.868	48 +2 **Cd** Cadmium 112.414
78 +4,+2 **Pt** Platinum 195.085	79 +3 **Au** Gold 196.967	80 +2,+1 **Hg** Mercury 200.592
110 unk **Ds** Darmstadtium [269]	111 unk **Rg** Roentgenium [272]	112 unk **Cn** Copernicium [277]

Figure 23: A section of the periodic table

Secondly, value is comparative. One thing is more or less valuable in comparison to another thing. There's a very simple test: take two objects (say, a car and a house) and decide which one you would rather have if you were only allowed to pick one. That's the one that is more valuable to you. Someone other than you might make the opposite choice – in that case, the other object is more valuable to them. Houses are of no use if you desperately want to go somewhere else. Cars are inferior to houses if you and your family want somewhere safe and warm to sleep.

Finally, value is transitive (with some transaction losses). If you know or suspect that someone values or might value an object, it has value to you too, because you may be in a situation to trade it with them for something you want more. But there are three issues: the opportunity for a trade is not guaranteed (reducing the value of the object to you), there may be expenses associated with storing the object until you can trade it, and trading has a cost – in time spent if nothing else – further reducing the value of the object to you.

So why am I going on about value? Because, as I said, in my experience the Internet is full of people who think that things have value in and of themselves.

Next, let's look at price. In "The Picture of Dorian Gray", Oscar Wilde wrote, "Nowadays people know the price of everything and the value of nothing"[73]. The concept of "price" is simply a way of putting a number on value to make it easier to perform comparisons between different valuations. The point that Wilde is making, is that if you are only thinking about price, you are forgetting the purpose of pricing – namely quantifying value.

With pricing, at best you can perform a statistical valuation on something – people in Finland, as of today, seem to think that 1.50€ is a reasonable price for a kilo of bananas and that 1.00€ is reasonable for a kilo of onions. So we can conclude from that, that bananas are generally considered 50% more valuable than onions. Unless that is, you desperately want to cook onion soup.

And this is why I find statements such as the following to be thought-provoking, but ultimately meaningless:

Gold has intrinsic value

Gold has uses in electronic circuitry, scientific experiments conducted in laboratories, and presumably quite a few other practical cases that I am not aware of because I am not a chemist or industrial engineer. So gold has some *utility* to us. But the price of gold does not correlate with any of these. We have a lot more gold stored in vaults than we would ever need for industrial purposes.

The main contribution to the value of gold is the fact that people have faith in it having value, and therefore use it as a store of other value. People are Tolkienesque dragons in this respect. Gold attained this status as a store of value long before it had any utility. It was just stuff that people found lying around and thought was pretty and scarce.

Note that being shiny, malleable, and durable, and hence used in jewelry is not a practical application – it is an expression of people signaling wealth (or possibly their marital status in some cultures). Doing so may have value to them, but it is certainly not an intrinsic property of gold. Gold is just gold. It doesn't care that we find it pretty or get excited because it's scarce. The price that we put on a kilo of gold is a collective illusion bolstered by thousands of years of history.

The euro has inherent value because it is backed by the European Central Bank[74]

Feel free to swap out the words "euro" and "European" for the currency and central bank of your choice.

I have never met anyone who thought that euros were valuable because they were "backed" by the European Central Bank, but then again I have never met a central banker in person. Actually, in everyday life in Europe, I have met very few people who even knew that there was such a thing as the European Central Bank and less who cared.

My former neighbor, a hard-working Finnish taxi driver, cares about euros because he gets paid in them by his passengers, and can then use them to cover his mortgage, electricity and water bills, and use the remainder to buy food from the local supermarket in order to feed his family. If he has a good year and there isn't a pandemic going on, he can use them to take a holiday to the Canary Islands. He doesn't ponder on the topic of the European Central Bank and its connection to the euro for a moment. He would probably be more impressed if the euro was backed by his favorite Finnish band (they're called *Eppu Normaali,* and started out playing punk music).

As far as I am concerned, the euro has value because people around me think it has value. If, for whatever reason, they no longer think that, then they will start trading with gold, rare seashells, or squirrel skins instead. Which will also only have value because people think they do. Note the use of the word "think" in the preceding two sentences.

This statement is almost meaningful:

The dollar has inherent value because it is backed by the United States military

If I am stronger than you, and for some perverse reason give you an ugly glass vase and tell you that you are to protect it, and that if I find out that it is broken at some point in the future then I will administer a severe beating to you, and furthermore, if you believe me, well … then you are going to look after it.

As such it will have "value" to you – but that value is not intrinsic (a fundamental property of the vase). The vase, in and of itself, has no value. It's ugly, so no one wants it. It is the continuation of the existence of the vase in one piece that has value to you. It is a value that has somehow been created and subsequently adheres to the vase. I could equally have given you a seashell, or a candle-stick, or a letter. How can it be that these different objects end up having the same inherent value? Because inherent isn't intrinsic – it flies in from the outside due to some kind of understanding between the different parties who are valuing the vase and sticks to it.

So the difference is that "intrinsic value" means the value resides in the object itself (and this applies both to real objects and virtual objects), and "inherent value" is value that is associated with the object due to circumstances outside of the object, but somehow gets attached to it. Does that sound like rigorous economics to you, or is it rather social psychology, or even philosophy?

The only place where I see the terms "intrinsic value" having any kind of sensible meaning is purely from an accounting point of view: if, for example, a contract has a payout of $100 and costs $10 to set up, then the contract has an intrinsic value of 90$. Even under that interpretation, saying that gold, or the euro, or the dollar has intrinsic value is meaningless. Gold has a market price, but it does not have an intrinsic value, even under the accounting definition. Dollars and euros have a comparative price, but their value lies purely in what they can get you – food, a roof over your head, and perhaps a bit of enjoyment in life.

Food and shelter. Now those have intrinsic value (or do they?), but unfortunately the former is perishable, and the latter is difficult to carry around and barter with. And that's why we allocate "value" to other things instead. It's about portability, fungibility, unforgeability, ease of determining authenticity, and ultimately it's about a circular faith in the faith of others assigning the same value to things that we do.

Where does the money come from?

I mentioned earlier that I would talk about the method whereby money, cryptocurrency, or tokens are created. It is necessary for this stuff to come into existence somehow, and there are a number of different ways to go about it, some of which are more sophisticated than others. If only it was all as simple as finding a gold nugget on a river bed.

Firstly, I would like to look at how money is currently created in our financial systems. It is truly the most amazing and brazen accountancy trick ever pulled.

Another use for the Gutenberg press

I will begin with cash – paper money – for which making more is very easy indeed. You simply print it using a printing press and then find some way to distribute it. In fact, it is so easy to produce paper money that counterfeiters have been doing so for centuries, and have developed all sorts of techniques for introducing it into society. There are plenty of movies out there showing you how.

For the central banks it is even simpler because they can't be prosecuted for doing what the counterfeiters do, even though the methodology is identical.

Generally speaking though, the central bank runs the printing presses (or a subsidiary organization does so on their behalf), they stack the bills onto pallets and ship them off to the high street banks. The balance at the central bank of each high street bank accepting notes is reduced by an equivalent amount, and those notes can then be passed on to the customers through ATMs.

Those days will soon be over because cash is on the way out.

The banking shell game

For fiat currency within the ledger-based and subsequently digital accounting systems of governments and banks, the traditional method for the initial creation of money occurs mainly through two intertwined long-established processes. I am just summarizing below and glossing over a lot of the subtleties and regional differences because I do not want to bore you with a thirty-page thesis on monetary policy and financial systems.

The central bank can create more money at will, or rather at a computer key-stroke, but if they do so they have to get it into the economic system. There are two main methods used to achieve this. One is when the government borrows the made-up money from the central banks by selling them government bonds, with the promise of repaying it later (usually with interest, although amusingly there are now "zero yield bonds"), and with repayment backed by the expectation of future money raised through taxation. Bonds are basically the government borrowing some or all of the foreseen profits of future gross domestic production to be able to spend them now. That puts some of the made-up money into the economy, because governments like to spend on real stuff like building bridges, roads, and hospitals. They also hand out benefits that are then used by people to purchase food and rent somewhere to live, which also keeps the economy moving.

The central bank also shifts a lot of the made-up money to banks, either by lending it to them, allowing them to buy reserves in the central bank with other assets, or even selling on the bonds they got from the government and then buying them back again. Banks like using existing reserves, because their assets and liabilities stay the same – they are exchanging rather than building up their debts.

So how do banks get the cash to buy bonds or other assets that they can then use to obtain more cash from the central bank? The banks produce loans that you or I take out in order to buy a house or fund our latest start-up. They are allow to lend out much more than they own because the loans are backed by only a fraction of the deposits and the value of the bonds the banks hold. This multiplies the initially created supply, and gets the money into the real economy in the process.

And the central bank controls the rate at which all this happens by setting the fractional reserve limit, which equates almost directly to a multiplier on the cash they originally created.

In summary, in the real world money is created out of thin air, and most of it is in the form of numbers in accounting spreadsheets and bank databases, not tangible rectangles of printed paper. And there is a further problem. If you are responsible for the creation of the money supply and borrowing from the future to kick-start it: when the future finally arrives, due to the interest you are charged on the debt you have used, there is guaranteed not to be enough money in the monetary supply to pay it back[75].

Magical internet money

I have had quite a few discussions with people who are unhappy about the fact that cryptocurrency blockchains allow the creation of money out of thin air, oblivious to the fact that our everyday money is created from precisely the same stuff. And I actually have no problem with either situation – money does not need to "be valuable", it needs to "store value". There are good arguments to be made that the best money actually has no real value in and of itself. If the community using it has come to a common understanding of what is to be used as money, consciously or sub-consciously, then it can fulfill its purpose.

Stating that conventional money is backed by the military power of a nation, or a central bank misses the key point of modern finance. It is not about kings or emperors raising armies and seizing gold anymore. It is an accounting trick and a very effective one at that. Blockchain money uses a different trick.

In the various blockchains out there, a number of alternate mechanisms for generating cryptocurrency are available. The most well-known is the "block reward" introduced by Bitcoin, in which by successfully mining the next data block of transactions for the blockchain, the miner gets to create some cryptocurrency as a pay-out for their effort.

In other blockchains, the founders simply create all the coins in the very first block for themselves and then hand them out as and how they see fit – usually through airdrops to try to encourage others to see value in the project too. Personally, I am not so impressed by the second approach, but it has made a few people very wealthy. I hope they use their wealth wisely.

Bartering is inefficient

Let's take a step back, and look at money and stores of value from a historical perspective. Back in the bad old days, people had to barter goods because there was no money. On the next page is a list of items from the Dungeons & Dragons Players Manual[76] in a bartering table, allowing goods of one type to be exchanged for good of another type. The number in each cell shows you how many items from the top row you require to obtain an item from the first column.

	Backpack	Holy Symbol	Lantern	Standard Rations	Rope	Large Sack	Mirror
Backpack	1	0.2	0.5	1	5	2.5	1
Holy Symbol	5	1	2.5	5	25	12.5	5
Lantern	2	0.4	1	2	10	5	2
Standard Rations	1	0.2	0.5	1	5	2.5	1
Rope	0.2	0.04	0.1	0.2	1	0.5	0.2
Large Sack	0.4	0.08	0.2	0.4	2	1	0.4
Mirror	1	0.2	0.5	1	5	2.5	1

Figure 24: A bartering matrix of comparative values of items

So, for example, if you want a backpack, and you have a number of large sacks, you can trade two and half large sacks to get a backpack. Or in practice, you'll have to hand over three, because who wants half a sack?

It is a pain in the neck to memorize this simple bartering table, even though there are some efficiencies – for example, the diagonal is always 1 (a lantern is worth one lantern), and similarly numbers at (x,y) in the table are 1 divided by the number at (y,x).

However, there are further complications. For example, what if you have some mirrors, and you want a lantern, but the trader with the lantern doesn't want a mirror? You may have to trade two mirrors for ten lots of rope and then trade the rope for the lantern. So now you have to know the relative value of mirrors, lanterns, and rope!

Finally, imagine if, instead of seven items, you had a list of a hundred items. Now you need to memorize a matrix with 10,000 entries. And although I have been unable to find a reliable source, there are indications that Amazon at the time of writing advertises over 10 million products on their site. So that would require at least a hundred trillion entries for the exchange matrix.

Even though there aren't that many things you can buy and own in Dungeons & Dragons, just like real life it generally eschews bartering. It uses money instead, in the form of gold pieces. Turn the page to see the actual price table.

Item	Cost (in gold pieces)
Backpack	5
Holy symbol	25
Lantern	10
Standard Rations	5
Rope	1
Large Sack	2
Mirror	5

Figure 25: A price table

That is a lot simpler and quicker to use than a bartering matrix and carries exactly the same information.

Dungeons and Dragons gold pieces are being used as money here – things that have no value in and of themselves, as you can't use these game coins for anything other than buying stuff in the game. Instead, they are acting as a unit of account to get around the problems of bartering, and they also work as a store of value, because you do not have to spend them immediately. When you are playing the game you can hold on to them until you have enough to buy that double-handed broadsword you've always had your eye on.

Fixed prices

In the Western world, we are used to walking into a shop and paying the price written on the label or tag next to the product that we want. Very few people would think of making their way to the checkout counter at Walmart or Tesco and begin bargaining with the cashier over the price of a tin of beans. Fixed prices are, however, a relatively recent phenomenon[77]. Anyone who has tried to buy souvenirs in a shop in Hurghada, Egypt, or Sousse, Tunisia will quickly discover that bargaining is an art that requires practice. I remember sitting on an airplane back from Tunis, and two women seated behind me were comparing identical handbags that they had purchased. Everything was fine until one found out that she had paid ten times the price the other had, and then spent the rest of the journey sitting there with a very sour look on her face.

Bargaining is a form of bartering intermediated by money. And although your local supermarket may have fixed prices, they are effectively bargaining on your behalf against the other supermarkets in the neighborhood in order to obtain your custom, which is why the prices in different shops vary.

We tend to think that price is determined by valuation: cost plus reasonable profits. But what are "reasonable profits"? The margins on various goods vary tremendously, as the percentage profit on an iPhone is substantially higher than that on a bag of flour. On commodity goods, the profits tend towards zero, whereas branded products and unique items can support much higher gains.

Ultimately price is discovered by putting goods or products on the market, and seeing what the buyers are willing to pay. That expensive handbag that the woman on the airplane bought was priced at a level that she was happy with at the time. It is only in retrospect that she became unhappy, and as she is unlikely to ever return to the store she got it from, the vendor did well out of the exchange.

Even though they are essentially just pieces of paper, we sure feel sad when we hand over more banknotes than we need to.

Rounding up

What is truly remarkable about Bitcoin is that it has become a significant store of value with many similarities to gold in merely ten years, purely through word of mouth, or rather through the peer-to-peer network. Normally it takes a large nation with a lot of natural resources and a significant army to be able to conjure up a financial tool or instrument in such a short period of time.

However, there is one area in which Bitcoin shines – as Nakamoto put it: it has "one special, magical property: [it] can be transported over a communications channel. If it somehow acquired any value at all for whatever reason, then anyone wanting to transfer wealth over a long distance could buy some, transmit it, and have the recipient sell it."[78]

Gold requires armored trucks in order to be transported from one place to another, and traditional payment remittances require an intermediary or broker. Cryptocurrencies are like cash or gold that you can email. And as we will discover in later chapters, there is much, much more that can be done with them.

The Truth is a Harsh Mistress

> Facts just twist the truth around
> *David Byrne, 1980[n]*

Back in the nineties I used to lecture mathematics to first year computer science and engineering students at South Bank University, next to the strangely named Elephant and Castle district of London[*]. Very early on in the course I would cover the subject of Boolean logic, propositional calculus, and truth tables in computing from a mathematician's viewpoint. You wouldn't think that something that sounds so dry and abstract would be the course in which the most vehement and agitated discussions and arguments would take place, but there were times that people stormed out in anger, swore at each other, and even threatened to get physically violent.

---

[*] The name "Elephant and Castle" is sometimes thought to be an English corruption of the title of a Spanish princess, derived from the term "La Infanta de Castilla", or possibly from an old public house in the area that took its name from the crest of a medieval cutlery manufacturing guild, which adopted a castle on the back of an elephant as its brand in a reference to the ivory used in the handles, and to portray some measure of magnitude of the organization, but the true origins are unknown.

To understand why, you will have to pay a bit of attention in the next few sections, because it does involve mathematics. You can just skip this chapter, but I promise you, it is not the kind of mathematics you had to deal with in high school.

Truth tables

In this section, I am presenting a cut-down version of the course notes that I used to deliver to South Bank University students[79]. There is a point behind all of this technical stuff, so please bear with me – here is the basis underpinning computer logic for first year undergraduates (although it is actually simple enough for ordinary young teenagers or bright middle-schoolers to understand).

The initial part of the topic never caused any trouble, namely logical "AND", "OR" and "NOT". Some of the students found it trivially self-evident and hence boring, and the rest cottoned on pretty quickly. For NOT they may well have had a point:

NOT Truth Table	
A	NOT A
True	False
False	True

Figure 26: Truth table for logical NOT

In a truth table the facts that we are given are on the left hand side, and the outcome is on the right.

If it is true that "I have one bitcoin", then it is false that "I do not have one bitcoin". And if it is false that "I have one bitcoin" then it is true that "I do not have one bitcoin". This is what is shown in the third and fourth rows of Figure 26 (row one contains the title, and row 2 the headings). Could it get much simpler than that when it comes to the truth? Most people consider this kind of truth to be self-evident.

How about AND? Again, a truth table shows how it works, and it makes sense in English, so the students had no problem with that:

AND Truth Table		
A	B	A AND B
True	True	True
True	False	False
False	True	False
False	False	False

Figure 27: Truth table for logical AND

A AND B is only true if A is true and B is true (as shown in row one). If A is "I have one bitcoin" and B is "I have one ether", then A AND B is "I have one bitcoin and I have one ether". And that is only going to be true if both parts of the statement are true. And you thought computer scientists were working on clever difficult stuff?

The next table did cause some problems. It is logical OR:

OR Truth Table		
A	B	A OR B
True	True	True
True	False	True
False	True	True
False	False	False

Figure 28: Truth table for logical OR

An OR statement is true if either part of the statement is true. So, "I have a bitcoin or I have an ether" is true if "I have a bitcoin" is true, if "I have an ether" is true, or if both are true.

It is the "both" that usually caused some problems. Most students were happy with the definition, but some complained that if I have a bitcoin and an ether (okay, they didn't complain about that, because bitcoins and ethers didn't exist back then, but I can't remember what example I used), then that was an AND truth and not an OR truth according to them. And other students would say, "but it is still true" and they would argue a bit, some of them would get a little bit angry, and then I would introduce the truth table for "either/or but not both", or "XOR" as it is called in computer-speak, and everything would go calm again:

XOR Truth Table		
A	B	A XOR B
True	True	False
True	False	True
False	True	True
False	False	False

Figure 29: Truth table for logical XOR (exclusive OR)

However, this table does illustrate that simple concepts in logic can have more complex interpretations in the real world, even among a small group of young aspiring computer scientists and mathematicians. And the fact that budding computer scientists can get angry about something like abstract logic explains a lot to me about the human condition and how badly we deal with conflicting views about messier things such as politics and religion, or even simple things such as how to put your cutlery in the silverware drawer. More on that later.

Back to the lecture room – so then all hell would break loose with the presentation of the following table:

IMPLIES Truth Table		
A	B	A IMPLIES B
True	True	True
True	False	False
False	True	True
False	False	True

Figure 30: Truth table for logical IMPLIES

From a Boolean logic perspective, IMPLIES is just a truth table, like all the prior ones, with no meaning attached to the word "implies". But in human language, "implies" carries extra implications. In everyday speech there is meant to be some kind of connection between the A part and the B part. It is supposed to be meaningful, whatever that means. Often there is a sense of causality, that is to say a possible connection to the passing of time: A happens, and because of it B happens. If I let go of the vase, then it falls to the floor and smashes into tiny pieces. If the vase smashes into tiny pieces, then my wife is upset.

In logic, that is not the case. Boolean logic is disconnected from time, from connectivity, causality, and even from meaning. When it comes to logical conjunctions such as OR, AND, XOR, and even IMPLIES, it doesn't matter what A and B represent. You just check that the truth value (True or False) for A and B gives the right results for the truth table that applies, and it is sorted. Mind you, I'm told that doesn't make up for precious broken vases.

But enough about my incompetence when handling family heirlooms - let's look at a a more general concrete example: if "the sun is a star" (statement A) is true, and "water is wet" (statement B) is true, then according to the IMPLIES truth table, the statement "the sun is a star implies that water is wet" is also true.

Hang on a minute. The sun being a star has nothing to do with water being wet! What is going on there? Well, it is just the truth table being applied. That is what you do in Boolean logic, and therefore in Computer Science. Can you think of a better way to define IMPLIES in a truth table? Feel free to grab pen and paper take a moment to see if you can do better. I bet you can't.

In the meantime the South Bank University students have started shouting at each other, one of them has left the room, and a few have risen from their chairs.

But it gets worse. Any false statement implies that a true statement is true. Seriously – think of something that is obviously false and call it A, and then think of a second thing that is obviously true and call it B, check in the truth table in figure 30 to determine what the resulting truth value is, and then construct the English sentence that is "A implies that B".

So back to the prior example: the statement "the sun is not a star implies that water is wet" is actually a true statement, even though "the sun is not a star" is false, and "water is wet" is true. Again, just check the truth table in Figure 30. It's not looking so great anymore, is it?

At this point I have to calm the student down, tell them that we are finishing early, and that I expect their answers to the worksheets on the table outside the hall are to be completed and handed in by the end of the week. It's amazing what the combination of the thought of leaving a lecture room and the formal requirements associated with completing a degree course can do to defuse tensions. Perhaps the United Nations should consider this. And I didn't even get on to the fact that if A is true and NOT A is true at the same time, then everything is true. Unfortunately, dear reader, you still have a few more minutes of a lecture on logic left.

So here's the thing with formal logic – it doesn't tell you whether the "atomic statements" (things like "the sun is a star" or "I have one bitcoin") are true. What it does tell you is whether compounding these atomic statements with operators such as AND, OR and IMPLIES will be true, given the truth of the original statements.

Okay, so what does that mean? Well, for example, A IMPLIES B is the same as (NOT B) IMPLIES (NOT A). Let's use A to mean "I am happy" and B to mean "I am smiling". Then the statement "*I am happy* implies that *I am smiling*" is supposed to have the same truth as "*I am **not** smiling* implies that *I am **not** happy*". That sounds like it might be correct, so let us construct a truth table:

\	\	Contrapositive Truth	\	\	\
A	B	A IMPLIES B	NOT A	NOT B	NOT B IMPLIES NOT A
True	True	True	False	False	True
True	False	False	False	True	False
False	True	True	True	False	True
False	False	True	True	True	True

Figure 31: Truth table for the contrapositive

This rule is called the contrapositive – the truth of an if/then statement is the same as the truth of the statement reversed with the two parts negated. This is proved through the truth table in figure 31 – the two gray columns have the same values given the same A and B input values.

Note that simply reversing the A and B does not necessarily give the same truth value. "I am smiling implies that I am happy" is not the same as "I am happy implies that I am smiling". I could be faking a smile while hurting on the inside. Something that some readers may be doing, having reached this point of the chapter.

Perhaps a simpler example is the proof that a double negative is the same as a positive, that is, NOT (NOT A) is the same as A. Feel free to construct your own truth table to prove that one. Hint: you can use the blank table below:

	Double Negative Truth Table
A	NOT A	NOT (NOT A)
True		
False		

Figure 32: Do-it-yourself truth table for double negative

Go on, channel your inner logical punk spirit and give it a try, and then compare the first column with the last one. They will be equal if you do it right. You only have to write four words into the four empty spaces, so it is not much effort. And if you do it right, you pass the course with flying colors and get to pat yourself on the back. Ain't that not the truth?

On meaning

Although a formal approach to logic such a the kind that is used by computer programs allows you to do all sorts of clever manipulations of statements and deduce all sorts of follow-on truths, as mentioned before, formal logic does not tell you whether a particular simple or initial statement is true or not.

It is like the law decreeing that *if* the defendant murdered the old lady with the axe, *then* he is guilty under the law and must serve a life sentence in jail. But the question still remains – did he commit the murder? Without determining the truth of that first part, the rest is effectively irrelevant.

If you start thinking about the idea of the possibility of "fundamental truths" – those basic A and B statements – then we leave the world of formal logic, and find ourselves embroiled in philosophy.

But first it should be noted that, as they are running on computers and manipulating transactions (financial, or data, or otherwise), blockchains do not magically make everything true. If you feed in nonsense or stuff that is just plain wrong, you get stuff out that is nonsense or just plain wrong too. This is commonly known in the industry as GIGO: garbage in, garbage out.

And after all that formal logic here's my final question: if even mathematical logic doesn't appear to be intuitively true until you spend years studying it, and even then can cause arguments and tantrums, then how can more ephemeral concepts such as "truth" truly be understood? To move beyond a formal concept of truth requires an understanding of underlying meaning, and meaning transcends formality.

Clever Covenants

> Running it, back it up.
> Is it too evil to find?
> *Dadabots, 2018[r]*

Smart contracts are possibly one of the most misunderstood concepts in the blockchain world, and yet you have in all likelihood encountered the simple equivalent of them in the banking world. They have been hiding in your bank statement for years.

Direct debits (or pre-authorized payments) and standing orders are similar to smart contracts in very many ways, in that smart contracts are essentially programmable money. But there are some subtle limitations, vulnerabilities, and complexities that need to be considered, as well as the possibility of all sorts of new manners of managing automated financial matters. It's pretty exciting and risky stuff. More on some of the nuts and bolts surrounding DeFi can be found in the chapter "DeFining Finance" on page 273.

There is one big problem with smart contracts at the moment - a well-meaning business development manager or the CEO (or if you work at the wrong company, the CTO) will read a Forbes article about them, and start having too many wild ideas.

"What if we use a smart contract to handle the warranty on our new dishwasher line?" or "How about farmers pre-sell their goods to the supermarkets using a smart contract?" are two suggestions that I have heard made in all seriousness in the past. On the surface, they sound plausible, but when you dig deeper they reveal both flaws in business thinking and the limitations of what smart contracts can realistically achieve. More about them later in this chapter.

We will start with a bit of history interspersed with some technical talk before we dive into applications.

Scripts and balances

Smart contracts all started with a rather prescient decision by Satoshi Nakamoto when designing Bitcoin. The simplest way to keep track of balances (and the first thing any standard developer would think of doing) is to ensure one basic rule is obeyed: whenever one balance increases, another balance or set of balances must decrease by the same amount. It's kind of like the equivalent of the conservation of energy or mass in the world of physics but transferred to finance. In practical terms – if I have 1000¥ in my wallet and you have 2000¥ in yours, and I then give you 500¥, my wallet should contain 500¥ afterward, and yours should contain 2500¥. The total amount of 3000¥ has to stay the same. Of course, this happens naturally with cash.

The only situation that is different is when money, cryptocurrency, or tokens are being created or destroyed on purpose, as discussed in the earlier chapter, "On Value" on page 167.

Nakamoto had better ideas on how to ensure that a Zen-like balance is maintained, and implemented a simple scripting language in Bitcoin to handle transactions.

The first idea was to use scripts – short computer programs run in a very basic program interpreter on each and every blockchain node, using something called a "stack-based state machine", which you can think of as a very limited kind of computer.

The script for each transaction is run on every single node and should return exactly the same result. If you think that this does not sound very efficient you'd be right: it isn't – thousands of computers running a basic computer program on a cut-down emulator in the hope that all of them come up with the same answer does not make sense in traditional centralized computing terms. However, the problem being addressed is not efficiency, it's consensus. And consensus comes at a cost – that's one of the reasons why parliamentary democracies or the United Nations are not cheap either.

The whole underlying idea is to ensure that everyone has the same "single view of the truth" – again, with cash this happens naturally. If I wave a 100€ note in the air in a Finnish bar, everyone in the room including the bartender will agree that I can afford to buy a round of drinks. No need for complicated consensus algorithms or smart contracts there! The problem is that when I'm waving a small piece of plastic that looks like a credit card, or a mobile phone that I claim has Apple Pay installed on it, the evidence that I can actually afford the round is much slimmer.

But back to programmable money: instead of updating balances, the scripts within the scripting language of Bitcoin usually perform a few calculations and cryptographic actions, and either return "true" or "false". If the result is "true" the transaction is valid and can be included in the blockchain. If it is "false" it gets discarded by the miners and nodes. The most common scripts check that the transaction has enough bitcoin to afford what is proposed and that the transaction has been cryptographically signed, which ensures that it has been submitted by a party that has the right to authorize it. They are, in effect, the digital equivalent of checks.

The second insight was the observation that it is the flow of currency that is ultimately important, and not the units. As a result, there is actually no such thing as a bitcoin (or a satoshi). Instead, there are "unspent transactions" and "spent transactions", and "inputs" and "outputs" to transactions. This is not the simplest thing to get your head around, and I have spent quite some time trying to come up with a clear explanation as to how this works. The best analogy I have been able to invent involves cups of sand, and so they are the topic of the next section.

The lone and level sands

Imagine traditional money as being equivalent to marbles. You have a pocket full of them, and when you want to pay for something you want, you hand over the right number of marbles to the shopkeeper, they put them in their pocket, and hand over the goods you want. Simple stuff – you lost some marbles, the shopkeeper gained an equivalent amount, and you have an item from the shop.

The way bitcoins move about is a bit different. For starters, you can't actually point at one particular section of the blockchain and say, "See, that's how many bitcoins I have."

Figure 33: A 5 bitcoin unspent transaction

For Bitcoin, you can imagine that when you have five bitcoin, for example, what you actually have is a cup containing 500 million grains of sand. Each grain of sand represents a satoshi (the smallest unit of currency in the Bitcoin world – and a hundred million satoshis is equal to one bitcoin). The cup is standing upright holding the sand, and is what is called an "unspent transaction".

When you decide to send one bitcoin to a friend, what you are doing is tipping the cup upside down, so that all the sand pours out. This means that your cup, which used to be full and was hence an unspent transaction, is now empty and is therefore a spent transaction. This sand pouring event constituting your overall transaction to your friend is recorded on the blockchain in perpetuity.

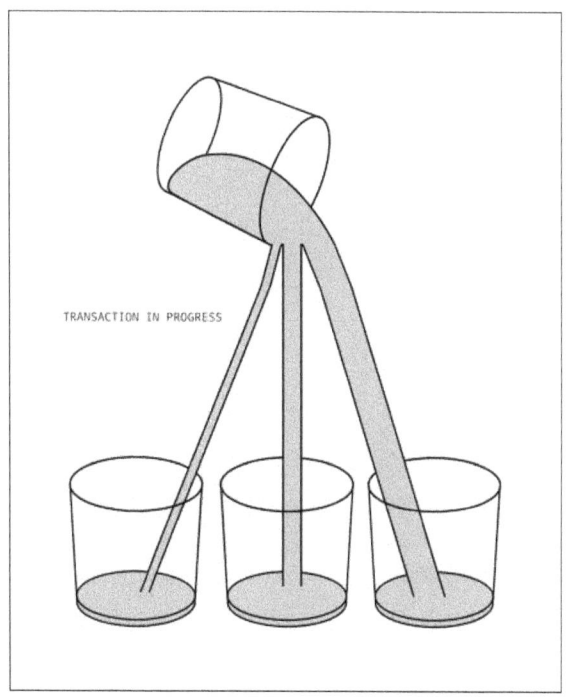

Figure 34: A transaction in progress

The second part of your overall transaction is about where that sand goes. You specify that other new cups, initially empty, get created and placed under the flow of sand. So if you're transferring one bitcoin to your friend, that's a hundred million grains of sand. A cup associated with your friend's Bitcoin address gets put under part of the stream of sand so that it catches that one hundred million.

Now, there are still another four hundred million grains of sand pouring down. So your transaction also creates a second new empty cup, associated with a new Bitcoin address that your wallet creates for you, to catch most of that sand.

The reason why you don't catch all of the remaining sand in your own new cup is because you need to pay a transaction fee in order to encourage a miner to actually include your transaction in a new block. So you catch the four hundred million grains minus, for example, ten thousand grains.

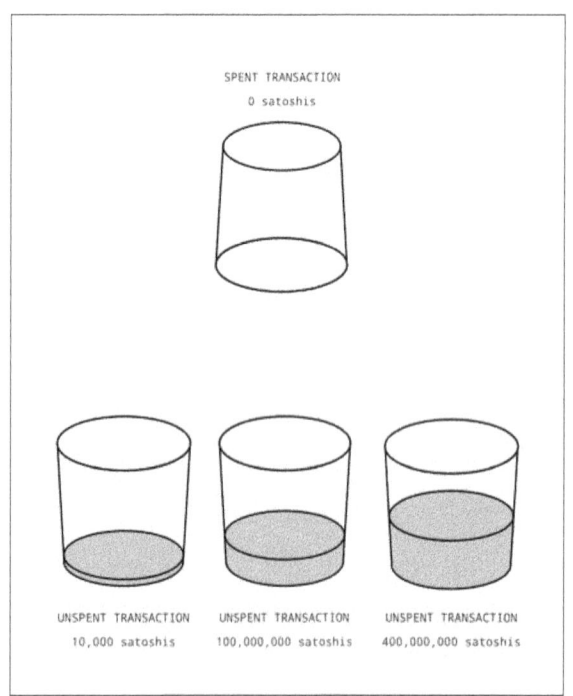

Figure 35: Transaction complete

When a miner includes your transaction in the new block and therefore actually permanently records that you've sent a bitcoin to your friend, they also specify their Bitcoin address in order to catch those ten thousand unclaimed grains of sand.

So now we have three new unspent transactions – the cup of sand that your friend received, the cup of sand that contains your change, and the third cup containing a little bit extra left over to tip the miner for recording the whole process.

It is not the simplest way of ensuring balance is maintained, but it's what Satoshi Nakamoto chose. Ethereum, for comparison, uses the simple "count the marbles" ledger approach that I talked about at the beginning of this section.

In order to know the balance of a given Bitcoin address, you have to search through the entire blockchain for all transactions that feed into it, and all transactions that have been spent out of it and add (or subtract) them all in order to get the final balance.

At the time of writing, there is about a quarter of a terabyte of data that needs to be parsed on the Bitcoin blockchain in order to determine the current state of all those unspent and spent transactions. Fortunately, the Bitcoin Core software parses the blockchain files in the background and keeps a second traditional database (currently LevelDB is used) for storing all the transactions, so this can all be computed very quickly.

Turing completeness

The thing is, although the Bitcoin scripting language and the transaction flow system allow you to do a number of clever things, they have their limitations. Here are some of the things you can implement with Bitcoin scripting:

- multi-signature transactions, where a number of people have to sign off on a transaction before it's valid. This is kind of like large purchases in a company requiring the CEO and the CFO to approve it before it goes through,
- time-locked transactions, in which payments do not become valid until some time in the future,

- transactions that include a data payload, which allows you to push a small list of bytes onto the blockchain. These can be used to publish a document hash, URL, or a newspaper headline onto the Bitcoin blockchain,
- quirky cryptographic or algebraic puzzle transactions that challenge other Bitcoin programming enthusiasts to solve them, with a bitcoin reward for finding a solution[80].

Although these all sound quite intricate, any developer quickly hits a wall as to what can be done, because the scripting language is not Turing complete. If you are interested, feel free to dig into the Chomsky hierarchy of formal grammars[81] in order to truly understand what that means.

If you're not interested in formal grammars, here is a quick summary: stack machine languages such as the Bitcoin scripting language are like memorizing a few phrases from a tourist guide when visiting a foreign country, which allows you to interact in a basic but effective way with the locals when on holiday, whereas a proper Turing-complete programming language is like actually learning to speak the language fluently, and being able to have a proper conversation. In a proper conversation you can actually discuss ideas, and go back and reference things you talked about earlier. And proper software developers like to be able to express themselves fluently.

How to stop going round in circles

There is an issue with Turing-complete programming languages called the "halting problem". When you have a simple linear script that, for example, compares two values and tells you whether they are the same or different, you know that the script will run and then stop. Such scripts are like a cooking recipe, which is followed from start to finish and has a specified run-time.

But more complicated programs can contain loops, where an action is taken again and again until an event happens that causes the loop to terminate. This means you can produce a program that may never terminate. Imagine a recipe that has a line, "add a pinch of cayenne pepper and taste. If the dish is not spicy and hot enough, repeat the previous instruction." If the chef following that recipe was unable to taste any heat from capsaicin, had an infinite supply of cayenne pepper, and furthermore was obsessive about following written instructions, then they would continue to add pepper to the dish until the end of their days. Computers often act just like such a bizarre chef.

Here is an example of a computer program, written in Sinclair BASIC, that obviously will never terminate without outside intervention:

```
10 PRINT "HELLO"
20 GOTO 10
```

And here is a more subtle one, in pseudo-Python, where it is not obvious at a glance if it will ever halt or not:

```
n = 1
while isNotPrime( (3^n) + 6 ):
    n = n + 1
    print("Still not stopping")
```

If programs like the ones above can be deployed as smart contracts, there will be trouble on the blockchain. All the nodes start running them, and never stop, bringing the whole system to what appears to be a standstill. For your desktop or laptop, the halting problem can be solved by rebooting it, but it is not feasible to power down every single blockchain node each time a non-halting smart contract is encountered.

In 2013, Vitalik Buterin published the Ethereum whitepaper, which described his solution to the halting problem on a blockchain[82]. The same mechanism is still used today in Ethereum, and it is elegantly simple: you charge whoever deploys a smart contract a fee, depending on the size and complexity of their program, and then you charge the users of the smart contract another fee whenever they use it. If the money runs out, the carousel stops spinning, and the program halts.

In Ethereum the fee for deploying or running a smart contract is called "gas". Gas is bought with the native cryptocurrency of the blockchain, namely ether. Of course, being Ethereum, it is slightly more complicated because there is a third number involved, namely the "gas price", which determines how much one unit of gas costs in ether. If you call a smart contract, you have to provide gas to do so, and if one smart contract calls another then it supplies gas to do so too.

You can probably guess that the standard analogy for smart contracts is one of a car – the car is the contract, the gas is like the petrol that is put into the car, the gas price is the current cost of petrol, and the ether that is used to buy the gas is like the dollars or euros that are spent at the petrol pump to buy the fuel.

Where does the gas that is burnt for running smart contracts go? To the miner who mines the next Ethereum block, as a reward. It is similar to the transaction fees in Bitcoin. Furthermore, there are smaller rewards for miners that mine what are called "uncles" – blocks that would have been in the canonical blockchain if only they had been found earlier than the winning block. After all, every node and miner on the network is running a copy of the smart contract, so there should be a reward for a few also-rans.

Why have a gas price and gas, rather than using ether directly? If the aim of having a "transaction fee" in Ethereum is the same as in Bitcoin, namely to provide an extra incentive to miners to include transactions and contracts in the blocks they mine, and also to allow people who are desperate to be able to jump the queue and get their transaction processed quicker, then surely simply using ether directly should be fine?

Well, no. This is where the car analogy breaks down and needs to be extended: two drivers driving two cars of the same make and model with the same size petrol tank arrive at a rural petrol station at the same time. Who does the pump attendant serve first? The answer is the driver who is willing to pay the highest price per liter for petrol.

Each command in a smart contract has a standard gas cost associated with it. If you look at the lines of code in the contract, you can work out almost exactly how much gas the contract will use to run unless it gets caught in a loop. So two identical contracts will require exactly the same amount of gas under the same conditions.

What if one person wants to deploy the contract immediately, and the other person is not in a hurry? Then the first will set a high gas price, and the second will set a low gas price. Let's say the first gas price is twice the second gas price. This means the cost in ether of deploying the first contract will be twice the cost of deploying the second contract, even though the lines of code are exactly the same.

That's the cost of wanting to go first.

What can these smart contracts do?

To answer the question posed in the above, I may as well go straight to the source and quote Buterin:

> In general, there are three types of applications on top of Ethereum.
>
> The first category is financial applications, providing users with more powerful ways of managing and entering into contracts using their money. This includes sub-currencies, financial derivatives, hedging contracts, savings wallets, wills, and ultimately even some classes of full-scale employment contracts.

The second category is semi-financial applications, where money is involved but there is also a heavy non-monetary side to what is being done; a perfect example is self-enforcing bounties for solutions to computational problems.

Finally, there are applications such as online voting and decentralized governance that are not financial at all.

— *Vitalik Buterin*[82]

Back in 2013, when Buterin was traveling the world, from Toronto to San Francisco, Israel, London, Amsterdam, Los Angeles, and Las Vegas, and dreaming up Ethereum, his head must have been spinning with all those thoughts.

Dishwasher warranties

I mentioned earlier in this chapter that using a smart contract to pay out a warranty for a defective dishwasher is not a good use case for smart contracts. Let's have a look at why that is.

Your dishwasher breaks down. The normal process to follow in such an event is to call the helpline. They then schedule a local repair person to visit your house to inspect what went wrong. If the cause was a manufacturing defect, they may mend it, or submit a proposal to the manufacturer to refund you your money, and take away the offending machine. Or, as is more likely, they will claim it is your fault for not using the dishwasher properly, and offer to repair it for a hefty fee.

How is a smart contract going to detect that your dishwasher suffered a fault and determine that it was a manufacturing error? You cannot allow the customer to make such a declaration, as word will soon get out that your product can be effectively be obtained for free – buy it, submit a claim on the blockchain, and get your money back.

You could fit every dishwasher with a diagnostic Internet of Things device, but the device would have to have network connectivity, and a well-tested blockchain wallet embedded in it securely. At the moment, the cost of fitting every dishwasher with such a device would swamp the cost of providing a helpline and paying out on the few devices that go wrong. Perhaps this may change in the future, but for now, even a simple cost/benefit analysis on the back of an envelope clearly shows that this is not a viable solution.

Finally, you can have an engineer go round to the house to check out the situation after the customer has called or emailed the manufacturer. In which case, you are back to the original method of handling reported defects, but you have tacked on a smart contract to the whole process for no clear benefit to anyone.

Summary

Sometimes the early days of the World Wide Web are used as a comparison for the power and significance of blockchain technology, with blockchain set to transform what we can do with the abstract concept of "value" in the way the web revolutionized how we handle the concept of "information". Extending the comparison, if Bitcoin is the HTML of the Internet of Value, then Ethereum is the Javascript of that system.

Early web pages were static and designed for transferring information, such as scientific papers, from a publisher to a reader. By adding a programming language to the web browser, and providing more tools to programmers on the webserver side, web sites developed from simple information presenting systems to the more complicated ecosystem we are now used to, where real-time multi-player games, online banking, shopping, user-generated content such as blogs and social media, and all the other bells and whistles of Web 2.0 or dynamic HTML are now possible[83].

The reasons why programmers should be as excited as Buterin was about smart contracts are because:

- they take the "programmable money" idea that Bitcoin introduced to another level of sophistication and flexibility. Unlike Bitcoin scripts, the programs persist, can be called time and time again, and are written in a Turing-complete language;
- they can store data in a more flexible manner, in that it can be changed later (although a record of the former values still remains, and storing data on the chain can be expensive), so they have memory; and
- they can call other smart contracts, allowing for chained actions and modular programming.

And the reason why programmers should be concerned is:

- smart contracts can potentially involve millions of dollars of your wealth and other people's wealth, which means that one bug, exploit, or mistake can result in the loss of a fortune in mere seconds.

Government Without Leaders

> Now I guard a system, built on abuse
> Lock and key, our man's need for certainty
> *K-Bomb, 2015°*

As an undergraduate, I was once at a formal dinner and the captain of the college chess team was seated opposite me. We were good friends and knew each other well, so I suddenly said "pawn to e4" and he immediately responded, "pawn to e5". Then we continued: "Knight to f3" ... "Knight to c6", "Bishop to b5" ... "Bishop to a6", and so on.

After a few more exchanges neither of us knew the state of the board, but we kept proposing realistic sounding moves for the next two courses of the meal, looking thoughtful, laughing when a particularly good move was supposedly made, and so on until one of us declared checkmate. I can't remember which of us it was, so it was probably me. Sometimes I can be that arrogant.

Of course, the game was total nonsense. But the people at the table didn't know that and were terribly impressed. Even though they were all Cambridge students, and hence extremely bright and sharp-witted. Just remember that if there are occasions when you feel over-awed by someone's intellect, there is a chance that they're just remarkably good at bluffing. On the other hand, they really might be extremely smart.

The rules of chess are formal, and that makes it an excellent game to code up in a computer program. A chess computer would have immediately spotted that my friend and I were breaking the rules of chess.

Although a game of chess that takes place on a board may be bound by clearly defined formal rules, the community or society that it takes place in will have a whole different set of traditions and regulations, many of which are not even written down anywhere. They emerge and evolve over time. The chess community uses terms such as "grandmaster", gives names to different openings, and ranks players with a scoring system such as the Elo rating, but those things are not a part of the core rules of the game. Etiquette during play is a further example of the unwritten rules that do not form part of the core concept that is "chess".

I guess what I am trying to say here is that chess, or for that matter blockchain, is not just about the formal system and the rules. It is as much about human interaction with those rules. If chess hadn't fired the imagination of generations of people, it would have been resigned to the dustbin of history shortly after its invention. And similarly, blockchain is about a lot more than just lines of code. When you have a society or a community that has decided to abide by a set of rules, the rules require legitimacy, and this is obtained through trust and faith in the means of governance, or in some cases through fear and ignorance. Unfortunately, there is plenty of evidence that most blockchain systems do not explicitly deal with questions of governance from the very beginning, as their white papers are almost always exclusively focused on technology[84].

Now for a short political interlude.

Checks and balances

One of the most astounding developments in the organization of human societies is the devolution of power from a single individual at the top of the hierarchy – a tribe leader, emperor, or king if you will – to separated branches and institutions of government. Although holding various powers within their own domain of influence, each branch may also have the right to veto the actions of the other branches, and similarly, be restrained by them.

Charles-Louis de Secondat, Baron de La Brède et de Montesquieu, commonly known simply as Montesquieu (although I like to call him Monty) is the political philosopher who in 1748 anonymously published the classic work on checks and balances in governmental power structures, namely "The Spirit of Law"[85]. The British parliamentary system and the USA's government and legal structure as arising from its constitution are both heavily based on Monty's thoughts, implementing the separation of powers into different institutions in order to provide safeguards against despotism. And despotism is something that blockchain enthusiasts should be aware of because it is the antithesis of what blockchain stands for.

> **Despotism**: *the rule of a despot (= a ruler with unlimited power, often one who is unfair and cruel)*
>
> — *the Cambridge Dictionary*[86]

I am not going to claim here that companies such as Facebook or Google, or financial institutions such as our banks, are consciously and intentionally going out of their way to be cruel towards individuals, or that they set out from the beginning to maliciously take advantage of ordinary people, but the fact is that within their sphere of influence they can act as despotic rulers if we allow them to. Political sociologists have plenty to say on the motivations that lie behind why citizens permit themselves to be ruled in a particular way, but as this is a book on blockchain and not political sociology, I won't start enumerating them all. Instead, here is an extremely brief analysis of how modern-day data harvesters such as social media companies end up acting as despotic rulers who do not have the best interests, or indeed any interests, of their users in mind.

For these companies, it seems to me that it boils down to a combination of user convenience and ignorance. There is a desire among people to have and maintain access to free communication channels with friends, family, and colleagues, combined with a lack of knowledge (often wilful) as to what companies are actually doing with the data they harvest when we use these communication channels. The motto is *carpe notitia* – seize the data.

Just this week, my attention was drawn to a paragraph in the terms and conditions presented by some Intel driver and support software, asking for permission to collect information about what websites you visit. How would knowing that you regularly go to Pinterest pages with pictures of cats help Intel improve their graphics driver software? It won't, but Google and Facebook have proved that such data has tremendous value, and so it is not surprising that every other corporation is trying to get in on the act.

There is truth in the statement that "if you are not paying for it, you're not the customer; you're the product being sold"[87]. And just remember: companies do not think of products as people.

Corporate hierarchies

Traditional companies may not be despotic, but sometimes it can sure seem like it to lower pay grade employees. Although checks and balances exist in companies too – for example, the board of directors generally has the power to hire and fire the CEO – most of the implicit structure of corporations is military or feudal in its architecture. Junior employees report to senior ones, who are beholden to directors, who in their turn are subservient to vice presidents, and so on up the chain. Company boards only meet infrequently, so on a day to day basis, the CEO is king.

This can have some bizarre consequences – one company I worked for had a CEO who sent every employee regular emails containing his "thoughts", which sometimes involved his vision for the company, but more often described his opinions on random topics such as the quality and portion sizes of peanuts served on first-class airplane flights. Another CEO in a different company I worked for sent me and the entire technical writing team on a one week trip from the UK to Boston, Massachusetts to work on a graphic novel capturing the "company spirit". Admittedly it was great fun, but any team-building gains could probably equally have been attained with a day out at a paintball range or a cooking class, and at a fraction of the cost.

To be fair, there are disruptive new companies experimenting with alternate approaches to the traditional corporate hierarchy, but the fact remains that most of us are brought up in cultures with clear linear chains of authority, and old habits such as those die hard. Perhaps we are brainwashed from an early age to want to fit into such organizational structures, or perhaps it's hardwired into our DNA – but as human beings, we have one advantage over most of the animal world. We can analyze what it is that we do, examine why it is that we do it, and then question if it is the right thing to do. And if we are really self-aware, then we can even make changes that stop us from doing the wrong things again and again.

Blockchain and governance

The implementation of a public open blockchain may prevent transaction censorship and provide for digital ownership that cannot be revoked by any other party, however, there is no guarantee that these properties will carry over into the evolution of the systems that spring up around the blockchain, that is, the governance mechanisms.

Looking at Bitcoin, for example, we see a number of groups that wield different powers: the development team, the node operators, the system users, coin owners, and the miners.

In permissioned blockchains there will necessarily be some centralization that is absent from open permissionless blockchains –

after all, not all participants on a permissioned blockchain are created equal. Nevertheless, in order to avoid becoming merely a clunky and cumbersome implementation of a centralized database, in a permissioned blockchain the authority in charge has to relinquish some power to other parties in order to achieve anything of note. This kind of yielding does not come naturally to traditional corporations.

There have been attempts to draw parallels between the familiar structures of Western democracies and the categories of participants on a blockchain[88], typically the legislative, executive, and the judiciary, and also the often overlooked electorate, who are meant to have the final veto over the appointment of the other three. It is difficult to precisely fit the groups involved in running a blockchain like Bitcoin into an analogy using the British or United States governments, but there are some clear parallels. And even though the analogy may not be perfect, it serves two purposes – firstly, it gives us a handle on how blockchains are constructed by groups of people, and secondly, it provides a measure of how decentralized a given blockchain ecosystem really is. More on that after the summary that follows.

The executive

The development teams behind blockchains have many properties in common with the executive branch of government. After all, they are the ones who take action and do stuff. Once the "what needs to be done" has been decided on, it is the developers who work on "how to do it".

Most blockchain projects are implemented in open-source code, and some people are under the misguided impression that in open-source projects anyone is free to make changes. In practice, the repository that the code resides in will most likely be under the control of one or a few people, who decide what is accepted and folded into the source-code base, and what is rejected.

Other programmers are generally able to submit suggestions that include their own code, and if they are rejected, can make a copy or clone of the project in their own repository, which they, in turn, will have complete control over. This is known as "forking"[89].

A distinction has to be drawn between the code, and the protocol that it implements. A blockchain will have all sorts of standards: the format of transactions, the peer-to-peer network protocol, the consensus system that is used, and the parameters that define the structure of the blockchain. Protocols are standards, and as such are set down by the next branch in the list. The developers provide a reference implementation of those standards that others can copy, for example by implementing the standards in a different programming language. However, controlling the reference implementation has significance – usually, that implementation will have the most instances out there in the real world. There may be generally accepted protocol enhancements and improvements, but until they make it into the reference implementation, the network software as a whole may well reject them.

One final point: members of the development team are generally not elected, unlike the executive in modern democracies. Instead, they are appointed, for example when Satoshi Nakamoto handed over the reins of the Bitcoin project to Gavin Andresen in late 2010[90].

The legislative

In the previous paragraph, I already started to touch on the role of the legislative branch: the group that decides what the protocols and standards should be, and when they should be altered or enhanced. They may also recommend specific code changes, for example, when a protocol has not been implemented in accordance with the meaning behind the standard that was proposed. This branch of government is possibly the most important, and yet in many blockchain projects consists of an undocumented or partially documented hodge-podge of processes and organizations: the means of submitting "requests for comments" or "improvement proposals" and the existence of foundations or committees that vote on them, and if they have funds, distribute them to development teams in order to incentivize the implementation of these proposals.

Initially, software architects play the role of the legislative. In the early days of any open-source blockchain project that someone or some group of people has dreamed up, it is highly likely that when you investigate, you will find that the developers were also the designers of the system. As it matures and becomes an ecosystem, and as the considerations of non-technical participants become significant, the two roles start to separate.

In my opinion, in permissioned blockchains it is essential for the project proposers to ensure that the different members of the consortium the blockchain is meant to support have the opportunity to act as legislators. A commercial blockchain project is somewhat different from a traditional monolithic software offering, in that there are many clients or customers, and their interests are often not completely aligned (although they have to be somewhat aligned – after all, the whole point of such a blockchain is to foster co-operation and trust).

Blockchain requires a rethink of traditional client and service provider relationships because everyone takes on a bit of each role.

The judiciary

The miners, stakers, or validators (as I will refer to them from now on in this chapter) have some attributes in common with the branch in politics and government known as the judiciary, as they too stand in judgment. Are given transactions, and therefore resulting data blocks to be added to the chain, or not?

What I initially started to write at this point is that a lot of trust is put into the validators, but of course, that is not actually the case. Traditional judges are trusted. They are expected to be fair and impartial, with the idea being that the education required, the process of selection, the experience gained over a career, and the august reputation that come with being appointed as a judge will somehow safeguard against any corruption. Although these guarantees may work in the majority of cases, there are plenty of precedents indicating that they are not failproof. Judges have been bribed in the past, and they have made mistakes.

Blockchain dispenses with all of this and goes straight to the root of all reliability – profit. How can you bribe a validator if they are already making the maximum returns they can under the system? On a blockchain there is a clear *quid pro quo* – expend the required capital on a mining rig, or coins, and the law of large numbers will ensure you get your reward as long as you play the game for a reasonable amount of time. Furthermore, all "judgments" that are made by validators are visible and can be audited using the blockchain data itself.

Validators have an interesting power over blockchains, which I can't quite explain. When it comes to proof-of-work based blockchains, it seems that whenever they undergo a fork due to contention over the direction the project should take, it is the chain that attracts the most validators that is generally perceived to be the truer implementation of the blockchain's vision. Or perhaps it is the one with the highest market capitalization in a fiat currency. The two seem to go hand-in-hand.

The civil service

In the United States, the civil service is the collection of appointed positions in the executive, judicial, and legislative branches of the government, whereas in the United Kingdom it is considered part of the executive only.

I would put it that the operators of nodes, namely people who have hardware running the software are like the civil service. By forwarding transactions and blocks, and storing a copy of the canonical data chain, node operators ensure the smooth running of the network. This gives them, as a group, the power to accept or resist change. If the developers roll out an update, but none of the node operators install and run it, the executive has been over-ruled.

It is interesting that on blockchains such as Bitcoin and Ethereum, node operators are not incentivized through any kind of cryptocurrency reward. Instead, there are a number of reasons why someone would run a node. One reason is to use it as their primary wallet and transaction service, although the Bitcoin Core wallet software is a bit of an afterthought. Another reason might be for research purposes, or as part of a commercial activity, for example, companies that investigate transaction patterns to track down criminal activity, or merchant service providers that confirm when payments have settled on the blockchain.

The oligarchs

I struggled for a while to find a suitable word for the group of people, often known as whales, who hold substantial amounts of a given cryptocurrency and thus have a disproportionate level of influence. I think "oligarchs" fits the bill. The existence of bots that act like the paparazzi by monitoring blockchain transaction activity and sending alerts to Twitter when large quantities of a given cryptocurrency move is a testament to this.

In a proof-of-stake system, there is the risk that oligarchs can scoop up the lion's share of block rewards due to the simple fact that they have more coins to stake, and therefore have a higher probability of getting to produce the next block. All sorts of variants of proof-of-stake have been proposed to mitigate this, most of which introduce the concept of "staking time" – the longer a coin has been sitting there locked up as a stake, the higher the probability of its owner being selected as the next block miner, or rather forger in the terminology of proof-of-stake. Once selected as a block generator, the staking time for the locked-up coins is reset.

The electorate

The users of a blockchain are like an electorate. Regardless of how regularly and enthusiastically the developers add features to a blockchain, and no matter how many nodes are running and how many miners are slaving away at securing the system, if no one is submitting transactions, then the chain serves no purpose. And it is the users who provide the transactions.

There is one significant difference between an electorate in a democratic nation and a set of blockchain users, which is discussed further in the section titled "Voting with your virtual feet". That's the reason why this section is so short.

Measuring decentralization

How can these characterizations of the parties involved in developing, deploying, and improving a given blockchain help us in our assessment of the real level of decentralization present? It is simple enough: are two or more of the different branches rolled up into one? If a small number of people are both the developers of the system, the holders of the majority of the coins, and hold exclusive control over feature changes to the software and alterations to the base protocol, then there are no checks and balances in place. Blockchain decentralization is not just about the current implementation in code that ensures ownership of assets as recorded on the decentralized ledger, but also about how the code is going to adapt and change in the future, and more to the point, who controls that future. There is no point in putting your trust in how the system is implemented in the here and now if it could arbitrarily be altered in the future by a despotic ruler.

Did Nakamoto foresee the separation of powers in the Bitcoin blockchain ecosystem? It is hard to say. There is nothing specific in the 2008 paper, and I have trawled through the posts Nakamoto submitted to Bitcointalk (most of which are about coding issues) and have come up empty-handed.

However, just as startups tend to have the founders acting both as board members and executives before the investors enter the scene and take majority control of the board, so it was that in the early days of Bitcoin the code developers were also the miners, the node operators, and the users of the system. Prescient though Nakamoto may appear in hindsight, my initial suspicion was that the original architect of the first blockchain was not thinking in terms of a formal political division of powers, but was focused simply on the technical implementation of the two holy grails of decentralization and disintermediation and that any resonance with political theory is either accidental or, more likely, an emergent property.

Later on, I started to wonder more and more about the fact that Nakamoto remains anonymous, walked away from Bitcoin just at the point that it was really starting to take off, and has (to the best of our knowledge) never spent any of the vast number of bitcoins that he or she owns. Through these three actions, the Bitcoin founder effectively removed themselves from the role of executive, legislative, judicial, and oligarchical leader, and in the process freed up the system to have the same properties at the community level that it has at the technical level.

Again, it seems that Nakamoto is either extremely smart and insightful or very, very lucky.

Voting with your virtual feet

In real life, governments can rely on geographical, logistical, and cost based restrictions to maintain their control over a population. Things have to get really bad before a revolution or diaspora is the result of national mismanagement. And yet history shows us that governments achieve this with surprising regularity.

In the virtual world, fragmentation and separation are much simpler to execute on. As a user of a blockchain, moving from one system to another is surprisingly easy, involving just the downloading of new wallet software, and using an exchange to convert the tokens from one blockchain into those of another. If the move is due to a fork, then the digital assets are automatically copied across, which is even easier.

Similarly, many blockchains use the same basis for securing the system, typically proof-of-work as outlined by Nakamoto. Deciding to mine one blockchain rather than another is merely a matter of changing one parameter in the mining software. Hence many mining pools implement dynamic chain mining, in which they analyze and compare the currently expected cryptocurrency rewards against the market price in fiat, and switch from chain to chain as the situation changes in order to maximize their profits.

As for deploying a fork or a new blockchain system: due to the generally open-source nature of such projects, anyone with enough technical knowledge can copy the code, make the desired alterations, and then launch the new system. It is then just a matter of marketing to ensure that a significant user base is encouraged to move from the parent chain to the fork.

Blockchains have less lock-in than banks or nations. On the one hand, this is a good thing, in that it provides the freedom to move from one to another at will. The downside is the proliferation of blockchain projects, of which there are so many that no one single person can comprehend them all anymore.

On-chain governance

So far I have looked at human organizations that provide governance of blockchain systems. Real people are necessary (for now) as blockchains provide us with utility and we, in turn, provide them with meaning and direction. But that meaning has not been locked down yet, and possibly never will.

However, this being the world of blockchain, there has been plenty of research into how much of the governance process can be moved from informal socially defined rules to automated token and smart contract-based management. Some people, such as the blockchain governance researcher Vlad Zamfir, have expressed severe concerns about moving towards on-chain governance systems[92]. But what exactly is "on-chain governance"? Here is one definition:

> *"On-chain governance" refers to the idea that the blockchain nodes automatically upgrade when an on-chain governance process decides on an upgrade and that it's time to install it.*
>
> — *Vlad Zamfir*

This definition adds two things – governance fundamentally concerns the change of blockchain node software (although it can also affect mining software if, for example, the consensus protocol is changed), and it adds the word "process".

So what then is an "on-chain governance process"? It can be many things. At the most fundamental level, the process could be designed into the very base protocols of the blockchain itself. A non-democratic solution is to bake automatic update functionality into the blockchain node software, but this removes power from the node operators and passes it to the developers.

Another example of base-level on-chain governance is proof-of-stake. It uses the native cryptocurrency of a blockchain to decide which block to add next. This could be extended to allow coin holders to vote, on the chain, whether a given upgrade or change should be accepted or rejected. Once again, in such a case power moves away from the node operators, this time to the oligarchs.

At a higher level, smart contracts issuing governance tokens can be deployed. This approach is already used in distributed autonomous organizations and decentralized finance code. You can make the system as complex and convoluted as you like, and I have no doubt that there are blockchain developers out there doing precisely that.

Ultimately, regardless of whether it is on-chain or off-chain, blockchain governance leads to forks. If it is handled badly, those forks occur in the community, rather than just in the software.

Knives, Forks, and Spoons

未開の土地に火をつけて
Naoko Yamano, 1983[p]

My wife and I had an argument early on in our marriage about how the cutlery (or silverware, as it's called in the United States) should be arranged in the cutlery drawer. Simple things like this, if left unresolved, can tear apart even the strongest relationship. So we spent a significant amount of time discussing the issue.

For all of my childhood the correct way, from left to right, was: "knives, forks, spoons". She, on the other hand, considered the natural order to be "spoons, forks, knives".

In the end, after some discussion, we actually came up with a rational and logical decision as to the proper way to store the cutlery. At the end of the chapter I will let you know what it is, how we reached our conclusion, and in the process saved our marriage. Because, ultimately, it is the little things that make or break a relationship.

Blockchain forks

There are three common problems within blockchains where the continuation of the chain can hit a speed bump. For this section, I'll discuss them in terms of the Bitcoin proof-of-work scheme. Similar things can happen with other consensus systems, but for the purposes of this discussion, Bitcoin works fine as an example system.

A *fork* occurs on a blockchain when two (or more) groups of blockchain participants have different views of the "single view of the truth" - that is, there is no longer a single view. And therefore there is no longer any truth. We see this kind of thing all the time in human history – for example, both human languages and human religions have experienced many "forks" in the past, and it's one of the reasons why we have so many variants of them.

Forks can happen accidentally, or they can happen on purpose. We will look at accidental forks first, and then forks that happen intentionally, and also how (or even if) they can be resolved, in the next few sections.

Accidents happen

As anyone can package transactions into a block, perform the proof-of-work computations, and possibly find a new block that is totally valid, occasionally two or more people find a valid block at roughly the same time. Because messages in a peer-to-peer network take time to propagate around the whole network, some miners on the network may see one valid block first, and some may see the other.

This means that you can end up with two or more different groups mining away at different heads of the blockchain, and producing different branches of the chain. That's something that needs to be resolved.

And actually, it's exactly the situation that Nakamoto's proof of work was designed to fix.

And sometimes they don't

Sometimes the blockchain developers need to make an improvement to the protocol or fix a bug. These improvements may require all the miners and blockchain nodes to upgrade their software. A significant change in a software package is often called a "fork" by software developers – again because the software has the possibility of going in one of two different directions. Or, if a significant group does not like the change, then the software splits into two factions, both of which continue their own separate way.

There are two types of intentional fork, and they are explained in the story I now present to make all of this forking stuff less abstract and hence more understandable.

A Minecraft analogy

Minecraft[93] is a 3D virtual world game made up of cubic blocks, in which players can, among other things, dig into the solid part of the world with a pickaxe or other tool, thereby making tunnels and caves.

In this section, I use an analogy based on Minecraft to explain the different types of forks that a blockchain can experience, which should shed some light on what is going on.

To start with, imagine that the blockchain is a tunnel, winding its way through a large mountain in Minecraft. The miners on the blockchain are Minecraft characters armed with pickaxes, and the end of the tunnel is the head of the blockchain, where the miners are busy trying to extend the tunnel. And the transactions are carved into the walls, floors, and ceilings of the tunnel as it is extended.

Figure 36: Illustrating Minecraft blocks suitable for mining

The current difficulty of mining the blockchain is set by how hard the rock at the end of the tunnel is. It takes time for the miners to hack away at blocks at the end of the tunnel to remove them, and through a clever formula (known as the "current difficulty") the blocks that the mountain is made of can dynamically be made softer or harder.

When you are at the end of the tunnel, there are five different blocks you, as a miner, can decide to try to mine. The one ahead (A), above (B), to the left (C), right (D), or below (E). Different miners may each pick a different one of those blocks to mine.

Oh, and no one knows in advance which of those blocks is the easiest to remove. You just have to hack away at one and hope that at some point you've damaged it enough so it disappears. That's the equivalent of the probability of mining a block with proof-of-work on a blockchain. Sort of.

With the above setup, which I'll call *Tunnelchain*, we can now analyze the different kinds of blockchain fork that can occur in proof-of-work blockchains.

Temporary forks

Imagine that about half the miners are hacking away at blocks to the left, and the others are working away at the right. Because mining is a probabilistic process, there is a small chance that both groups will destroy the stone they are working on at the same time. Now there are two possible directions the tunnel can go in. Miners from each group start hacking away at the next rock-face to continue their branch or fork of the tunnel. This kind of event happens naturally all the time in proof-of-work blockchains, so it's nothing to be worried about.

The odds are that one group of miners will remove their next block of rock before the other. Let's say it's the left one. So now the left branch is two squares long, and the right branch is only one square long. Some of the miners in the shorter branch will notice this and move over to help with mining the left branch because it's more likely to eventually become the "canonical tunnel" in the long run.

As a result, that branch quickly extends to three squares, so it is substantially longer than the right branch. More and more miners give up on the right branch – remember that mining a branch that ultimately fails means no block rewards, and there's no financial incentive to keep hacking away at something that is obviously going to fail.

Eventually, everyone has given up on the right-hand branch and is working on the left-hand one. Through this, the left-hand branch becomes the one true tunnel, and the right-hand one is a dead-end, which everyone ignores from now on.

And that's how temporary forks in a proof-of-work blockchain arise and are resolved through the consensus algorithm.

Selfish mining

Sometimes a miner may mine a block, but keep the fact that they have done so secret. This is called "selfish mining"[94].

But why would anyone do that? Miners are almost exclusively motivated by the possibility of obtaining a block reward, so there has to be a financial reason.

And the reason is this – there you are at the rock face, surrounded by all the other miners, and a block dissolves as you hit it with your pickaxe. You could announce this to everyone, which means you would get the block reward (currently 6.25 bitcoins), and all the miners would switch to mining your branch of the tunnel.

Or, you could make a false wall, hide the fact that you have successfully mined a block, and continue mining the next block along your branch of the tunnel in secret. No one else is digging along your path, but if you manage to mine a second block and a third block, and so on, you can then announce them all at once and get all the rewards. Think of the profit!

But wait! What happens if someone successfully mines a block in a different direction? Then you immediately announce your block too. Now there's a 50/50 chance that your block will be selected. If you've managed to mine two blocks down your path, then announcing both will pretty much guarantee everyone chooses your branch. And if you've mined three or more, you can continue to keep your path secret until another branch looks like it's gaining on you, before you announce.

The result of this is that anyone who joins the selfish mining group wastes less time and energy because they aren't mining on a branch that is already known to be doomed. But the downside is that mining becomes centralized in this "mining pool".

The debate is still open on whether selfish mining is going to undermine the decentralized nature of proof-of-work blockchains.

The 51% attack

Now imagine that a large group of rogue miners get together and decide to subvert the system. The honest miners are continuing to mine the block ahead (block A), and the rogue miners start mining the block to the left (block C), but as with the selfish miners, they hide the fact that they are doing so by putting up a fake wall concealing their activity.

If the rogue group has more than half of the mining power, unbeknownst to the rest of the world, their fork could be growing longer and longer than the publicly mined tunnel along route A.

This allows the rogue miners to submit transactions along the public tunnel that spend their coin while submitting similar transactions that spend that same coin back to their own addresses. People who are looking at the transactions on the public tunnel see confirmations of those transactions as the public tunnel gets longer, so they may send goods or cash to the rogue miners for receiving the coins.

And then, after a while, the rogue miners reveal the alternate branch. Down comes the fake wall, the honest miners notice that the path starting where rock C used to be is now the longest, so they stop mining branch A and switch.

And with that, all the transactions along branch A are no longer valid. People who accepted those transactions as payments suddenly find that they no longer hold that coin. They've been conned by a 51% attack!

Soft forks

A "soft fork" is defined as an upgrade to the software that means that:

- the old nodes will accept blocks produced by the new nodes; however

- the new nodes might no longer accept blocks produced by the old nodes.

It is a restriction on what makes blocks produced after the soft fork acceptable – the set of possible acceptable blocks is reduced. So what does this mean in terms of our Minecraft analogy?

Imagine that after the tunnel is 74,638 meters long, a majority of the miners decide that from now on it is not permissible to mine blocks to the left (blocks like block C in figure 36). For the tunnel so far, that is for the first 74,638 meters, left hand turns are acceptable, but from now on they are not.

You can see that this is a restriction that limits the kind of digging that can take place from the point that the soft fork occurs. Perhaps it is instituted because the miners have noticed that the tunnel is getting dangerously close to the left side of the mountain and will soon break through and out into daylight. Or possibly they're just biased against left-handed people.

From now on, whenever one of the old miners manages to mine a block to the left, the new miners will ignore it. As long as the new miners are in the majority, the path to the left should fail to be mined further in favor of up/down/forward/right directions, and with any luck, the old miner will see the error of his way and will adopt the new restrictive rules.

After all, it's in his or her best financial interest. No one wants to waste their time mining blocks that don't result in a reward.

Hard forks

A "hard fork" is somewhat harder to define, mainly because there are two distinct different types. One involves a significant change to the software used, and the other (the *rollback*, discussed in the next section) involves a concerted change to the data stored on the blockchain.

If a major software change is introduced that changes the protocol:

- the old nodes will generally not accept blocks produced by the new nodes, and
- the new nodes will definitely no longer accept blocks produced by the old nodes.

In a hard fork, the set of acceptable blocks is either expanded or even drastically redefined.

So how does that work in the context of the Minecraft analogy?

The software developers decide that from now on, tunnels should be round and not square because circles are so much more efficient and aesthetically pleasing.

They release new "pickaxe" software that produces and validates round extensions to the tunnel rather than square ones and, after a lot of advertising and announcements, release it when the tunnel reaches a specific length. Let's say it's at a point where the tunnel is 252,450 meters long.

The idea is that when the change-over point is reached, all the miners shift to the new pickaxes, and the tunnels are round from then on.

If everything goes well, and the community agrees that round tunnels are actually better, then up to and including 252,450 meters into the mountain the tunnel is square, but from 252,451 meters the tunnel is round, and everybody is happy.

However, if a significant group disagrees, then they may continue mining square tunnels, and the blockchain permanently forks. You have the square miners digging off in one direction, and the round miners in another, never to meet again.

They may even adopt different names: Tunnelchain Round and Tunnelchain Square.

Rollbacks

In a rollback, a concerted decision is made by the majority of the miners to ignore what is technically the longest and strongest branch of the blockchain in favor of a lesser branch.

The most famous occurrence of this was the Ethereum rollback after the DAO hack, which resulted in two forks of Ethereum – namely, Ethereum Classic, which consists of miners that decided against the rollback, and Ethereum proper, or foundation, or something (it was never given a different name, presumably as it is the branch that Vitalik Buterin, the main founder of Ethereum, considers to be the "one true Ethereum").

The Ethereum Classic miners continued to mine blocks that were found after the DAO hack, whereas the Ethereum miners started mining from before the hack, and a special smart contract was added that paid back lost funds from the hack to the original contributors.

This kind of fork is very simple to explain in Minecraft terms. Imagine that the tunnel has led to a place on the map that is considered to be an unpleasant environment by a large number of miners. Perhaps there are lots of lava pools around, cave spiders, or something else undesirable.

As a result, a large number of the miners agree that they should backtrack a couple of hundred meters, and start digging in a different direction. So that's what they do. All the transactions that were recorded in the path that led to the lava or spiders are now invalid for people following that group. The rollback group starts creating its own new path, which soon grows longer and longer. But some of the miners disagree, and continue mining through the lava field and cave spiders.

And now the one single tunnel has become two: Tunnelchain Classic and Tunnelchain Rollback.

Split those coins!

An interesting side-effect of a blockchain fork is that all the transactions up to the the fork are valid on both chains. This is because they both have the same history up to the split. If you held some cryptocurrency on a blockchain before a split, then after the split you now hold it on both.

This is because the private key that controls the coins that came into your ownership before the fork now controls the coins on both forks of the chain. It can be used to sign a valid transaction on either one.

But there is a caveat – unless one of two chains institutes a further soft fork to alter the format of valid transactions, for example by including a new marker in the binary code that constitutes the transaction, then a transaction submitted to one chain can be submitted to the other chain too. This is called a "replay attack" or "replay bug". If a transaction submitted to the nodes maintaining one blockchain is subsequently submitted to one of the nodes maintaining the second chain, then it's equally valid on both, and so the transfer of cryptocurrency happens on both.

And for some reason, the transactions always make it across the two different networks. Perhaps there are some people out there who think it's funny to pick up transactions on one network and replay them on the other, even though they don't personally stand to make any kind of profit or gains from doing so. It really only takes one entity to do so. I have no idea if it is accidental, or on purpose, but it is as though there are two islands, and whenever one island comes down with the flu, just one single person thinks it might be a good idea to row across to the other island and cough on the first person they meet[*].

The next section describes a real "replay attack" issue that exists between two Bitcoin-based forks.

Identical Banks

When the Bitcoin Cash crew decided to split from the Bitcoin main blockchain on 1 August 2017 (although I should add that they consider themselves to be the "real" Bitcoin), they purposely changed the format of transactions to ensure that replay attacks could not happen by adding the requirement that an extra few bits

---

* I wrote this sentence about three months before Covid-19, so it wasn't meant as a metaphor for the present day.

of data were included in Bitcoin Cash transactions to distinguish them from the Bitcoin main system.

But when Bitcoin SV split from Bitcoin Cash on 15 November 2018, the Bitcoin SV crew refused to change their transaction format, claiming that despite the name change, it was *they* who were really the one true Bitcoin blockchain, and therefore should not have to. And Bitcoin Cash took the approach that they had already made the change to distinguish themselves from the earlier Bitcoin blockchain (yes, I know, it's confusing – three Bitcoin blockchains?), and so it wasn't their responsibility to make the change either.

Note that the assessment as to which chain is the original one, and which is a branch is a subjective one. Although I am not going to judge, I cannot help noticing that the chain that I refer to as Bitcoin in this book, as I am writing this, has a fiat cash value that is more than fifty times higher than the other two.

Squabbling and infighting aside, here is an analogy to explain what happens with blockchain forks such as the Bitcoin Cash and Bitcoin SV split, in which neither party agreed to change the format of their transactions, and hence replays of transactions are possible:

Imagine that you have an account with a bank (let's call it the BCH Bank), and you have $1000 in your account. The bank undergoes what effectively amounts to an internal civil war, and splits in two.

One part of the bank continues to operate under the name "BCH Bank", but the other half of the bank re-brands to the name "BSV Bank". Both new branches still agree that you have an account with them and that it contains $1000. Bonus! You now have two accounts, and effectively got some free money.

However, neither bank re-brands nor re-issues their checkbooks. And the individual blank checks in your checkbook folder do not contain any reference as to whether they are BCH or BSV Bank checks. Sounds crazy, right? But effectively, that is what actually happened.

As a result, if you write a BCH Bank check and cash it, the same check can then be re-cashed at the BSV Bank. And vice versa. This means that if you go and buy a new dinner service at a store that accepts BCH checks, the store owner can turn around, take a photocopy of your check (and we're in the digital world, so a photocopy is indistinguishable from the original) and cash one check at the BCH Bank and the other at the BSV bank. This means you've paid twice for the same dinner service!

Fortunately, there is a way out. Each check contains references to all the previous transactions with each bank. If the history of your accounts in both is the same, then every new check can be reused (or in the terminology of blockchain, replayed). But – if somehow, you can get a transaction logged with one bank, but not the other, then the two accounts become "split", and subsequent checks issued using one account can no longer be replayed and cashed at the other bank.

All you need is to receive a small amount of cash at one of the banks and not the other. So, for example, you need someone who has an account at BCH Bank, but not BSV bank, to send you a small number of pennies.

So where can we get some cash that is only valid at one of the banks? The answer is simple: from a miner.

Once the two chains split, different miners started spending their mining capacity on producing blocks for the different chains. And the block reward that they obtained is only spendable on the chain that is was mined one, because it wasn't found on the other chain at the same time.

So, for example, if a miner finds a block for Bitcoin Cash, the block reward from that discovery is only recorded on the Bitcoin Cash blockchain, and hence cannot be replayed on the Bitcoin SV chain. That reward (or even just part of it) can subsequently be used to free up conjoined coins that were mined on the original chain before the split, by creating transactions that are unique to just one of the chains.

How to store your cutlery

I promised at the beginning of this chapter that I would reveal the order in which we now store our cutlery in our kitchen drawer in my family home. The definitive answer is here:

| **Forks** | **Spoons** | **Knives** |

Figure 37: My great new cutlery arrangement

The reason is that this is the way they are placed on the table: fork on the left, knife on the right, and spoon above the plate. No other ordering makes more rational sense.

But if you think about it a bit more, the problem with this arrangement is that it moves the reasoning one layer deeper but doesn't resolve it in any true absolute sense. Knives may be placed to the right of a plate because most people are right-handed, and want to cut with their right hand (much to the annoyance of left-handed people like myself, who spent years of their childhood being chastised for tearing food with their knife rather than cutting it), but the fork could equally be stored above the plate. Or all cutlery could be put on the right side of the plate in any order. Furthermore, desert forks are traditionally placed above the plate, and oyster forks are put on the right, so that breaks the logic of the arrangement.

It's just like mathematics or particle physics: every time you think you've reached the bottom, there is another layer beneath it, or another subatomic particle or concept which underpins your reasoning, and isn't fully explained.

Or worse still, it leads to contradictions and mystery. And forks.

Fair Gambling

> If you like to gamble
> I tell you I'm your man
> You win some, lose some
> all the same to me
> *Lemmy Kilmister, 1980[q]*

Until the mid-1990s, the Internet and the World Wide Web were the preserve of tech heads and academics. The first business boom was in two areas, sometimes considered to occupy the underbelly of society: pornography[95] and gambling[96].

The former may have been a driving force behind the adoption of the Internet, but also home video, DVDs, digital cameras, and even the printing press[97]. Unfortunately, blockchain does not easily lend itself to disseminating images or videos, no matter how desperate you are to view pictures of naked ladies. However, the latter – gambling – offers a lot more potential. But let's back up and look at a couple of issues concerning gambling and in particular the problems that online gambling needs to overcome.

Born to lose

The Gambler's Ruin problem looks at the probability of a gambler with a finite bankroll (and let's face it, all bankrolls are finite), who can't quit playing (and let's face it, hardened gamblers can't quit playing), either breaking the bank of a casino or going bankrupt[98]. It turns out that if the gambler's initial stake is small compared to the casino's resources, and if the bets made are therefore small, the gambler is almost certain to lose all his or her money.

The problem equates to something called a "random walk", which can be easily visualized. Imagine that you are standing a hundred paces away from a cliff edge. You toss a coin, and if it comes up heads you take a step away from the edge. If it comes up tails you take a step towards the edge. If you keep on playing and playing, eventually you will fall off the cliff, no matter how lucky you are at the beginning because, quite simply, that's the only condition under which the game will stop – unless you're one of the fortunate few who have more money than they can realistically spend in a lifetime. Comparatively speaking the casino has a bankroll that it's effectively infinite.

As a result, from a player's perspective, the only sensible choice is not to gamble. And if you must gamble, you should place all your stake in one go. Of course, that's not as much fun.

From the casino's perspective, it's somewhat different. Although individual players are unlikely to break the bank there are a lot of them. Like ants, any individual player is insignificant, but the sheer combined number of them means that precautions have to be taken to prevent them from carrying off the proverbial picnic. Therefore casinos institute two things: a maximum bet size (the house limit) and the vigorish (or house edge – namely a slight bias in favor of the casino winning).

The house limit ensures that the casino cannot be bankrupted – by only allowing bets up to a percentage of the casino's cash reserves they can cover any loss they make. If the casino is unlucky, by dropping the maximum bet at high stakes tables if their reserve funds dwindle, they can continue to ensure the covering of their losses. Finally, they can bar any high-rollers from continuing to play if they are on a winning streak (and hence possibly cheating).

The vigorish ensures that they make a slow but steady profit over time, due to the amusingly named "weak law of large numbers".

The weak law of large numbers

Also known as the law of averages, the weak law of large numbers was first proved by Bernoulli, and the proof was published after his death, in 1713[99]. It is actually a fairly intuitive law. In simple terms, the more often you conduct a random experiment (for example tossing a coin, rolling a die, or spinning a roulette wheel), the more the average of your results tends towards the real average of the underlying system.

This mathematical law has important applications because over time it allows you to work out what is going on in a "black box" system in the real world by taking more and more samples. For example, if you want to know the average weight of frogs in a large pond, you don't have to collect and weigh all of them. Measuring the weight of one frog has a high chance of giving you a value that's far from the average, but as few as thirty or forty frogs can get you very close to the actual average, provided you pick your sample frogs in a random and unbiased way and not only from the shallow south end of the lake.

You can apply the weak law of large numbers to an online casino too. If the casino is cheating, then by gathering enough data concerning the outcomes of games played you can quickly build up a body of evidence showing whether the game is biased or fair.

Proving fairness

A big problem that online gambling sites therefore have is proving to the players that they are not cheating. And there are plenty of tricks that can be used to make it seem as though the site is fair, but still edging up the profits for the owners. For example, look at the table below – it shows a game being played ten times, in which the player is betting sums on numbers on a digital "roulette wheel" coming up odd. As is normal with European roulette, the house edge is 2.7%, because if zero comes up, everyone loses (except those who placed a bet on it). The player bets 1 chip on some occasions, and 2 on others.

Bet placed	Number on table	Win or loss?	Return
1	11	WIN	2
2	35	WIN	4
1	1	WIN	2
2	26	LOSS	-2
2	22	LOSS	-2
2	2	LOSS	-2
1	3	WIN	2
2	17	WIN	2
1	14	LOSS	-1
1	13	WIN	2

Total bet	Number of wins	Number of losses	Total returned
15	6	4	7

Figure 38: Wins and losses in a "fair" game

The numbers the roulette table produced were generated totally randomly. In the game, the player ends up eight chips down, even though they won six times out of ten. So what's going on? Was it just bad luck?

If the numbers produced are analyzed it can be shown that they really are truly random. Okay, not with the short list that I provided above, however, I did generate them in a truly random fashion. But in this particular case, my online casino has "shuffled" the order of a few of the numbers to ensure that high bets are more likely to lose, and low bets are more likely to win. As a result, the game is heavily biased against the player, and yet on the surface it all looks above board. What can be done to prevent such a bias?

Hash functions to the rescue (again)

One solution is to publish the list of numbers beforehand so that everyone knows that they are genuine. That way anyone can check they are truly random and have not been shuffled about or manipulated through some other trickery. But hang on, if my casino publishes all the roulette results beforehand, then the players will know exactly what to bet on each time, and that's not fair either!

A good compromise is the following:

1. Publish a cryptographic hash of the list of random numbers on a public forum at the beginning of the week. Because the hash is made public, everyone knows that a week later you cannot go back and change it.

2. Publish each number as it is used. This ensures that a list of the numbers your roulette table "selected" can be produced by anyone who is interested.

3. Finally, provide the actual list of numbers at the end of the week. That way, anyone can check that the actual list hashes to the published hash and that the list was used in the correct order.

Actually, the last step is just a courtesy and is not required, because step 2 allows anyone to construct the list over time, which someone probably should, just to make sure that the casino doesn't publish a false list at the end of the week.

If you have been paying attention for the last 238 pages, your neurons should be firing, because a number of blockchain checkboxes are being ticked here. We have the requirement for an immutable record of publication, we have cryptographic hash functions, and we have transactions of value – either from the punter to the casino or vice versa. This makes online gambling seem like an ideal use case for blockchain. The only problem remaining concerns true randomness. And the world of chance suffers from two problems – true information of value looks just like random noise, and deterministic systems cannot provide true randomness. To understand why you have to have a basic understanding of something called entropy.

Entropy

Whenever people talk in-depth about randomness, the term "entropy" invariably crops up, eyes start to glaze over, and people begin to feel like they are sitting in a dull physics or chemistry class. There is a reason for this – our scientific understanding of the properties of randomness arose from the study of gases in containers. And not the fun experiments involving actual gases in real containers, such as hydrogen and oxygen in a test tube going "bang!" when you put a lit match near them, but the theoretical study of things called ideal gases.

The thermodynamics textbook "States of Matter" by Goodstein, which examines the contributions of historically significant scientists to the formulation of the concept of entropy and our understanding of it in mathematical terms, starts with the quote:

> *Ludwig Boltzmann, who spent much of his life studying statistical mechanics, died in 1906, by his own hand. Paul Ehrenfest, carrying on the work, died similarly in 1933. Now it is our turn to study statistical mechanics.*
>
> *— David Louis Goodstein*[100]

The ironic thing is that entropy is actually all about possibilities. What could be more uplifting than that?

Randomness

What does it mean for something to be random? It's pretty simple – something is random if we can't predict what is going to happen next. Randomness is unpredictability. Paradoxically, although the next specific event in a sequence of events may be unpredictable, the mathematical tools of statistics and probability have provided us with formulas that, under common circumstances, allow us to make predictions about the overall behavior of these unpredictable or random systems, even though we can't say exactly what is going to happen next.

And the second weird thing is that in a random system or set of events there is often this sense that there is actually something structured and formal going on underneath that, if only we knew what it was, would allow us to move from randomness to predictability. It is like the fabled philosopher's stone that is supposed to convert anything it touches to gold. Academics, market traders, business executives, gamblers, and all sorts of other people are all eternally looking for the means to make some kind of predictive sense of the chaotic maelstrom that they operate in.

Tossing a balanced coin in a fair manner appears to be random. So do the decimal digits of π. And yet the former is ruled by the laws of dynamics, and the latter appears to be a fundamental construct of the universe we live in. There is always this sense that if we knew more, then these apparently random objects would become entirely predictable, and hence no longer random. There is a small but real possibility that a mathematician may stumble upon a formula that allows us to immediately compute the *Nth* decimal digit of π without having to churn through all the previous ones using something called the Chudnovsky algorithm[101].

In the meantime, one predictable thing is that the world is full of unpredictable things. An example would be the exact location of all the atoms of hydrogen and oxygen in a test tube on a chemist's laboratory workbench at a specific time, just before they go bang.

It's a gas gas gas

In a physical system, such as a solid, liquid, or gas, entropy is a property that tells us how many different possible configurations the system can have. A solid such as ice floating in your gin and tonic has a regular cubic crystalline structure, and each water molecule is tightly bound within that structure – it can wobble about a bit, but it cannot wander about and move from the center of the ice cube to the edge. As a result, there are not many states the ice cube can be in, and so it is said to have low entropy. You can easily predict where a given molecule is going to be over time because it can't really move anywhere. I have simplified ice quite a bit here – it turns out that there are actually sixteen known crystalline forms it can take[102] – but given that most of them require the ice to be in the core of the planet Neptune, a place where no one is able to enjoy a late evening cocktail, hopefully you get my point.

Liquid ice, or water as we usually call it, does not have a crystalline structure. The individual molecules can slide over each other, but they still hang around in close proximity. Water doesn't climb out of the glass it is poured into, but unlike ice, it is harder to know where a particular water molecule is going to be in the near future, let alone an hour later. So we say that water has higher entropy than ice.

If you boil the water, you get a gas called steam. The water molecules are bouncing about in the available space, and hardly interacting at all. Gases spread out to fill the room and beyond. The hotter the gas, the faster the molecules are moving around, and the harder it is to predict where a given molecule is going to end up. Steam, therefore, has even higher entropy than water.

You should now have a hand-waving qualitative concept of what entropy is in the physical world. The final step is to look at Boltzmann's entropy equation, which puts an actual number to the entropy of a system. Here is how Boltzmann originally formulated it, and how it is engraved on his tombstone:

$$S = k \times log\ W$$

In this equation, S is entropy, k is the Boltzmann constant, and W is the number of possible permutations for the system. Don't worry about the specifics of the equation: what we are interested in is the fact that when you look at it you can see that entropy is logarithmically proportional to possibilities.

Taking logs is to raising powers what division is to multiplication. So logs measure the order of magnitude of something. Imagine three systems – the first has ten possible configurations, the second has a hundred and the third has a thousand. The entropy of the second system will be twice that of the first, and the entropy of the third will be three times the first:

$log(10) = log(10^1) = 1$

$log(100) = log(10^2) = 2$

$log(1000) = log\ (10^3) = 3$

Another way of looking at entropy is that as the complexity of a system increases exponentially, the entropy increases linearly.

I mentioned earlier in this section that entropy was first pinned down through the theoretical study of ideal gases, and gases in real life are far from ideal.

However, if we move away from the real world and into the virtual world of bits and bytes, then we kind of are in an ideal world – a world of ideas and information.

Signals and noise

I have just talked for over a page about the entropy of gases, and by now you are probably wondering why. The reason is that it is simpler to get an intuitive understanding of entropy when we are talking about physical things like ice, water, and steam because we have everyday experiences with them. However, the same concept of entropy exists in the subject of information theory, underpinning much of what makes the components of blockchain work.

In the 1940s, Claude Shannon came up with a novel approach to digital information[103]. Previous attempts had looked at information as order or structure. Shannon turned this on its head, proposing that true information appears random. The less predictable and more disorganized the message appears, the more information it contains.

Although initially counter-intuitive, when you think about it more, it starts to make sense. Imagine a Morse code signal arriving through your radio to your headset. If it is the same pattern repeated over and over again, once you have spotted the pattern you are not gaining any more information.

Here is an example using an ordered pattern consisting of repeating signals of dot-dot-dot, dash-dash-dash, dot-dot-dot:

... --- ...   ... --- ...   ... --- ...   ... --- ...

There is no point in listening to it for hours on end – nothing further is being added. It doesn't contain much information (although what it does contain could indicate something extremely distressing is happening).

The following pattern appears to be random:

```
..  -.  .-  ....  ---  .-..  .   ..  -.  -  ....  .   --.
.-.  ---  ..-  -.  -..  -  ....  .  .-.  .   .-..  ..  ...-  .
-..  .-  ....  ---  -...  -...  ..  -  .-.-.-  -.  ---  -
.-  -.  .-  ...  -  -.--  --..--  -..  ..  .-.  -  -.--
--..--  .--  .  -  ....  ---  .-..  .  --..--  ...-.  ..
```

It could be purely random, or it could contain very surprising information indeed.

For a string of length x containing letters or digits from a set of N characters, where each character is equally likely to be selected, Shannon's information entropy equation simplifies to the following expression that allows us to calculate the information entropy E:

$$E = log_2(N^x)$$

Take coin tosses for example. They can come up heads or tails, so $N = 2$, because the set of possible characters is {head, tail}.

Imagine you toss a coin ten times. Shannon's formula categorizes this as having $log_2(2^{10})$ = 10 bits of information or entropy. Each bit records the result of each coin toss, so it seems almost trivial.

A slightly more complicated, but still comprehensible example is given by a blogger called Zimbles[104], who notes that through asking five or six questions with "yes" or "no" answers, you can determine a randomly selected card (but we have to agree that aces are low). Imagine someone selected the seven of spades:

1. Is it red?   No.
2. Is it spades?   Yes.
3. Is it less than 9?   Yes.
4. Is it less than 5?   No.
5. Is it less than 7?   No.
6. Is it the eight of spades? No.

After these six questions, we know that the card must be the seven of spades.

Hang on, I said "five or six questions", and finding the seven of spades took six. When can it be five? Well, what we are doing here is called a "binary search algorithm" – you split the group in two, and check whether the target is in one half of the group or the other, and keep doing so until you find what you are looking for. If there were sixteen cards in a suit, this method would always take six questions. But there are only thirteen cards in a suit, so if our card had been the queen of spades, the questions would have gone on like this after question 2:

3. Is it less than 9? No.
4. Is it less than a queen? No.
5. Is it the king of spades? No.

Therefore we have determined that it is the queen of spades in five questions.

Now let's look at this with Shannon's equation. In the card case, our string has length one – it is a single playing card. The set of possible characters is the cards in the deck, and for a traditional pack of cards, there are 52. So without even fully understanding the formula, we can just plug in the numbers: $log_2(52^1)$, which any decent calculator will tell you is about 5.7. That is between five and six, slightly closer to six, and matches our practical investigation really well.

Note that Shannon's entropy formula looks very similar to Boltzmann's one – both give a result that is equal to the log of a measure of possible outcomes or states.

There is a story that Shannon was discussing his ideas with John von Neumann, and in particular what to call his theory. Shannon had been considering "information" or "uncertainty", but von Neumann immediately responded with the following:

You should call it entropy, for two reasons. In the first place your uncertainty function has been used in statistical mechanics under that name. In the second place, and more important, no one knows what entropy really is, so in a debate you will always have the advantage.

— John von Neumann[105]

Strong passwords and private keys

Here is another example: you have a list of 2000 English words, and you select twelve of them to be your mnemonic phrase. For example:

carpet baby bicycle betray shift approve barrel phrase measure prevent image brand

What is the entropy of that phrase[*]? Just plug the numbers into the formula:

$$E = \log_2(2000^{12})$$
$$= 131.589$$

Instead of a mnemonic passphrase, let's say we are using a binary string of ones and zeroes as our private key. How long does it need to be to contain the same entropy as the phrase? We use Shannon's entropy formula again:

$$131.589 = \log_2(2^x)$$
$$= x$$

---

[*] Actually, this is not completely accurate in the cryptocurrency world, where the last word contains some entropy and a checksum, so in that case the entropy is slightly lower.

So the private key needs to be 132 bits long to be at least as strong as the mnemonic phrase, provided both are truly selected at random.

If a hacker can test a single potential private key in a nanosecond, on average it will take over two duodecillion attempts to brute force either password, which amounts to 6 sextillion years of trying.

To put that in context using understandable numbers: it takes five thousand billion times the age of the universe so far. No one has that much spare time.

How to choose a winner

A core concept in an open permissionless blockchain is the addition of data to the end of the chain of blocks in a decentralized manner. But what exactly does that mean?

Firstly, anyone who wants to participate in the process should be allowed to, provided they have the resources and inclination to purchase the required hardware to "mine" blocks. Otherwise it's not open and permissionless. And secondly, the system has to ensure that the task of adding blocks is randomly allocated to different parties from block to block, otherwise, it is not decentralized.

The first requirement can simply be met by making all the code and protocols publicly available, thus enabling anyone with spare time and cash to study them, purchase suitable computing hardware and network connectivity, and spin up a node and a miner.

The second requirement is somewhat trickier. Current solutions rely on two principles – making sure the participants have "skin in the game", and selecting the next block generator through some random process. The most common methods for ensuring skin in the game are either external, for example, the investment in proof-of-work mining equipment, or internal, by requiring those participating in block generation to stake a number of cryptocurrency coins – the staked coins are then locked up and cannot be used.

It is the random process for selecting the next block generator that poses the biggest problem. Satoshi Nakamoto hit on an ingenious method for running the lottery that is Bitcoin mining by using proof-of-work to produce the randomness, but it is worth taking a few steps back in history to look at the work of Nick Szabo, Adam Back, and Hal Finney. There are plenty of other names I could reference: Wei Dai, David Chaum, Cynthia Dwork and Moni Naor[33] ... the list goes on and on, so I have to draw the line somewhere.

Szabo came incredibly close to inventing Bitcoin as early as 1998, publishing details in 2005[106]. His ideas have at their core the concept of creating digital objects of value, with the value arising from the fact that the object creator had conducted work to create them, namely through expending computer power and hence energy. Evidence of the value used to generate the objects involved Finney's reusable proof-of-work ideas[34] and Back's HashCash[107]. However, one thing was missing. In Szabo's system, anyone could at any time start mining the digital gold, so the more people that joined the system, the more bit gold would be produced, and the less valuable it would become. Szabo started to patch his system by proposing that each bit gold piece should be timestamped, and that earlier gold would be considered more valuable than later gold. The problem is that bit gold would then no longer be fungible, so then another patch was proposed – effectively a mixing service to bundle together quantities of bit gold from different years into tranches of similar value.

Randomness through proof of work

Nakamoto took a different approach – have a known cap to the total amount of bitcoins that can ever be produced, and use a lottery to determine who gets a portion of that total amount every ten minutes or so. Just as with a traditional lottery, the jackpot is paid out regardless of whether one single ticket is sold, or millions.

So how is the winner decided in a random manner? It cannot be done hermetically on the blockchain itself, for the blockchain data has already been determined. Any scheme relying on the prior blockchain data is open to manipulation – Sybil attacks and carefully constructed blocks can allow a suitably wily party to take control of the mining process and ensure that they are picked each time to create the next block, forming a vicious cycle of centralization controlled by that party.

Instead, Nakamoto relied on the unpredictable nature of hash functions. As previously discussed in "Hash Functions" on page 63, the only way to find out the result of hashing some data with a good hash function is to actually perform the work, that is compute the hash. In Bitcoin it is the SHA-256 hash function applied twice to a proposed block, making the process a bit like buying a lottery ticket, or perhaps a scratch card. If the outcome isn't small enough, you buy another card again and again (by adjusting the nonce), until you find one that produces a small enough number, or until someone else wins before you do.

With Bitcoin proof-of-work, Nakamoto found a way of injecting entropy into the deterministic blockchain system from the random outside world by effectively encouraging people to engage in a lottery, with rewards on the blockchain forming the incentive to play. Very clever stuff indeed.

Randomness and proof-of-stake

In proof-of-stake backed blockchains there is no longer a group of people outside of the system performing hashes and generating random numbers, and hence a different source of randomness has to be found to ensure that the blockchain is truly decentralized. At the time of writing, Ethereum has just launched version 2.0, which moves its public blockchain from proof-of-work to proof-of-stake, using random choice to select the next block generator. How have they managed to introduce chance into their deterministic system? As is usually the case with Ethereum, it's complicated, decentralized, and involves smart contracts. There are many moving parts to the solution, but in this section, I will be looking at one particular aspect in detail: how the random numbers are generated.

Ethereum 2.0

First, here is a short primer on how Ethereum is moving from proof-of-work, that is, randomness by lottery, to proof-of-stake.

Entropy is introduced to the new incarnation of the Ethereum blockchain by a parallel chain called the beacon chain. It runs alongside the main transaction chains, and is used to … hold on, did I just say "chains"?

Yes, I did. Ethereum 2.0 is an attempt to solve congestion problems caused by things such as too many cryptokitty sales or wildly popular DeFi contracts swamping the transaction pool by splitting the main chain into multiple parallel chains, called shards. There are going to be a whole bunch of these to start with – some estimates say 64, and with the number set to increase over time.

That means that there needs to be some kind of way of synchronizing the various shards because there will be occasions when a smart contract on one shard needs to interact with a contract on another shard. This is done by the beacon chain providing a regular time pulse for Ethereum activity, and a record of the overall state of each shard. It is a bit like the various members of a band listening to the drummer in order to keep the beat of the song. The beacon chain also allocates committees of validators to the various Ethereum shards where they, well, validate blocks. The Ethereum crew never does things in a simple manner. This validation is performed by people, or rather, their computer hardware running the right software.

The first step is to ensure that people actually participate on the beacon chain. There is quite a steep entry requirement – 32 ether (about $14,000 at the time of writing), as well as the expense of purchasing and running a validator node. The reason for the high stake is because if you muck about too much or drop off for a while, the remaining validators can punish you by "slashing" your stake, that is, removing your access to some or all of the cryptocurrency you locked up in order to become a validator in the first place. This should prevent any serious and obvious sabotage, but there is still the problem of randomly allocating different validators into different shards to vote on whether each shards' next block is valid. And the beacon chain blocks need validating too. There is a lot of validation to be done in Ethereum 2.0.

Anyway, if you are interested in delving into the inner mechanics there is a rather thorough overview of the architecture available here – [108]. I think that's enough about the complexities of Ethereum 2.0 for now though.

Do not worry: if the previous paragraphs seemed a bit complicated that is because they are. All you really need to know is that we have groups of validators, and they are going to select the one validator that assembles the next block at random, and then the remaining validators sign the block to give it the seal of approval. Then the committee members are shuffled about for the next round of block approvals.

All of this has to be done randomly, because otherwise, you could end up with groups of colluding validators manipulating one or more shards, effectively making them centralized and under the control of the colluding group. And so, finally, we have enough background information to look at the solution Ethereum has adopted to get randomness from the outside world into the blockchain without relying on a centralized "oracle": the RANDAO, or random number generating distributed organization[109].

Randomness by committee

Obviously, we cannot select one entity to be the centralized provider of randomness on a blockchain – even if they play fair and genuinely select real random numbers, they will know before everyone else what each number is going to be. And if large sums of money are at stake, the temptation will be there to manipulate the system with non-random inputs.

However, if a committee of unconnected entities could somehow select the random number together, then we could truly have reliable, decentralized randomness. That is how the RANDAO works.

Recall the XOR operation from the chapter "The Truth is a Harsh Mistress" on page 184 - the output from that operation is 0 if both inputs are the same, and the output is 1 if they are different.

Just as there is a symbol for addition, namely +, there is a symbol for XOR, which is ⊕, so here is the table again, written slightly differently:

Input A	⊕	Input B	=	Output C
0	⊕	0	=	0
1	⊕	0	=	1
0	⊕	1	=	1
1	⊕	1	=	0

Figure 39: XOR table using binary arithmetic

If Alice picks input A and Bob picks input B, and they do so randomly, and if they both reveal their choice at the same time, neither of them can know in advance whether the result will be a one or a zero.

Of course, getting two people to conspire is easy. If Bob and Alice agree that Alice will always choose zero, then the output is always equal to Bob's choice. It would be better to have more people contributing in order to generate the numbers. Fortunately, you can ⊕ add many numbers together. In fact, the rule then becomes: count the number of ones – if it's odd, the output is one, and if it's even, the output is zero. Imagine four people each choose a four-bit random number:

Alice:	0	0	0	0
Bob:	1	0	1	0
Chen:	0	1	1	1
Deepak:	0	0	1	1
	⊕	⊕	⊕	⊕
Result:	1	1	1	0

Figure 40: Four people generating a random number

In this table, the choices of the four participants are written in rows, and the columns are XORed together to produce the final result. Alice is colluding with Bob, but Chen and Deepak are truly independent, so the output is once again random.

Here is the next problem: what if the four participants each reveal their number in turn? Given that Deepak is going last, he can pick a number to make the output whatever he wants. For example, in the above table, if Deepak had chosen 0010, then the result would have been all ones (try it for yourself).

The solution to this is for all the participants to first publicly reveal the result of putting their individual choice through a hash function. Once all the hashes have been revealed, none of the participants can alter their choice (re-read "Hash Functions" on page 68 if this is not clear to you). Surely that solves the problem of the last person altering their number?

Well, no. There is still one further thing the last person can do, and that is to choose whether or not to reveal their number. Revealing it will give them one result, and not revealing it will give another, so they can decide which of the two they prefer and have an unfair advantage. You could punish people who do not reveal their number by taking away some of their stake, but that would also punish people whose computers went down due to a power cut or failure in internet service, which seems a bit unfair. Oh dear, will these problems never end?

For now, they end with the final piece of the puzzle: make calculating the result of mashing together of all the inputs difficult, so difficult in fact that takes a long time to compute the final random number. That way the last participant cannot determine whether showing their number in time is beneficial or detrimental, so they might as well put their cards on the table and reveal it. In Ethereum this is done through something called a "verifiable delay function" or VDF. If you want to learn more about VDFs, there are plenty of articles about them on the Internet[110].

Of course, we are talking about computer science and mathematics in this section, so there is no guarantee that there are not other sophisticated hacks or attacks that have been overlooked. But it all seems robust and trustworthy for the time being.

The arrow of time

There you have it – randomness is complex, especially in the decentralized world. What can we take away from all of this?

As far as we can tell, time moves in one direction, and because we can only hypothesize what the future will bring, life is full of unexpected events. That's what makes it interesting. I think Shannon put it perfectly in the last sentence of his 1951 paper, thrillingly titled "Coding - Theorems for a Discrete Source With a Fidelity Criterion", so it is appropriate to use it as the final sentence of this chapter:

> *Thus we may have knowledge of the past but cannot control it; we may control the future but have no knowledge of it.*

> — *Claude E. Shannon*[111]

Rise of the Autonomous Machines

> He's gotta a degree in economics
> Maths, physics, and bionics
> *Damian O'Neill and Michael Bradley, 1980*[f]

These days, if you follow leading-edge technology in the media, you don't have to look far to find someone touting a solution featuring "Virtual Reality meets 5G and the Internet of Things, plus Artificial Intelligence and Blockchain thrown in for good measure".

They invariably make me laugh. It is as though someone read about the aqualung, guided missiles, synthetic fertilizers, and solar panels, and therefore thinks that in the next few months anyone with a bit of drive, vision, and funding can set up a self-sustaining colony on Mars, so why shouldn't it be them?

Just blockchain and IoT, on the other hand – now there is an idea that I truly believe has legs.

The use cases for blockchain in logistics, supply chain, enterprise resource planning, and provenance of goods or data are starting to mount up, but these are only specific instances where blockchain can provide significant cost and time savings to industry. In this chapter, I provide a more general analysis of how I believe blockchain in combination with IoT should be positioned to revolutionize all of these areas.

Back to the ship of Theseus

To start with, please cast your mind back to page 122, when I talked about the ship of Theseus. I quickly moved on to talking about the identity of human beings, but did you notice that the philosophical question about identity was centered on an object, not a person?

Here is the funny thing – you do not have to be a conscious being to have an identity. Ships, cars, and airplanes can have an identity. A location, such as a field outside of the university town of Cambridge, can have such a strong identity that people write poems[112] and songs[113] about it. I won't dig further into this idea other than to point out that even an equation, or an idea, can have something close to an identity.

For this chapter I will be talking about IoT devices, which have one big advantage over a field when it comes to identity: they can actually do stuff. And when stuff is being done, it helps if you can work out who is "doing the doing", if you get what I mean.

An IoT overview

An explosion in the reliability, robustness, and affordability of a wide range of sensors, combined with significant improvements in power consumption, processor power, and data connectivity has resulted in the possibility of tracking, tagging, monitoring, and identifying pretty much anything we produce these days. We've come quite some way from slapping a bar code on a can and scanning it manually in the shop.

I would encourage IoT practitioners to explore how blockchain can apply to their data flows and specific use cases to determine whether blockchain is the right tool to solve their problems – and whether it is truly the missing link in their IoT deployment.

— *Maciej Kranz*[112]

Factories are being upgraded all the time. IoT devices can often be bolted on to existing machinery, and linked together to provide essential data for optimizing production processes and mitigating equipment failure or malfunctions.

However, having "all the data" at your disposal is not enough. A supermarket may, through a forensic process of sifting through shipping and production manifests, be able to work out exactly when and how the potato salad they wanted to sell was contaminated with salmonella, but it is a time consuming and costly process. Similarly, sensors in a factory may report that an assembly line is producing at half the expected rate, but ultimately an engineer has to determine and then authorize what action should be taken. When you drill down into the processes taking place, you eventually reach the assessment that a trade-off is being made. Do I investigate the potato salad situation, or just dump the spoiled stock? Do I fix or replace a machine part, or shut down the whole line and re-route raw material inputs?

A trade-off essentially comprises a form of negotiation or bartering. And key to the concept of negotiation or bartering in any society, ecosystem, or environment is the concept of a marketplace. This is where we move away from engineering and into the philosophy and sociology of economics.

The relevance of markets

Identity, reputation, a medium of exchange, contracts, reliable bookkeeping, and the authority to act are all separate and yet essential components in the provision of a corruption-free, fair, and accountable marketplace. We have touched on all of those in previous chapters, and those of you who have as a result spent some time thinking about blockchain's capabilities will probably already see where I am going with this.

> *To give real service you must add something which cannot be bought or measured with money and that thing is sincerity and integrity.*
>
> *— Donald A. Adams[115]*

Identity: You need to know who you are trading with. A blockchain provides the possibility for IoT devices to register their digital certificate simply by publishing it on the chain in an initial registration transaction, allowing other parties to subsequently verify that they are indeed dealing with the device they think they are, and to determine who the owner of the device actually is. The registration can happen in a fully automated manner.

Reputation: You need to be able to identify bad actors and rank good actors in the marketplace. This is therefore an enhancement of the identity component, together with some form of voting mechanism that allows parties in the system to label individual devices as positive contributors or drains on the system. Votes can easily be provided in a blockchain ecosystem by simply issuing tokens for them.

Medium of exchange: Probably the most obvious application of a blockchain, and certainly the most successful to date, the concept of cryptocurrency has been well-examined. In a blockchain system where all parties are identified, there is no need for proof-of-work, and hence micro-payments are feasible through such a cryptocurrency.

Contracts: Although I have previously asserted that I cannot see smart contracts replacing lawyers in the near or even distant future, for simple agreements at the level of the "direct debit" or "standing order", current smart contract technology is eminently suitable for an automated implementation. Moving on from these simple proven smart contracts, in the realistic future, we can envisage more complicated standing orders in which payment is only made on receipt of a service. The complexity of financial interactions that can be achieved with smart contracts implementing "decentralized finance" is the topic of chapter "DeFining Finance" on page 312.

A parallel with the real world would be an enhanced standing order for a magazine subscription, based on detection by a device in your house that this month's issue had actually been delivered. Parallels into supply chain and logistics are fairly obvious.

Reliable bookkeeping: Due to the fact that the blockchain ledger is immutable, it is feasible to perform regular automated audits of all transactions that have taken place. Furthermore, analytics run on the ledger would allow for further optimizations of the system, resulting in more cost savings. Blockchain provides the next step forward in double-entry accounting.

If you look at the history of the American capital market, there's probably no innovation more important than the idea of generally accepted accountancy principles

— Lawrence Summers[116]

Authority to act: It is not enough just to know who you are dealing with, you also need to know that they have the authority to make the decisions they are proposing. In the computer technology world, this is known as IAM (identity and access management), and it is traditionally managed by having a user database with associated permissions. For example, a system administrator account has a much higher authority to act on the system (it may be allowed to delete or update all data entries) than a standard user account (which may only be allowed to read data entries made by others). Again, functioning as a distributed database, a blockchain can track IAM and the consensus protocol of the system can enforce the permitted actions.

Putting it all together

When you consider all the above parts in isolation, you are left with a collection of interesting components. But as is usually the case for blockchain, it is only in combination that it becomes apparent that an ecosystem can function like a bazaar or a confederation of guilds. That is to say, it is effectively a virtual network of "merchants", "bankers" and "craftsmen" realized in software, working in a specific area. In the blockchain example, "bankers" are the combination of the medium of exchange and the ledger, "craftsmen" constitutes the IoT devices and the data they produce, and "merchants" consists of the companies and software services that allow the system to produce useful work.

And the beauty of a virtual bazaar is that swathes of activity can be automated.

The automatic bazaar

Now we're ready to make the final leap, dig into the fun part, and really start playing with ideas. What could be done with an automatic bazaar? What if there was a possibility of a simple, truly rational market, because the participants have no emotion, and are just looking to optimize their returns. What is more, they are able to take the big picture into account, and profit from it.

> *Markets can remain irrational longer than you can remain solvent.*
>
> — *A. Gary Shilling*[117]

For starters, devices can join, receive funding for work that they perform, make purchases and sales, and then pass the profits on the device owner. A basic example would be fitness bracelets that can submit anonymized data to aggregators, who sell it on to research institutions, pharmaceutical companies, or insurance companies, and pass part of the profit back to the bracelet owners. There are hundreds, if not thousands of cases like this.

Permissioned data sharing in an automated manner allows data analytics to be performed in an ethical way, which should increase data accuracy and therefore the real value of the data shared.

Factory devices can bargain with each other in an open marketplace, deciding which machines should receive raw materials, more electricity, determine maintenance priorities, order replacement parts, all without manual intervention.

Supply chains could not only be interrogated for product integrity at any stage, but sales and routing could be determined algorithmically, with raw materials being produced, transferred, and transformed in the most market-optimized manner. Automated bidding, for example through a Dutch auction on a blockchain, would allow for an improved general production life-cycle, with each stage of the production and shipping process being involved. As a result, the whole chain can be optimized (and some of the value of the improvements passed back as compensation to participants losing out due to the loss of a local optimization maximum), for the benefit of all.

And that last example should give you an insight into the true value of an automatic bazaar. At the moment trades are executed for a locally maximized profit. There are some financial instruments out there (hedging, or insurance, or derivatives) that allow for two-step transactions, in which one of the transactions is made at a lower profit, but the second transaction results in a substantially higher profit that offsets the first loss. Within an automatic bazaar, the potential for multiple transactions to be packaged and optimized for an overall gain would become a reality.

On the downside – we mere humans may well soon lose track of what is going on, if we haven't already.

Independent Sacrificial Offerings

> Wanna grow up to be
> be a debaser
> *Charles Thompson IV, 1989*[u]

Although it isn't technically "blockchain", in this chapter I will take a short look at coin offerings, which fall into the "crypto" side of things – the issuing and trading of digital assets, hopefully for a profit. Crypto enthusiasts generally don't actually care about what is going on under the hood, but as their activities are enabled by the properties of blockchain, I am guessing it is of interest to some to know what is going on in that space. I regularly get asked for advice by random people on the Internet as to which new shiny token or cryptocurrency they should spend their hard-earned cash on. I have no idea which cryptocurrency or token is going to skyrocket or collapse this week. If I did, I wouldn't be filing blockchain technology patents or writing books, I'd be trading.

I haven't bought any Initial Coin Offering tokens from a single ICO sale, because it was never clear to me what was on offer in the ones I reviewed, other than the hope of selling them on for a profit.

Actually, that's not completely true. I did buy some bitcoin (not enough, unfortunately, which is why I still have to work), and some ether, back in the days when it wasn't known that Bitcoin and Ethereum were, theoretically speaking, ICOs.

In the next decade, I have no intention of investing in Security Token Offerings, Initial Exchange Offerings, or any other activity in the token space ending in O that may be thought up in the future. Again, it turns out that I do have some other coins and tokens, because in the past some companies and organizations "airdropped" tokens into Ethereum addresses that held my balances of ether, as a way of advertising their project, but I didn't buy them – I got them for free, which is probably why their total worth is about $20.

There is a lot of controversy in the token-backed fundraising scene, and this chapter is just my personal take on the whole thing. You are welcome to spend your money or time as you like, and of course, are free to disagree with me if you want to.

In the next chapter, "DeFining Finance" on page 273, I will leave the confusing world of market psychology and pump-and-dump schemes, and look at some of the mathematics and software engineering that enables decentralized finance. If, like me, you are into blockchain and not into crypto, feel free to assume that I have done the reading on the latter so you don't have to, and skip to the next chapter.

Definitions

I'll start with a definition of what an ICO, STO, and IEO are:

ICO: Initial Coin Offering. An alternative to raising funds from investors, venture capitalists, or by a company going public (through an Initial Public Offering, or IPO).

The company publishes a white paper, puts up a fancy website with animated moving network diagrams in the background, and issues a new virtual coin, for example by instantiating a new ERC20 token on Ethereum.

The coin is then sold on cryptocurrency exchanges or directly to investors. It is therefore an unregulated form of crowd-funding.

STO: Security Token Offering. An ICO in which the issued coin is called a token, and is backed by an asset, typically a security. There should therefore be stocks, or bonds, cash, gold, or some other traditional asset of value that the token represents stashed away somewhere, and a contract ensuring that the security and the token are linked.

Security token offerings are therefore clearly bound by securities laws and in the United States, in particular, the Securities and Exchange Commission takes a very dim view of people who fail to comply with Federal regulations. They don't care if bringing down an unlicensed securities offering harms the unaccredited investors in the project, or how noble or revolutionary the proposal is. As far as they are concerned, the law is the law, and that is all there is to it.

IEO: Initial Exchange Offering. An ICO, in which the token sale is overseen by a cryptocurrency exchange. The idea is that an experienced entity (the exchange) manages the ICO, and takes a cut from the funds raised in compensation. The company raising funds using an IEO accepts the fact that they have to pay a commission as they are supposedly gaining credibility from the reputation of the exchange.

The flip side of the coin

When you invest in an ICO, what do you actually get? The answer: a digital asset that you own, and can hold onto, or sell onward, as and when you see fit. However, there is a big caveat:

ICO tokens are not shares and probably never will be

When I buy a share in a company, I know that I am eventually going to get a proportion of the profits as dividends. A company that has been through an IPO has a clear structure, plan, financial records, management and an executive that don't hide behind pseudonyms or fake personalities, as well as a corporate track history. And even with all of that due diligence in place, things still go wrong in the traditional IPO space.

So why would someone buy an ICO token?

- Because the token is expected to have utility at some point in the future, at which point it should be more valuable (the greater use theory), or

- Because at some point in the future someone else is expected to buy it for more money than was initially spent on acquiring it (the greater fool theory), or

- Because they are an idiot who didn't do their research.

Many ICO tokens that I looked at back in 2017 did not seem to be tied to anything useful or valuable. A lot of them were simply veiled (or not so veiled) requests for cash, with nothing substantial or relevant offered in return, often from people who were not even real.

I did get a lot of spam about ICOs though, encouraging me to buy into them or even offering to help me launch one with my blockchain company (for a fee). I politely declined at first, then set up a spam filter.

Insecurities

To me, STOs look like an attempt to continue the ICO game, because as I write this, in the majority of cases I have examined they are merely ICOs in disguise.

For example, given that a security token represents an investment contract into an underlying investment asset, it is *vital* that:

- the STO documentation explains how the real asset backing the token is actually going to be tied to the token, and
- there is a way of being sure that for each STO token there actually is a genuine backing asset.

I looked at three in detail, and there was no contract or legally binding agreement from the founders that the STO token actually had to be redeemed by the asset on request, which either suggests a significant lack of understanding on the project founders' part, or that it is a scam.

British pound notes state on them "I promise to pay the bearer on demand X pounds", where X depends on the denomination. This used to mean that a five pound note could be exchanged for gold to the value of five pounds of sterling silver at the bank of England. As of 1931 the British pound is no longer linked to precious metals, so apparently the statement means what it says in a purely tautological way – you can take a five pound note to the Bank of England and they will exchange it for a different five pound note if you ask[118].

However, the British pound has one advantage over modern STOs, namely over half a millennium of historical use.

Futility

Utility tokens made more sense to me - some of them were an attempt to repeat the early Ethereum success, but with a specific practical application. However: again, for every conceivable project out there, there appeared to be multiple utility token offerings. It's not rationally possible to assess the chances of success for any particular one, so again investing makes no more sense than playing the lottery.

In this section, I am looking specifically at blockchain projects that aim to tokenize an existing industry. I am not considering projects that aim to provide a brand new service or add extra functionality to blockchain technology.

I regularly get people asking me to have a look at their token project. They're usually very upbeat, have a nice looking website, and a cheerful set of team member head-shots. Surprisingly often their business idea is an initial coin offering, and not only that, but one with tokens that have no real utility beyond what could be offered by Bitcoin or some other existing cryptocurrency.

Being generous, I think in many cases these enthusiasts are not even aware that what they're promoting is a 2017-style ICO. Usually, they're not asking me to buy anything, and the belief is that with their new shiny token they are going to revolutionize a particular industry or cause.

They're probably wrong, and possibly even inadvertently breaking the law.

Ask yourself the hard questions

The first and most important question you need to ask when you are thinking of tokenizing an industry or investing in a project that intends to, is:

Why is this being done with a token?

Could everything be done equally well with a centralized database, like standard loyalty point schemes? Are the cost savings to the token holders going to be minimal compared to the traditional way of operating? In that case, there's nothing about blockchain or a distributed ledger that adds anything to what is on offer. It should be about the benefits of decentralization, not decentralizing just for the sake of it.

The second question is to look around at what is already out there, and ask:

Does a token I could use to provide this service already exist?

Why is a new token being created? Sometimes the initial founders intend to issue a large proportion to themselves, which means they are simply trying to print money. In which case it's not about a great idea at all. It's just a get-rich-quick scheme.

The third question is about the industry to be improved (or if the project is insanely optimistic, disrupt):

Are the project administrators uniquely connected and qualified to revolutionize the industry selected?"

Do they have a world-class network of connections in to that industry? Are they highly experienced in operating in the industry? Are they so intimately connected to the daily ins-and-outs of working in the business that the flaws and inefficiencies of it cause them great irritation?

Someone who has spent their life selling second-hand cars in upstate Wisconsin is probably not the person who is going to revolutionize farming practices in countries with low-income economies.

The fourth question you need to consider is:

How many other people are doing this?

In-game currencies, stocks on a blockchain, tracking intellectual property rights, reward points for watching adverts, incentivizing going green - there are tens if not hundreds of projects like this out there. Pick a random profession or business, and I guarantee that within an hour you can find three relatively mature start-ups that are hoping to tack tokens onto it.

Here's an example - I picked dentistry at random, and a quick search shows there's already something called *dentacoin*. But why do dentists need their own coin? Isn't Bitcoin good enough for them? Will there be a separate coin for orthodontics - *orthodentacoin*? Perhaps there's even space in the market for *franco-orthodentacoin*, specifically for French-speaking orthodontists?

Obviously not. But is the project you are considering the equivalent of a *franco-orthodentacoin*?

These days your token project should check most, if not all, of the boxes that blockchain's properties provide, and your project should do so in a novel industry-relevant way.

In summary

Here is a checklist of the kinds of things that should be considered when proposing a project crowd-funded by tokens. Will the project:

- return control to the end-user,
- remove the inefficiencies and "rent charging" of traditional projects that drain rather than add value,
- allow otherwise infeasible automation of processes,
- improve access and usability,
- reduce risk and reliance on third parties,
- prevent counterfeiting and false accounting practices?

If the project provides all of the above, in an area that the founders are intimately familiar with, they won't need to issue themselves with half (or even more) of the available tokens to become rich, and then watch as the project quickly folds.

If you are thinking of investing in such a project, conduct an analysis using the above checklist yourself. It could save you a lot of money.

The centralized IOU

What do you get if you combine an ICO with a cryptocurrency exchange? An Initial Exchange Offering. Now you have all the risks and problems of an ICO, and you are paying commission to a middleman in the form of an exchange. Talk about the worst of both worlds.

The less said about IEOs the better.

So what now ...

Well, that was a lot of negativity. Perhaps it's time to be a bit more positive.

I still believe that the functionality offered by blockchain should eventually result in significant advances in current financial products and open the door for new products, but I just have a layman's understanding of these things: bonds, securities, mortgages, or capital loans. It's not an area I have spent much time on.

However, as someone who owns a few shares in various companies (I used to own one single TSLA share for example, just so I could say I own a Tesla, but thanks to the stock split on 28 August 2020, I now own five), I think blockchain-issued stocks on a decentralized stock exchange with direct seller-to buyer-trading would be neat.

Another possible example I'd like to see is real-time dynamically updated and continuous stock issuance for early-stage companies. At the moment startup funding is done in rounds and the cash is handed over in tranches. I could see an independent blockchain oracle receiving company financials on a month by month basis and a smart contract that issues more shares on the open decentralized market based on how the company's revenue growth is proceeding, which I think would be closer to what ICOs should have been.

However, there's still the concern that the oracle could be manipulated by an unscrupulous CEO – although to be fair, that also happens on a regular basis with earnings reports in traditional listed companies.

Anyone here remember Enron and Arthur Anderson[119]?

DeFining Finance

> Ik ben verzekerd van succes,
> Tegen brand en voor mijn leven.
> *Ernst Jansz, 1982[v]*

In the previous chapter, I looked at how anyone can create a token these days, and how it resulted in the ICO gold rush of 2017, how tokenization works, and touched briefly on some of the craziness that happened after sales and marketing-focused entrepreneurs got in on the game.

In this chapter, I am going to be looking at the successor to the ICOs, namely Decentralized Finance, or DeFi for short[*]. It represents the latest phase in the apparently never-ending waves of excitement and hype, which in the crypto world invariably leads to scams and pump-and-dump activity. I would not be at all surprised if in a couple of years' time another craze hits the scene. I predict it will be called DeFi 2.0.

Once again, Ethereum is at the center of it all, although other smart contract blockchains are catching up. I happen to love the

---

*   Disclaimer: in this chapter I mention some DeFi projects by name as illustrative examples of the methods used. The reader should not take this as an endorsement of the reliability, legitimacy, or security of these projects.

concept of Ethereum, but it does seem to attract a mixture of madness and brilliance like nothing else. And just as ICOs before it, the rising excitement in this corner of the blockchain world is going to end up with a few people making a fortune and a lot more people losing a fortune. Hopefully, at the end of it, we will yet again have learned some lessons that can inform us in the future, but they will be expensive.

DeFi is supposed to be about developing improved financial services accessible to the masses and the unbanked and hopes to cater to all sorts of niches and unusual markets that are badly served by "one size fits all" banking. Not all of these niches are small. As of late 2020, we are still in a gold rush era involving complex concepts and poor user interfaces, so some parts of this chapter will date badly.

I am going to provide you with a selection of information that should get you up to speed on what is actually going on at the nuts-and-bolts level of some of the components of DeFi. Unfortunately, I can only scratch the surface, as the offerings have become so varied and convoluted that it would take an entire second book to cover them all, and they are arriving at such a rate that by the time such a book were finished, it would be woefully out of date.

Nevertheless, if you've been wondering what automated market makers, stablecoins, flash loans, and other weird sounding terms are all about, some of the answers are to be found below. There is also a section highlighting the risks involved. After that, you can make up your own mind whether you want to look into it more yourself. If it all starts to sound a bit weird and pointless, hang in until the last section, where I pull it all together and provide a bit of meaning.

I will begin with a basic introduction to the traditional world of financial instruments to set the groundwork, so if you are one of those people who already know what a financial derivative is, and clearly understand the difference between an option contract on a future, and a future contract on an option, then feel free to skim through the first few sections or send me long ponderous emails pointing out where my quick summary is not quite right.

For the rest of us: let's get started.

Underlying Assets

Everything needs a foundation and in the finance world, when you follow the trail back through all the obfuscation and jargon, eventually there has to be something at the bottom of the pile that people value. That thing at the bottom is known as an "underlying asset". When the chips are down and people in the space want to cash in on all the financial cloud castles that have been built, it is the underlying asset they turn to, because there is meant to be a genuine demand or use for it.

An underlying asset could be as simple and tangible as a crate of oranges. At a slightly more abstract level, it could be gold (which as we discussed, does have industrial usage, but obtains most of its importance by being perceived as a store of value independent from any government), or the fiat currency of a nation-state (which has value in that it can generally be used to buy a crate of oranges, or more importantly, to pay taxes to said nation-state).

I would therefore like to propose the hypothesis that the original cryptocurrencies such as bitcoin in the Bitcoin blockchain system, and ether in the Ethereum blockchain system, have attained enough credibility and respectability to attain the status of an underlying asset for the crypto-world. There are enough people out there that now perceive them as valuable, and not just a handful of cypherpunks, technically literate followers of the Austrian school of economics, and libertarian computer programmers.

In the financial world, when there is an underlying asset, you can implement subsequent financial instruments built on top of it and then start trading them. This is what most of finance is really all about.

Derivatives

The financial cloud castles mentioned in the previous section were built for a reason. Take an orange farmer, for example. The farmer has committed land, effort, and time to cultivate those oranges. Growing fruit takes a while, so the farmer can calculate how much money has and will be spent on producing the crop. They can determine that at the moment the price of oranges on the open market means that it makes enough of a return to ensure the effort has been worthwhile.

But what if the bottom drops out of the market and for some reason oranges are suddenly worthless? Enter a financial instrument: the derivative, so called because it is "derived" from the underlying asset (and that caused me an immense amount of confusion when I first encountered it, because I tend to think like a mathematician, and in mathematics, a derivative has a very specific meaning that has no bearing on the financial term).

There is a specific derivative that provides the farmer with insurance. It is called a "future", and is a contract which guarantees that the oranges can be sold in the future at a set price once they are ripe, picked, crated, and shipped off to the orange juice processing plant. The fixed price is set well before harvest time, and as is always the case with insurance, there is a premium. However, for a farmer trying to balance the books for their endeavor, having a guaranteed income is worth that relatively small cost.

Other derivatives include:

- Options, which give you the right but not the obligation to buy or sell an underlying asset (at a premium), and so they are like renting the asset for a while.

- Swaps, which allow one bank to swap a floating interest rate instrument for a fixed-interest rate one with another party, so they are a bit like taking a fixed-rate mortgage on your house rather than gambling on interest rates not going up.

Derivatives are thus meant to provide a service and bring additional value and utility to the financial system.

Decoupling

Underlying assets can be cumbersome to trade. If you want to sell and buy gold on the open market, it is going to be a bit awkward to have couriers turning up on your doorstep with gold ingots on one day, and expecting to collect them again the next day. By having an abstract representation of the underlying assets in the marketplace, things become much faster and more convenient.

A side effect of this abstraction is that trading can become decoupled from the original asset, and financial instruments evolve into entities in their own right. There may be a farmer producing oranges at one end of the system, and a warehouse holding a Dutch auction for supermarket buyers at the other, but in the middle, futures can be changing hands over and over, and traders may be placing put and call options, without anyone on the exchange actually caring that it is oranges (or rather an abstraction of oranges) that are being traded.

Centralized exchanges

I can still remember that a couple of decades ago the satellite office of a Nasdaq-listed company in Cambridge I worked for had to buy a fax machine because the broker in New York who handled our share options would only take orders over that communication channel. You needed a broker because ordinary people couldn't buy and sell shares directly on the stock market floor, and your request to exercise an option and sell shares would be executed at some point in the next few days.

By the time I left that company, only two years later in 1999 at the height of the dotcom boom, our stock options were handled by an online electronic trading platform, which meant that we could sell them at a few minutes' notice. The exchange was still centralized but was no longer tied to a physical location – a trading floor. The electronic exchange acted as a "market maker", holding enough share reserves in the company stock to ensure its ability to absorb any requests to buy or sell, so in a way, it was acting as a derivative of the underlying asset of a physical stock market. Market makers provide liquidity in a given market, and in return for providing this service, they profit from the spread between asking prices and bidding prices.

Of course, the virtualization of a trading platform does not equate to decentralization. Technically speaking, the market maker and electronic trading platform act as custodians of the shares, just as a bank does for your money. Traditional stock markets and commodity exchanges have worked well for centuries (for some), evolving over time to adopt the efficiencies that technological advances have brought – the printing press, the telegraph, the radio, computers, and the internet – but the underlying paradigm is still the same. Commission is charged, arbitrage advantages accrue to some parties but not others, and ordinary people do not have full ownership or control of their assets. There are membership requirements, market opening and closing times, and anonymity is only granted to a select few insiders.

I did say it was going to be a quick and basic summary of the mainstream *status quo*, but with that out of the way, we can move on to look at what DeFi is attempting to solve in relation to these past solutions.

Crypto-capitalism

Many cryptocurrency holders would like to do more than sit on their assets while waiting for the price to appreciate. They want to profit from them by putting them to work. What is the point of having capital if you can't use it to be a capitalist? But until recently there were really only three main choices:

1. hodling: a slang term in the crypto-space for "holding", derived from a drunken typo made on the bitcointalk.org discussion forum[120], and which is similar to making a long-term investment in a stock,

2. day trading: in its simplest form, selling or buying cryptocurrency in exchange for fiat one day, and buying or selling it back again a few days, hours, or even minutes later after the price has shifted, and

3. the equivalent of foreign exchange trading on a cryptocurrency exchange: swapping one digital asset for another one that might go up in value.

The second and third choices used to involve signing up to a cryptocurrency exchange as centralized as electronic trading platforms for the stock markets. In the early days obtaining an account was as simple as supplying a username and password and sending some bitcoin or ether to a deposit address, but the downside of the complete lack of regulation was a series of crypto-exchange scams and collapses, the most famous being Mt. Gox in 2014[*].

Regulation has slowly caught up with cryptocurrency exchanges, many of which are now required to hold financial licenses, and apply Know Your Customer (KYC) and anti-money-laundering (AML) processes[121]. We can but hope that this decreases the number of exchange hacks and scams.

DeFi is now used as a catch-all phrase for various digital analogies to traditional financial instruments that can be engaged with in a decentralized manner. At a base level, DeFi relies on autonomous smart contracts to enable a connected system of such functionality. Finance is complex, and various pieces needed to slot into place in order for DeFi to come into existence. There are plenty of fundamental components out there on various blockchains, running in the form of decentralized applications (Dapps), and they

---

[*] Why anyone ever thought it was a good idea to send bitcoin to a cryptocurrency trading platform whose name was an acronym of "Magic: The Gathering Online eXchange" is beyond me.

come in all sorts of different configurations. In the sections that follow, I will look at some of the more noteworthy experiments to date in this space, but you should be aware that DeFi moves fast.

Crypto-loans

At this point, I have to confess that until five years ago I had never really thought about what loans actually achieve, despite having had several mortgages, a car loan, and an overdraft at my bank. Just as my childhood concept of money as "paper you can use to buy stuff" was naive, I also thought of loans as "money you borrow to buy things that you can't afford". Which, at its simplest is what they are, but there is so much more going on underneath.

Loans are about something called "liquidity", which is a financial or accounting term used to talk about how quickly you can exploit the value of an asset. Cash is the most liquid because you can spend it immediately. At the other end, you have something like a house, which is highly illiquid. Getting the market value for your home in a property sale can take several months or even years. If you want to sell it quicker, you usually have to set a lower price, but in a country like England, all the legal paperwork and surveys required mean that selling in less than a month is still unlikely.

However, if you own a house outright a bank will lend you a significant proportion of its market value using the property as collateral. A secured loan can turn an illiquid asset such as a house, into a liquid asset, namely cash.

But what about an unsecured loan? Again, it functions as a tool for converting an illiquid asset – in this case, your future earnings – into a liquid one, that is, cash in hand. Just as it takes time to sell a house, so it also takes time for next month's paycheck to arrive.

And of course, the bank covers the risk of you defaulting and makes a profit by expecting to receive more back at the end than they provided you with at the beginning. This also known by the shorter and more familiar term "interest".

Lending and charging interest are therefore the first and most obvious method that people think of when pondering how to profit from virtual asset holdings.

MakerDAO[122] and Compound[122] are examples of decentralized lending services. They are too complex to explain here, but rely on two basic premises:

1. ensure that the cryptocurrency loan is over-collateralized to provide confidence that it can always be repaid, and
2. automatically "repossess" the collateral if the over-collateralization drops below a certain percentage.

Stablecoins

From a trading perspective, volatility is not just good, it is essential. If a commodity or stock were to permanently stay fixed in price, there would be no profit to be made in trading it. The only purpose for buying a fixed-price stock would be to hold it over long periods of time as a reliable investment paying out a regular dividend, or for voting rights. A stable commodity would not need options or futures contracts as the commodity producer would already know what price they were going to get in the future. Both are, however, just thought experiments. Only in a deterministically predictable universe could you ensure that the supply of a commodity exactly matched the demand for it at any given time, or that there was perfect competition between companies, and we clearly don't live in a universe like that. So what is the problem with volatility in the cryptocurrency markets?

None for traders, provided they enter into the market with historical knowledge of the rates of price change that cryptocurrencies can experience. However, blockchain tokens do not directly translate across to securities such as stocks, or to commodities. Instead, they behave somewhat like gold, in that they also have currency-like properties. If a cryptocurrency or token is used for payment, then the user expects it to behave like money. In smoothly running economies we want our money to be stable – if the value of money decreases rapidly, for example, due to rampant inflation, then consumers will want to spend it quickly before it devalues, and similarly, if it appreciates rapidly in value then the same consumers will start hoarding it in the expectation that they will be able to buy more stuff with the same amount in the near future.

If you want to (or have to) be paid in cryptocurrency, don't want to participate in the roller-coaster ride of ups and downs in the market prices, and also don't want to have to immediately cash out your earnings to a fiat currency on an exchange, then a stablecoin will sound very appealing. This is because you are thinking of these virtual assets as money.

Money needs to maintain a stable value if it is to be used as a measure of the appreciation and depreciation of assets over time. These are some of the motivations for bringing stablecoins into the blockchain economy. There are a few others, for example enabling traders to sit out of the market for a while without having to cash out to fiat currency, which in many jurisdictions is a taxable event.

To further complicate things, the term stablecoin is used for different types of asset and currency representations.

The definition of a stablecoin is simple: it is a blockchain token that is pegged to something else. That something else may be a fiat currency, a commodity, a stock, gold, or even a cryptocurrency on another blockchain. As all these different things have diverse properties, you can already see that this stable holds a lot of coins, some of which are going to turn out to be racehorses, and others donkeys.

How can you peg the value of one item to another? In the real world, a fixed exchange rate amounts to a promise. Back in the days of the gold standard, the central banks promised to sell and buy gold at a set price designated in the national currency, and before World War I there were actual gold coins in circulation, with an understanding that copper and silver coins could be traded up for gold ones at face value, even if the market value of the metal in the coins was lower. Similarly, if a nation pegs its currency to the US dollar then that nation's central bank makes a commitment to always exchange the local currency for the dollar.

Stablecoins work in the same way – there is an understanding that the coin can always be redeemed for a fixed amount of the backing asset at any time. How can such a promise be made? It depends on what the stablecoin is supposedly pegged to, and how the decentralized contracts that deliver on that promise are designed.

On-chain stability

Pegging a stablecoin token to a cryptocurrency on a single blockchain that supports smart contracts is simple: deploy a contract that, on receiving a token of one type, mints one stablecoin token and hands it over. Oh, and the contract also has to honor the reverse, namely on receiving a stablecoin token it has to return one token of the underlying asset. I can create a smart contract on Ethereum that instantiates an ERC-20 token called Keircoin, which sends one keircoin to any address sending it one ether, and similarly sends one ether to any address sending it one keircoin. Keircoin would then reliably be pegged to ether.

Why I would do this is another question – after all, ether is already a usable native token on the Ethereum blockchain. On the other hand, people sometimes seem to like to buy birthday presents in the form of 10 euro gift tokens, pegged to the euro, and that are only redeemable in specific retail outlets. Please keep in mind that, personally, I prefer to receive 10 euro banknotes. They have all the properties of the gift tokens, and what is more, they can be spent in every shop in the country.

Cross-chain stability

How about pegging an Ethereum token to bitcoin? Every blockchain acts as its own hermetic system, and it is not possible under ordinary circumstances to create or destroy* bitcoin at will, so this is not a trivial problem. In blockchain parlance it is called "blockchain interoperability", and there are solutions out there called "atomic† cross-chain swaps" which solve one half of the problem[124]. They ensure that if I have bitcoin and you have ether, the transaction guarantees that the correct quantity of my bitcoin is only transferred to your Bitcoin address if the right amount of ether is transferred from your Ethereum address to mine. As they involve a time-locked transaction on the Bitcoin blockchain and four distinct steps that must be completed correctly, they cannot be executed that quickly.

Swap the term "ether" for "a token representing bitcoin on the Ethereum blockchain" in the preceding paragraph, and you have the first half of what is needed for a Bitcoin stablecoin on Ethereum.

The second half of the problem is as follows: after my atomic transaction to convert my bitcoin on the Bitcoin blockchain into the pegged stablecoin on the Ethereum blockchain has gone through, there has to be a guaranteed method for me to convert it back again at a later date. One solution is to eschew decentralization and rely on a custodian. This is how "wrapped Bitcoin" or wBTC on Ethereum works, which in my eyes makes it more like a token backed by a peculiar cryptocurrency exchange than anything else[125].

After all that, you may be asking, why would I want to use my bitcoin holdings on Ethereum? The answer is that it is about liquidity again – there might be a great trading opportunity on another blockchain that you want to take advantage of quickly without having to jump through the hoops of trading on a cryptocurrency exchange as well.

---

* Actually, there are two ways I know of to destroy bitcoin: one is to send it to a made-up address that no one knows the private key for, although that is more like locking it up and throwing away the key, and the other method is for a miner to fail to claim the transaction fee while minting a block. Neither makes commercial sense.

† This is atomic in the sense of indivisible, not radioactive.

What if you want to have a truly decentralized system? For that, a mechanism known as an automated market maker can be used, which is the topic of the next section.

Automated Market Makers

If you are going to have an exchange on a blockchain that mirrors the real-world price of an asset, there needs to be some way of getting that price into the blockchain in a trustworthy manner. Initial solutions involved things called an "oracle" – a trusted third party running a service that publishes those prices in the blocks on a regular basis. Unfortunately, making an oracle less centralized involves a lot of ugly hacks. However, there is a more decentralized method that uses the naturally arising greed of arbitrageurs to import the external price without requiring trust.

Magic chocolate vending machines

Imagine a chocolate vending machine that not only accepts money and distributes chocolate but also allows the reverse to happen. That's right – you can put chocolate into it, and it gives you back cash. Furthermore, in order to determine how much chocolate you get for the money you put in, or *vice versa*, the machine uses a simple formula.

Inside the machine, there is a balance with a fixed weight on one side, and a pile of chocolate and money on the other.

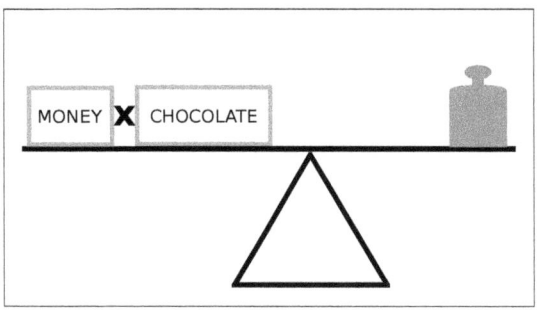

Figure 41: The internal balance of the machinery

The weight of chocolate in the machine times the amount of money in the machine has to stay constant. Let's start with a machine that contains 10 kilos of chocolate, and 100 euros. The product of those two numbers is 1000.

Someone comes along and puts 10 euros in. How much chocolate do they get out? Well, now there are 110 euros in the machine, so the amount of chocolate it holds has to decrease from 10 kilos to ... hang on, I can't do that in my head, so let's use an equation and a calculator:

$$110 \times x = 1000$$

Therefore x is 1000/110, or about 9.091 kilos. The machine has to dispense approximately 909 grams of chocolate to keep it in balance.

Now someone else puts 2 kilos of chocolate in. The machine's chocolate holdings go up to about 11.09 kilos, so to maintain balance the machine should only be holding 90.16 euros, and it's currently got 110 euros. As a result, it pays out 19.84 euros. Balance maintained.

So far so good, but what does it imply?

Arbitrage

The interesting thing is that the magic chocolate machine is not connected to the internet or any other provider of information, so it has no idea what the current market price of chocolate is, and yet it is happily buying and selling one for the other. Furthermore, its prices will match the market prices remarkably closely.

The reason for this is down to the fact that there are people interacting with the machine, and some of them will quickly notice if it is handing out chocolate cheaply, and start piling money into it to get a bargain. We call those kinds of people arbitrageurs. And the actions of the arbitrageurs push the price of the remaining chocolate up. Once the price matches that of the external market, the arbitrageurs will stop buying. If the external market price changes again, then they start buying or selling anew.

On smart-contract enabled blockchains such as Ethereum, magic chocolate machines are called Automated Market Makers, or AMMs for short. There are now plenty of them out there, using all sorts of pricing algorithms, but in essence the underlying mathematics performs the same function. They are decentralized and manage to bring real-world data onto the blockchain without having to use a trusted third party such as an oracle. Instead, relying only on the basic human desire to make a profit they keep an on-chain decentralized exchange in step with traditional of-chain marketplaces. I find this remarkable in its simplicity, as most mathematical equations are a lot more complicated than:

$$x \times y = k$$

An example of an AMM that is immensely popular at the time of writing and uses precisely this equation is Uniswap, founded by Hayden Adams and launched in late 2018[126].

Investing in the machine

Very few people would set up a magic chocolate vending machine out of the goodness of their heart and even less would stock it with chocolate and money unless there was a profit to be made. DeFi applications use various mechanisms to incentivize people to add funds, or "liquidity" as it is known, to the exchange. But liquidity is just the same as the supply of chocolate and money in the magic vending machine. This supply is called the "liquidity pool" because it is a pool of different investors' assets that provide liquidity to traders who can use it to quickly swap between different tokens on the blockchain. The investors supplying the tokens to the pool are also known as liquidity providers, but that is a name that looks at them from the traders' perspective. From their own viewpoint, they are investors or venture capitalists, in that they provide capital (their tokens) to the AMM (which is like a business or startup) in order to enable it to function. In return, they expect to make a profit.

The most common method for returning a profit to the investors is trading fees. By charging exchange users a small commission for their use of the service, and distributing a part to the developers and the rest to the liquidity providers, passive income is made from the capital or the upfront work of designing and deploying the contract. As we are in operating in the blockchain world, this is usually done through a mechanism using virtual assets called liquidity tokens. By providing a supply of the token exchange pair to the AMM you receive some of the liquidity tokens in return, and profits can then be paid out automatically to those token holders on a regular basis. As an AMM becomes more popular, more people use it, the amount earned in commissions increases, and so more people pile in to provide liquidity in the hope of making profits.

Flash loans

Let us suppose that you happen to notice that your local supermarket is selling pears at one euro per kilo. Furthermore, there is this guy who has an apple orchard, and who will swap apples for pears weight for weight. Finally, there's a market trader at the other end of town who pays two euros for a kilo of apples. This is a great triangular arbitrage opportunity. With just three trips and transactions, you can turn a hundred euros into two hundred euros!

You grab your wallet and head for the supermarket. Ten minutes later your wallet is a hundred euros lighter, but you have a hundred kilos of pears, so you head onward to the orchard. Another ten minutes and a jovial chat with the orchard owner later, and you have swapped the pears for apples. Now you make your final trip to the market trader.

Imagine your disappointment when you get there, and find that the trader is no longer accepting apples at two euros a kilo. Even worse, she has reversed the price and now it is a euro for two kilos.

Half an hour ago you were sure you could double your money, but instead, you have halved it. If only you could have conducted all of the transactions in the same microsecond.

Some DeFi protocols allow you to do precisely that. You can chain transactions into one single atomic transaction that only executes if every element in the chain can complete. If just one single sub-transaction would fail, then the entire transaction is invalid, and it is as though it never happened. As a result, the worst outcome is that you are exactly where you were when you started, minus a small fee for trying.

It is all very well if you spot a triangular, square, pentagonal, or even greater arbitrage opportunity, but wouldn't it be even better if you could somehow borrow virtual assets in order to leverage your profits? That is what flash loans enable. There are contracts and protocols on the Ethereum blockchain that allow you to start your transaction with a loan, continue with actions that trade and exchange the loan, and end with converting back to the original asset type to repay the loan, with a small amount of interest. In effect, this is a form of margin trading, except that no up-front collateral is required because you are guaranteed to repay the loan if you get to take it out in the first place.

The Aave protocol is an example of a DeFi offering that provides precisely such a service[127]. Investors provide virtual assets to a lending pool and receive tokens in return. The token holders get a share of the interest charged on loans as a reward for locking up their capital. Tokens can be traded or can be cashed in to unlock the locked-up capital.

Flash loans do have one unexpected side-effect: they can be used by sufficiently skilled DeFi traders to leverage profits derived from exploiting bugs in smart contracts to astronomical levels. If you see a small arbitrage advantage in the real world you will generally ignore it. After all, most of us do not have hundred million euro lines of credit with our bank that we can call on at a moment's notice, and just try going to your bank manager and asking for a one day loan of such a sum. You will be laughed out of the local branch office (if your bank still has one, that is).

However, if a DeFi project contains a bug that only yields the opportunity for small returns if exploited, flash loans give the trader the opportunity to throw millions of dollars worth of tokens or cryptocurrencies at it in a brief moment, resulting in serious profits for the trader, and the incidental demise of the project.

In this section, I have referred to the arbitrageur as a skilled trader. The cryptocurrency press usually calls them malicious hackers, because they are violating the spirit of the decentralized applications. For comparison – George Soros pocketed a billion dollars in 1992 by exploiting a bug in the British government's economic thinking and is now seen as a financial genius rather than a hacker[128].

Automated pyramid schemes

As is the case with any new technology, it can be used constructively or destructively. Today I was looking at the source code for a smart contract deployed on the TRON blockchain[129] that implemented a pyramid scheme.

Simply put, in pyramid schemes you pay an upfront fee and your returns depend on the number of people you subsequently recruit. The related Ponzi scheme is an illegal scam whereby the fraudster pretends that returns are being generated by investments, but in actual fact money submitted by later investors is used to pay improved returns to earlier investors[130]. In both scams, as long as more participants are recruited or investors arrive bringing more money, it flows up the chain or pyramid, the scheme keeps running, and the earlier investors are often so pleased that they even help market it further. As there are not an infinite number of people available in the world to keep the scam running, at some point investment dries up, the scheme folds, and the latecomers lose their contributions and gain nothing in return. In accounting terms, pyramid schemes and Ponzi schemes always have more liabilities than assets, so at some point, they must fail. Albania famously suffered from a spate of national-level pyramid schemes in the 1990s that brought financial ruin to the country and resulted in riots and thousands of deaths[131].

DeFi takes such scams to a new virtual level. In the case of the Albanian pyramid schemes, with the help of the IMF and the World Bank to rebuild the economy, and some support from neighboring countries, the government finally managed to regain control and wind up the fraudulent schemes. Because there were various companies orchestrating them, arresting and jailing the company directors brought the scams to an end. But with DeFi it is different – there is no "head" that you can chop off. The scam is autonomous, and if the smart contract running it does not have a kill or terminate function in it, it will keep running and interacting with future investors unless the entire blockchain is shut down[132].

Of course, the underlying principles of scams such as pyramid schemes and Ponzi schemes have been around for centuries. It is just that with new technology you can launch them more quickly, with more anonymity, and in the case of blockchains and smart contracts, in a manner that cannot be censored by the authorities.

Furthermore, setting up a real-world pyramid scheme or Ponzi scheme requires organization, incorporation, producing brochures, engaging in meetings or calls with potential future recruits or investors, and so on and so forth. An Ethereum-based smart contract pyramid scheme can be implemented in as few as 29 lines of Solidity code[133]. Yes, you read that correctly. The source code to the scam fits on a single side of one of the pages of this book, and you can deploy it in a couple of minutes at an expenditure of somewhere between $50 and $500 in ether depending on the current Ethereum gas prices.

Is such a smart contract scam really part of DeFi? We can use the "duck test" for that – if it looks like a duck, swims like a duck, and quacks like a duck, then it probably is a duck[134]. The contract is decentralized and it concerns the automation of the movement of cryptocurrency or tokens from one set of addresses to another in a deterministic manner. It's a duck.

As a side note, I can't help wondering if there will come a time when some government will pass a law that makes you eternally liable for any damage your smart contract causes and continues to cause throughout a blockchain's existence.

Risks

I mentioned at the beginning of this chapter that we would look at some of the risks involved in engaging with DeFi, and we have already covered pyramid schemes and Ponzi schemes. The rest of the list in this section is by no means exhaustive, but it should give you a starting point of other things to consider before investing.

Bugs in smart contracts probably constitute the most significant danger. They are often subtle and can hide in code for months or years with all sorts of unexpected and unwanted effects when discovered. There have been cases of badly coded smart contracts allowing anyone to terminate them without paying back the contents, thereby preventing assets locked in the contracts from ever being unlocked again[135]. Overflow errors are another example of potential problems that can arise. These are similar to a car odometer looping around from 999,999 kilometers back to 0, except that in the case of such a car the potential buyer will quickly notice that the battered old vehicle in front of them has seen many more miles than the odometer indicates. In smart contracts, on the other hand, such errors have allowed people to withdraw a fortune in stored tokens[136]. The list of bugs that have bitten DeFi investors over the last few years goes on and on and is worth a book in its own right.

Price manipulation in the cryptocurrency markets is suspected to be rife, especially for less established virtual assets where there can be individuals with large holdings able to flood the market and move prices at will. There have been so many pump-and-dump schemes over the years that it is not even worth enumerating them all here.

Sudden collapses in the market price of underlying virtual assets collateralizing DeFi loans can automatically trigger liquidation events in smart contracts for loans, and such events are invariably costly to borrowers. In the real-world lending business at least there is a due process with plenty of notice before the bailiffs turn up and start carrying off your possessions, but in the DeFi world you can go to bed thinking everything is fine, and wake up eight hours later to discover that all of your virtual assets are gone[137].

Traditional finance has spent centuries on ironing out errors and loopholes in the system, usually through regulation, and yet is still not flawless. In DeFi, regulation can really only take place by improving coding standards and through trial and error, and even so, there will always be bugs.

Evolution or Revolution?

If it feels like all of the decentralized finance systems described above are nothing more than using magical internet money to perform the equivalent of taking cryptocurrency loans on chance cards in some kind of virtual game of monopoly, simply to put non-existent houses on a digital Park Lane (or Park Place if you're used to the US version), then you may have a point.

However, there is something further to consider. In the chapter titled "On Value" starting on page 167 we already looked at how there are many similarities between traditional currencies issued by Central Banks and some cryptocurrencies, and between gold and other cryptocurrencies. Only the entities involved and the means of production differ, and open permissionless blockchain-based tokens and coins are far more amenable to investigation by anyone who is interested, and not just large auditing companies.

We all labor under a collective illusion that money, traditional or blockchain-based, is storing value for us and will always be accepted as payment, and it is that illusion that allows us to trade efficiently using it. Mainstream markets have decoupled from the underlying assets to such an extent that the world is full of people making or losing fortunes trading lumber, oranges, gold, or soybeans using financial instruments several steps removed from the physical assets they represent, and so decentralized finance systems and the more familiar markets actually have more in common than most people realize.

As time goes on, and better techniques are developed to "onboard" various asset classes into blockchain systems, the established financial markets are inevitably going to be either displaced or transformed. We may not be there quite yet, but all the technical pieces are falling into place, and that means that the social pieces will follow.

Just as stock markets and the trading floors of the exchanges could not resist the rising tide of online portals that enabled ordinary people without licenses, fax machines, or funny striped blazers to buy and sell all kinds of assets and financial instruments from the comfort of their own homes, so decentralized finance will eventually affect traditional centralized finance. At least, that is what I predict.

Whether it will be a revolution that sweeps away the old guard, or an evolution in which decentralized finance engages in some kind of merger with traditional finance, remains to be seen. It should be an interesting spectacle though, whatever path is eventually taken.

Selling Out

> Ah hah hah.
> Ever get the feeling you've been cheated?
> *John Lydon, 1978[w]*

As I write this there are an estimated 7,828,030,622 people alive on the planet[138]. Sometime in the early 2050s this is expected to exceed 10 billion[139]. That is a seriously large number of people, each of them with their own identity.

There will only ever be 21 million bitcoins in existence[*], and some of those have been proven to be irretrievably lost.

If we assume that Satoshi Nakamoto, for whatever reason, never plans to spend his or her coins, that only leaves about 20 million coins to share between the rest of us. This is a conservative estimate of the total number of lost coins: Chainalysis reckons that between 2.3 million and 3.7 million are actually missing in action[140].

A simple division – 20 million divided by 10 billion – shows that there are, at best, 0.002 bitcoins per person on the planet when we reach the middle of this century.

---

* The initial block reward was 50 bitcoins, the protocol sets that to halve every 210,000 blocks, and you cannot have fractional satoshis. This is enough information to calculate the maximum total.

The Credit Suisse global wealth report for 2018[141] puts the average *per capita* wealth of the planet at about $63,000. So if the unthinkable were to happen, and Bitcoin replaced all other means of accounting for wealth, then a single bitcoin could be worth $31 million.

Now I have to state that the aforementioned scenario seems extremely unlikely to me, however, it is interesting to look at how much one bitcoin should be worth if Bitcoin were to replace various other stores of value or financial institutions that we use (and assuming 20 million bitcoins are available):

If Bitcoin were to replace:	then 1 BTC should be worth:
Western Union[142]	$488
Paypal[143]	$6,000
Visa and Mastercard[144]	$33,100
All US dollars in circulation[145]	$85,000
All non-cash transactions for a year[146]	$241,000
Gold[147]	$386,500
All the wealth in the world[141]	$31,000,000

Figure 42: If Bitcoin were to replace other value storing entities

Admittedly, some of these do not really make much sense – for example, the value of a company does not represent the transactions it conducts – but the numbers above do provide a "scale" as to the significance (potential or realized) of cryptocurrency.

The great treasure hunt

Well done for getting through this book to the last section, where it is with great pleasure that I now announce a Bitcoin treasure hunt! Please excuse my exuberance, but I've had to announce these kinds of things at children's parties many times, and old habits die hard.

I have transferred eight lots of 0.002 bitcoin (the amount per person calculated at the start of this chapter) into eight different Bitcoin addresses, which are listed below.

```
14aFhno96fkt7knLWMDQ4j8yh8v5hBF4n1
181rPpfdUGFg4fVEdhDZEfDbBSqgigtoZR
1KZei2D5yz3UJ59LvXsC1Y9y4ktSgcnVwz
14utGQn5GdfPvUrHNLAwTmmP99QpXm9mg6
1DZ5NbUwDgxeJkKhQLgYcUUX36PtYso1pm
161YgNX2NrCzGunWvoV1hN3DuzWeuovBK3
17Y9czcbcCz433QXsy1SGQjwLb27BBtLLZ
1QFafw3weoWTRQhiLafRw2eyWbVmES6wfJ
```

Dotted throughout this book are various clues that, provided you think the way I do, will allow you to deduce the private key of every one of the above public addresses. There is no need to travel – you hold the source of each and every key in your hands at this very moment, as long as you have a physical copy, that is. Note that there are plenty of red herrings too.

You can go and check through any Bitcoin blockchain explorer that, at the time of publication of this book, those addresses did indeed hold that balance. Of course, if some of the addresses have been drained of their funds then you cannot truly know whether someone solved a puzzle associated with the address or just brute-forced them, but then – that's pseudonymity for you.

I will be able to monitor your progress through the magic of the Bitcoin blockchain. Because all transactions are transparently published on the blockchain, if you deduce a key and transfer out the coins, I will know.

And before I sign off, here is a hint:

Va znal pnfrf, lbh'yy unir gb unfu gur nafjre guerr gvzrf. Nsgre nyy, nf gur Fanex Uhagref fnvq, "Jung V gryy lbh guerr gvzrf vf gehr."

Good luck!

References

> Why did you have to leave so soon?
> Why did you have to walk away?
> *Billy Joe Armstrong, 1990[y]*

Acknowledgments

[1] Nawotka E. (2011), "Should Publishers Credit Editors, Proofreaders, Agents and Others in Books?", retrieved from https://publishingperspectives.com/2011/08/should-publishers-credit-editors-proofreaders-agents-and-others-in-books/ on 4 May 2020, Publishing Perspectives.

Introduction

[2] Titchmarsh E.C. (1950), "Godfrey Harold Hardy", Obituary in the Journal of the London Mathematical Society, vol. 25, part 2.
[3] Hoffman P. (1998), "The Man Who Loved Only Numbers: The Story of Paul Erdős and the Search for Mathematical Truth", Hyperion.
[4] Wikipedia, "1970s energy crisis", retrieved from https://en.wikipedia.org/wiki/1970s_energy_crisis on 25 August 2019.

[5] Layard R. (1982), "Youth Unemployment in Britain and the United States Compared" from "The Youth Labor Market Problem: Its Nature, Causes, and Consequences", p. 499, University of Chicago Press.
[6] The Balance, "2008 Financial Crisis" retrieved from https://www.thebalance.com/2008-financial-crisis-3305679 on 9 September 2019.
[7] Sayle A. (2017), "Alexei Sayle's Imaginary Sandwich Bar", episode 3, BBC Radio 4
[8] Arnold C. (2016), "A Brief History of Zines", retrieved from https://mentalfloss.com/article/88911/brief-history-zines on 27 August 2019, Mental Floss
[9] Dunn K. (2016), "How Punk Rock Kickstarted the Do-It-Yourself Record Revolution", retrieved from https://medium.com/cuepoint/how-punk-rock-kickstarted-the-do-it-yourself-record-revolution-39a41d78e12a on 27 August 2019, Medium
[10] O'Connor J. J., Robertson E. F., "Luca Pacioli", retrieved from https://www-history.mcs.st-andrews.ac.uk/Biographies/Pacioli.html on 9 September 2019
[11] Nakamoto S. (2008), "Bitcoin: A Peer-to-Peer Electronic Cash System", retrieved from https://bitcoin.org/bitcoin.pdf on 9 September 2019, self-published

Three Chords

[12] Moon T. (1977), "Three Chords", Sideburns Fanzine.
[13] Anderson C. (2004), "The Long Tail", retrieved from https://www.wired.com/2004/10/tail/ on 9 September 2019, Wired
[14] Jakobsson M., and Juels A. (1999), "Proofs of Work and Bread Pudding Protocols" in Secure Information Networks: Communications and Multimedia Security, Kluwer Academic Publishers: 258–272.

Weltanschauung!

[15] Black J. (2014), "The ancient invention of the steam engine by the Hero of Alexandria", retrieved from https://www.ancient-origins.net/ancient-technology/ancient-invention-steam-engine-hero-alexandria-001467 on 9 September 2019, Ancient Origins.

[16] Woods R. (2003), "Thomas Newcomen and the Steam Engine", retrieved from https://ethw.org/Thomas_Newcomen_and_the_Steam_Engine on 9 September 2019, Mechanical Engineering Magazine

[17] Pettegree A. (2015), "Brand Luther: How an Unheralded Monk Turned His Small Town into a Center of Publishing, Made Himself the Most Famous Man in Europe—and Started the Protestant Reformation", Penguin Press.

[18] Caruso C. (2019), " The five camps of crypto", retrieved from https://medium.com/@caseycaruso/the-five-camps-of-crypto-1aa8695b76bc on 23 September 2019, Medium

[19] Grigg, I. (2005), "Triple Entry Accounting", retrieved from http://iang.org/papers/triple_entry.html on 23 September 2019, self-published.

[20] Bloor R. (2018), "If Data is The New Oil, Then You're The Oil", retrieved from https://medium.com/permissionio/if-data-is-the-new-oil-then-youre-the-oil-2c90fb42135b on 23 September 2019, Medium

[21] He H. (2019), "The Lord of the Protocols", retrieved from https://medium.com/sesameopen/the-lord-of-the-protocols-cb48bea92bef on 23 September 2019, Medium

Blockchain City

[22] VanderPlas J. (2019), "The Waiting Time Paradox, or, Why Is My Bus Always Late?", retrieved from https://jakevdp.github.io/blog/2018/09/13/waiting-time-paradox/ on 21 June 2020

Buying Trust

[23] Braben D., and Bell, I. (1984), "Elite", Acornsoft.
[24] Schreiber, F. R. (1973), "Sybil", Independent Publishing Group.
[25] Gilbert S., and Lynch N. A. (2012), "Perspectives on the CAP Theorem", retrieved from https://groups.csail.mit.edu/tds/papers/Gilbert/Brewer2.pdf on 16 November 2019, MIT.

Hash Functions

[26] Cambridge Dictionary website, retrieved from https://dictionary.cambridge.org/dictionary/english/repudiation on 20 September 2020.
[27] Taycher L. (2010), "Books of the world, stand up and be counted! All 129,864,880 of you" retrieved from http://booksearch.blogspot.com/2010/08/books-of-world-stand-up-and-be-counted.html on 20 September 2020.
[28] FermiGuy (2014), "Physics Questions People Ask Fermilab" retrieved from https://www.fnal.gov/pub/science/inquiring/questions/atoms.html on 20 September 2020.
[29] Kimpton I., and Padilla A. (2012), "Cleaning up the cosmological constant", retrieved from https://arxiv.org/pdf/1203.1040.pdf on 20 September 2020.
[30] Bipartisan Policy Center (2020), "Deficit Tracker", retrieved from https://bipartisanpolicy.org/report/deficit-tracker/ on 20 September 2020.
[31] Holden J. (2013), "A Good Hash Function is Hard to Find, and Vice Versa", retrieved from http://citeseerx.ist.psu.edu/viewdoc/download?doi=10.1.1.225.2528&rep=rep1&type=pdf on 21 September 2020, Cryptologica.
[32] emn178, "Online Tools: SHA256", available at https://emn178.github.io/online-tools/sha256.html

[33] Dwork C., and Naor M. (1993), "Pricing via Processing, Or, Combatting Junk Mail", retrieved from http://www.wisdom.weizmann.ac.il/~naor/PAPERS/pvp.ps on 22 September 2020.

[34] Finney H. (2004), "Reusable Proofs of Work", retrieved from https://web.archive.org/web/20071222072154/http://rpow.net/ on 22 September 2020.

[35] Merkle R. (1982), "Method of providing digital signatures", retrieved from https://patentimages.storage.googleapis.com/69/ab/d9/2ff9f94fada6ea/US4309569.pdf on 23 September 2020, USPTO.

Part One on Identity: Who Are You?

[36] UK Government Publishing Service (2017), "Passports", retrieved from https://assets.publishing.service.gov.uk/government/uploads/system/uploads/attachment_data/file/633475/passport.pdf on 26 November 2019

[37] van Beek J. C. (2009), "ePassports reloaded goes mobile" retrieved from https://www.blackhat.com/presentations/bh-europe-09/VanBeek/BlackHat-Europe-2009-VanBeek-ePassports-Mobile.pdf on 26 November 2019.

[38] Lerner S. D. (2019), "The Return of the Deniers and the Revenge of Patoshi", retrieved from https://bitslog.com/2019/04/16/the-return-of-the-deniers-and-the-revenge-of-patoshi/ on 20 September 2020.

[39] The Tor Project, retrieved from https://www.torproject.org/ on 15 February 2020

[40] United Nations (1948), "The Universal Declaration of Human Rights", retrieved from https://www.un.org/en/udhrbook/pdf/udhr_booklet_en_web.pdf in an amusing illustrated version on 15 February 2020.

[41] Maxwell G., "CoinJoin: Bitcoin privacy for the real world", retrieved from https://bitcointalk.org/?topic=279249 on 16 February 2020.

[42] Rivest R.L., Shamir A., Tauman Y. (2001), "How to Leak a Secret." in: Boyd C. (eds) "Advances in Cryptology — ASIACRYPT 2001.", ASIACRYPT 2001, Lecture Notes in Computer Science, vol. 2248. Springer

[43] Department of the Treasury (2020), "Pilot IRS Cryptocurrency Tracing", retrieved from https://beta.sam.gov/opp/3b7875d5236b47f6a77f64c19251af60/view?index=opp on 20 September 2020.

Passwords are the Worst

[44] Diffie W., and Hellman M. E. (1976), "New Directions in Cryptography", in IEEE Transactions On Information Theory, vol. IT-22, No. 6, retrieved from https://ee.stanford.edu/~hellman/publications/24.pdf on 4 October 2020

[45] Clark J. (2011), "Bitcoin-thieving Trojans appear in the wild", retrieved from https://www.zdnet.com/article/bitcoin-thieving-trojans-appear-in-the-wild/ on 5 October 2020, ZDNet.

[46] The Bitcoin devs, "Issue #3: Encrypt wallet", retrieved from https://github.com/bitcoin/bitcoin/issues/3 on 5 October 2020, Github.

[47] Vryonis, P (2013), "Public-key cryptography for non-geeks", retrieved from https://blog.vrypan.net/2013/08/28/public-key-cryptography-for-non-geeks/ on 7 October 2020, personal blog

Part Two on Identity: Self-Sovereignty

[48] Plutarch (75), "Theseus", translated by John Dryden, retrieved from http://classics.mit.edu/Plutarch/theseus.html on 28 July 2020

[49] Quote from B J Neblett or Maya Angelou? You decide.

[50] El-Rjula T. (2020), "The Invisible Son: True story of a man who altered his mess into a global message", self-published

[51] Allende Lopez M. (2020), "Self-Sovereign Identity: The Future of Identity: Self-Sovereignty, Digital Wallets, and Blockchain", retrieved from https://publications.iadb.org/en/self-sovereign-

identity-future-identity-self-sovereignity-digital-wallets-and-blockchain on 10 October 2020, Inter-American Development Bank.

[52] Allen C. (2016), "The Path to Self-Sovereign Identity", blog post retrieved from http://www.lifewithalacrity.com/2016/04/the-path-to-self-soverereign-identity.html on 10 October 2020

[53] Universal Life Church (1998-2020), "Become an Ordained Minister", retrieved from https://www.ulc.org/ on 11 October 2020.

[54] Cambridge Dictionary website, retrieved from https://dictionary.cambridge.org/dictionary/english/sovereign on 18 October 2020.

[55] McCarthy N. (2918), "Dramatic rise in number of Britons losing citizenship", retrieved from https://www.statista.com/chart/17079/the-number-of-individuals-stripped-of-uk-nationality/ on 18 October 2020, Statista.

[56] Hill K. (2019), "Many are abandoning Facebook. These people have the opposite problem." retrieved from https://www.nytimes.com/2019/08/22/business/reactivate-facebook-account.html on 18 October 2020, the New York Times.

[57] lifeID (2018), "Self-sovereign identity bill of rights", retrieved from https://medium.com/lifeid/lifeid-self-sovereign-identity-bill-of-rights-d2acafa1de8b on 18 October 2020.

[58] Schutte M. (2016), "Schutte's critique of the self-sovereign identity principles", retrieved from http://matthewschutte.com/2016/10/25/schuttes-critique-of-the-self-sovereign-identity-principles/ on 18 October 2020, personal blog.

[59] Surowiecki J. (2005), "The Wisdom of Crowds", Anchor Books.

[60] United Kingdom Public General Acts (2000), "Regulation of Investgatory Powers Act", retrieved from https://www.legislation.gov.uk/ukpga/2000/23/contents on 23 October 2020

[61] In Search Of Satoshi (2018), "The Time Zones of Satoshi Nakamoto", retrieved from

https://medium.com/@insearchofsatoshi/the-time-zones-of-satoshi-nakamoto-aa40f035178f on 24 October 2020, Medium.
[62] Directed by Meyer N. (1982), "Star Trek II: The Wrath of Khan", Paramount Pictures
[63] European Union (2018), "General Data Protection Regulation (GDPR) Article 17 – the Right to Erasure", retrieved from https://gdpr-info.eu/art-17-gdpr/ on 24 October 2020

Cryptocurrencies and the User Experience

[64] Cambridge Dictionary website, retrieved from https://dictionary.cambridge.org/dictionary/english/user and https://dictionary.cambridge.org/dictionary/english/experience on 20 September 2020
[65] Cambridge Dictionary website, retrieved from https://dictionary.cambridge.org/dictionary/english/analogy on 20 September 2020

The Network Effect

[66] Marsden R. (2005), "Pushing the Envelope", retrieved from https://www.independent.co.uk/news/uk/this-britain/pushing-the-envelope-483256.html on 27 October 2019, the Independent
[67] Baran P. (1964), "On Distributed Communications: I. Introduction to Distributed Communications Networks", retrieved from https://www.rand.org/content/dam/rand/pubs/research_memoranda/2006/RM3420.pdf on 27 October 2019, the RAND corporation.
[68] Whitehead A. N., and Russell B. (1910, 1912, 1913), "Principia Mathematica", in three volumes, Cambridge University Press.
[69] Jelasity M. (2011), "Gossip", pp. 139-162, in "Self-organising software. From natural to artificial adaptation", editors Serugendo G., Gleizes M., Karageorgos A, Springer, Berlin-Heidelberg.
[70] Wikipedia, "Erdős number", retrieved from https://en.wikipedia.org/wiki/Erd%C5%91s_number on 4 November 2019.

[71] Peterson T. (2018), "Metcalfe's Law as a Model for Bitcoin's Value", retrieved from http://dx.doi.org/10.2139/ssrn.3078248 on 19 September 2020

[72] Wikipedia, "Birthday Problem", retrieved from https://en.wikipedia.org/wiki/Birthday_problem on 19 September 2020

On Value

[73] Wilde O. (2003), "The Picture of Dorian Gray", Penguin

[74] Draghi M. (2019), ""Bitcoin [...] is not something that pertains to the central bank"", retrieved from https://www.youtube.com/watch?v=wztu8yyCPZQ on 30 October 2019

[75] Douglas C. H. (1924), "Social Credit", Institute of Economic Democracy, Canada

[76] Gygax G., and Arenson D. (1974), "Dungeons & Dragons Players Manual", TSR Hobbies.

[77] Kent S. A. (2007), "The Quaker Ethic and the Fixed Price Policy: Max Weber and Beyond", retrieved from https://www.researchgate.net/publication/229523106_The_Quaker_Ethic_and_the_Fixed_Price_Policy_Max_Weber_and_Beyond on 31 October 2020, Sociological Inquiry 53(1), pp 16-28

[78] Nakamoto S. (2010), comment on "Bitcoin does NOT violate Mises' Regression Theorem", on Bitcointalk.org, retrieved from https://bitcointalk.org/index.php?topic=583.msg11405#msg11405 on 12 November 2020.

The Truth is a Harsh Mistress

[79] Winbourne P., Finlow-Bates K. (1994), "Unit Guide: Mathematical Contexts and Strategies", South Bank University

Clever Covenants

[80] Roche S. (2019), "Bitcoin Script Puzzles", retrieved from https://bitcoindev.network/guides/bitcoinjs-lib/bitcoin-script-puzzles/ on 27 October 2019, Bitcoin Developer Network
[81] Wikipedia, "Chomsky hierarchy", retrieved from https://en.wikipedia.org/wiki/Chomsky_hierarchy on 27 October 2019.
[82] Buterin V. (2013), "Ethereum Whitepaper", retrieved from https://ethereum.org/en/whitepaper/ on 9 November 2020.
[83] DiNucci D. (1999), "Fragmented Future", retrieved from http://darcyd.com/fragmented_future.pdf on 11 November 2020, Print Magazine.

Government Without Leaders

[84] Honkanen P., Westerlund M., and Nylund M. (2019), "Governance in Decentralized Ecosystems: A Survey of Blockchain and Distributed Ledger White Papers", Cloud Computing 2019, the Tenth International Conference on Cloud Computing
[85] de Secondat, Baron de Motesquieu C. L. (1748), "The Spirit of Laws", translated by Nugent T. (1752), retrieved from https://socialsciences.mcmaster.ca/econ/ugcm/3ll3/montesquieu/spiritoflaws.pdf on 15 October 2020
[86] Cambridge Dictionary website, retrieved from https://dictionary.cambridge.org/dictionary/english/despotism on 17 October 2020
[87] Lewis A. (2010), comment on Metafilter.com, retrieved from https://www.metafilter.com/95152/Userdriven-discontent#3256046 on 19 November 2020.
[88] Lundy L. (2019), "No such thing as decentralised governance", retrieved from https://outlierventures.io/research/the-crypto-trias-politica/ on 16 October 2020
[89] Github Guides (2017), "Forking Projects", retrieved from https://guides.github.com/activities/forking/ on 20 November 2020, Github.com

[90] Andresen G. (2010), "Development process straw-man", retrieved from https://bitcointalk.org/index.php?topic=2367.0 on 20 November 2020, Bitcointalk.org

[91] Sharma A. (2018), "Understanding Proof of Stake through it's Flaws", retrieved from https://medium.com/@abhisharm/understanding-proof-of-stake-through-its-flaws-pt-1-6728020994a1 on 20 November 2020, Medium.com.

[92] Zamfir V. (2017), "Against on-chain governance", retrieved from https://medium.com/@Vlad_Zamfir/against-on-chain-governance-a4ceacd040ca on 21 November 2020, Medium.com.

Knives, Forks, and Spoons

[93] Mojang, "What is Minecraft?", retrieved from https://www.minecraft.net/en-us/what-is-minecraft/ on 6 October 2019.

[94] Ieyal I., and Sirer E. G. (2013), "Majority is not Enough: Bitcoin Mining is Vulnerable", retrieved from https://www.cs.cornell.edu/~ie53/publications/btcProcFC.pdf on 6 October 2019, Cornell University

Fair Gambling

[95] Seriously, you were expecting a reference to pornography? Do your own search.

[96] Computer History Museum, "Timeline of Computer History: Networking and the Web", retrieved from https://www.computerhistory.org/timeline/networking-the-web/ on 26 August 2019.

[97] Strusiewicz C. J. (2010), "5 Ways Porn Created the Modern World", Cracked.com, retrieved from https://www.cracked.com/article_18888_5-ways-porn-created-modern-world.html on 26 August 2019.

[98] Cargal J.M. (1988), "Discrete Mathematics for Neophytes: Number Theory, Probability, Algorithms, and Other Stuff", chapter 33.
[99] Grinstead C. M., and Snell, J. L. (1997), "Introduction to Probability", chapter 8, retrieved from https://www.dartmouth.edu/~chance/teaching_aids/books_articles/probability_book/Chapter8.pdf on 28 October 2019, American Mathematical Society.
[100] Goodstein D. L. (1985), "States of Matter", Dover Publications.
[101] Wikipedia, "Chudnovsky algorithm", retrieved from https://en.wikipedia.org/wiki/Chudnovsky_algorithm on 31 October 2020.
[102] Baez J. (2012), "Ice", retrieved from https://johncarlosbaez.wordpress.com/2012/04/15/ice/ on 31 October 2020, personal blog
[103] Shannon C. E. (1948), "A Mathematical Theory of Communication", retrieved from http://people.math.harvard.edu/~ctm/home/text/others/shannon/entropy/entropy.pdf on 1 August 2020, the Bell System Technical Journal
[104] Zimbles (2017,)"Some quotes about Entropy I found", retrieved from https://anotherbloodybullshitblog.wordpress.com/2017/07/25/some-quotes-about-entropy-i-found/ on 2 November 2020, personal blog.
[105] Tribus M., McIrvine E. C. (1971), "Energy and Information", retrieved from http://www.esalq.usp.br/lepse/imgs/conteudo_thumb/Energy-and-Information.pdf on 4 November 2020, in Scientific American, vol. 225, no. 3, p. 180
[106] Szabo N. (2005), "Bit gold", retrieved from https://web.archive.org/web/20060329122942/http://unenumerated.blogspot.com/2005/12/bit-gold.html on 5 November 2020, personal blog post.
[107] Back A. (2002), "Hashcash – A Denial of Service Counter-Measure", retrieved from

https://www.researchgate.net/profile/Adam_Back/publication/2482110_Hashcash_-_A_Denial_of_Service_Counter-Measure/links/00b7d523761e012678000000/Hashcash-A-Denial-of-Service-Counter-Measure.pdf on 5 November 2020.

[108] Kim C. (2020), "Ethereum 2.0: How it works and why it matters", retrieved from https://www.coindesk.com/wp-content/uploads/2020/07/ETH-2.0-072120.pdf on 6 November 2020, Coindesk.

[109] Randao.org (2017), "Randao: Verifiable Random Number Generation", retrieved from https://www.randao.org/whitepaper/Randao_v0.85_en.pdf on 7 November 2020

[110] VDF Alliance (2020), "Open VDF: ASIC Introduction", retrieved from https://www.vdfalliance.org/news/open-vdf-asic-introduction on 7 November 2020.

[111] Shannon, C. E. (1959), "Coding Theorems for a Discrete Source With a Fidelity Criterion", retrieved from https://mast.queensu.ca/~math474/shannon59.pdf on 4 November 2020, IRE. Nat. Conv

Rise of the Autonomous Machines

[112] Plath S. (1981), "Watercolor Of Grantchester Meadows", in the Collected Poems, Faber.

[113] Pink Floyd (1969), "Grantchester Meadows", vinyl single, Emidisc

[114] Kranz M. (2018), "Why blockchain is the missing link to IoT transformations", retrieved from https://www.networkworld.com/article/3295903/why-blockchain-is-the-missing-link-to-iot-transformations.html on 17 September 2020, Networkworld.

[115] Ironically, given the nature of the quote, the internet variously credits this to Douglas Adams, and Donald A. Adams. I emailed Garson O'Toole at Quote Investigator, and just a few days later received confirmation that the quote actually originated from the

latter: https://quoteinvestigator.com/2020/09/17/integrity/ retrieved on 19 September 2020
[116] Summers L. (2001), "The Significance of Ideas and the Transformation in Economic Thinking", interview text retrieved from https://www.pbs.org/wgbh/commandingheights/shared/minitext/int_lawrencesummers.html on 17 September 2020, PBS.
[117] Shilling A. G. (1986), however, https://quoteinvestigator.com/2011/08/09/remain-solvent/ indicates that the quote may well have been around longer. It is often erroneously attributed to John Maynard Keynes.

Independent Sacrificial Offerings

[118] The Bank Of England, "Frequently Asked Questions", retrieved from https://www.bankofengland.co.uk/faq on 2 November 2019.
[119] Wikipedia, "Enron scandal", retrieved from https://en.wikipedia.org/wiki/Enron_scandal on 20 September 2020

DeFining Finance

[120] GameKyuubi (2013), "I Am Hodling", retrieved from https://bitcointalk.org/index.php?topic=375643.0 on 13 November 2020.
[121] Financial Action Task Force (2019), "Guidance for a Risk-Based Approach to Virtual Assets and Virtual Asset Service Providers", retrieved from https://www.fatf-gafi.org/media/fatf/documents/recommendations/RBA-VA-VASPs.pdf on 23 November 2020, FATF.
[122] MakerDAO (ongoing), "The Maker Protocol: MakerDAO's Multi-Collateral Dai (MCD) System", retrieved from https://makerdao.com/en/whitepaper/ on 26 November 2020, MakerDAO.
[123] Leshner R., Hayes G. (2019), "Compound: The Money Market Protocol", retrieved from

https://compound.finance/documents/Compound.Whitepaper.pdf on 26 November 2020, Compound Finance

[124] Lys L., Micoulet A., Potop-Butucaru M. (2019), "Atomic Swapping bitcoins and Etheres", retrieved from https://hal.archives-ouvertes.fr/hal-02353945/document on 25 November 2020, Proceedings of the 38th International Symposium on Reliable Distributed Systems, SRDS

[125] Kyber Network, BitGo Inc, Republic Protocol (2019), "Wrapped Tokens: A multi-institutional framework for tokenizing any asset", retrieved from https://wbtc.network/assets/wrapped-tokens-whitepaper.pdf on 26 November 2020.

[126] Adams H., Zinsmeister N., and Robinson D. (2020), "Uniswap v2 Core", retrieved from https://uniswap.org/whitepaper.pdf on 24 November 2020, Uniswap.org.

[127] Aave (2020), "Aave Protocol Whitepaper V1.0", retrieved from https://whitepaper.io/document/533/aave-whitepaper on 24 November 2020

[128] Dhar R. (2014), "The Trade of the Century: When George Soros Broke the British Pound", retrieved from https://priceonomics.com/the-trade-of-the-century-when-george-soros-broke/ on 24 November 2020, Priceconomic.com blog

[129] TRON Foundation (2018), "TRON: Advanced Decentralized Blockchain Platform", retrieved from https://tron.network/static/doc/white_paper_v_2_0.pdf on 26 November 2020.

[130] Kenton W. (2019), "Pyramid Scheme", retrieved from https://www.investopedia.com/terms/p/pyramidscheme.asp on 23 November 2020, Investopedia

[131] Jarvis C. (2000), "The Rise and Fall of Albania's Pyramid Schemes", retrieved from https://www.imf.org/external/pubs/ft/fandd/2000/03/jarvis.htm on 23 November 2020, the International Monetary Fund.

[132] Roan A. (2020), "Ethereum Smart Contract Ponzi Schemes", retrieved from https://medium.com/blockcentric/ethereum-smart-

contract-ponzi-schemes-9e43015b56f8 on 23 November 2020, Medium.com

[133] Roan A. (2020), "EthereumPonzi / contracts / Tree.sol", retrieved from https://github.com/alexroan/EthereumPonzi/blob/master/contracts/Tree.sol on 24 November 2020, Github.com.

[134] Wikipedia, "Duck test", retrieved from https://en.wikipedia.org/wiki/Duck_test on 2020 September 2020.

[135] Thomson I. (2017), "Parity's $280m Ethereum wallet freeze was no accident: It was a hack, claims angry upstart", retrieved from https://www.theregister.com/2017/11/10/parity_280m_ethereum_wallet_lockdown_hack/ on 25 November 2020, The Register.

[136] Biggs J. (2018), "Overflow error shuts down token trading", retrieved from https://techcrunch.com/2018/04/25/overflow-error-shuts-down-token-trading/ on 25 November 2020, Techcrunch.

[137] Igamberdiev I. (2020), "Black Thursday for MakerDAO: $8.32 million was liquidated for 0 DAI", retrieved from https://medium.com/@whiterabbit_hq/black-thursday-for-makerdao-8-32-million-was-liquidated-for-0-dai-36b83cac56b6 on 25 November 2020, Medium.com.

Selling Out

[138] Retrieved from https://www.worldometers.info/world-population/? On 4 December 2020.

[139] United Nations Department of Economic and Social Affairs (2017), "World population projected to reach 9.8 billion in 2050, and 11.2 billion in 2100", retrieved from https://www.un.org/development/desa/en/news/population/world-population-prospects-2017.html on 28 September 2019, UN Report.

[140] Chainalysis Team (2018), "Bitcoin's $30 billion sell-off", retrieved from https://blog.chainalysis.com/reports/money-supply on 29 September 2019, Chainalysis

[141] Credit Suisse (2018), "Global Wealth Report 2018", retrieved from

https://www.credit-suisse.com/media/assets/corporate/docs/about-us/research/publications/global-wealth-report-2018-en.pdf on 29 September 2019, Credit Suisse Research Institute

[142] Western Union market capitalization retrieved from https://ycharts.com/companies/WU/market_cap on 29 September 2019 as 9.771 billion USD.

[143] PayPal market capitalization retrieved from https://ycharts.com/companies/PYPL on 29 September 2019 as 120 billion USD

[144] Mastercard and Visa market capitalization retrieved from https://ycharts.com/companies/MA and https://ycharts.com/companies/V on 29 September 2019 as 662 billion USD.

[145] The total 2016 non-cash payments made retrieved from https://worldpaymentsreport.com/wp-content/uploads/sites/5/2018/10/World-Payments-Report-2018.pdf on 29 September 2019 as 482 billion, and 10% of Bitcoin estimated as replacing them.

[146] The Board of Governors of the Federal Reserve System, "How much U.S. currency is in circulation?", retrieved from https://www.federalreserve.gov/faqs/currency_12773.htm on 29 September 2019.

[147] Golden Eagle Coin, "Value of all of the gold in the world", retrieved from https://www.goldeneaglecoin.com/Guide/value-of-all-the-gold-in-the-world on 29 September 2019

Did I really end the most boring section of this book, namely the bibliography, with a reference to a random American website providing an estimation of the value of all the gold in the world, when I personally only own exactly 5 grams in the form of my wedding ring? I think I did.

Discography

> What they want, I don't know
> *Tommy and Dee Dee Ramone, 1976*[2]

Why not listen to the playlist (which consists of possibly the least cohesive collection of songs consciously assembled in 2020) as defined by the quotations at the start of each chapter? Or even better: why not do so while re-reading this book, and then recommending it to all your friends and relatives and then also buying them all copies?

Ahem, it seems like I got sidetracked into a sales pitch there. But if you'd like to listen to the music, you can visit this Spotify playlist that I assembled for your convenience:

https://open.spotify.com/user/1175682526/playlist/64u4UNTitsKjUPKSIOeHIG

And if you are one of those people who like to know all the facts, the complete discography that provided a backdrop to the writing of this book starts on the next page.

[a] Violent Femmes, "Kiss Off", track 2 on *Violent Femmes*, vinyl studio album, Concord Music Group, 1983.
[b] Sex Pistols, intro to "No Fun", b-side to *Pretty Vacant*, vinyl single, Virgin, 1977.
[c] The Jam, "All Mod Cons", track 1 on *All Mod Cons*, vinyl studio album, Polydor, 1978.
[d] Propaghandi, "A People's History Of The World", track 12 on *Less Talk, More Rock*, compact disc studio album, Fat Wreck Chords, 1996.
[e] John Cooper Clark, "Evidently Chickentown", track 1 on *Snap, Crackle and Bop*, vinyl studio album, Epic, 1980.
[f] Dead Kennedys, "Life Sentence", track 6 on *Give Me Convenience Or Give Me Death*, vinyl studio album, Alternative Tentacles Records, 1987.
[g] Trust, "Antisocial", track 1 on *Répression*, vinyl studio album, CBS, 1980.
[h] The Who, "My Generation", track 6 on *My Generation*, vinyl studio album, Brunswick, 1966.
[i] The All-American Rejects, "Dirty Little Secret", track 1 on *Dirty Little Secret*, Interscope Records, 2005.
[j] X-Ray Spex, "Identity", track 6 on *Germ Free Adolescents*, vinyl studio album, EMI, 1978.
[k] Patti Smith, "Free Money", track 4 on *Horses*, vinyl studio album, Arista Records, 1975.
[l] The Buzzcocks, "No Reply", track 2 on *Another Music In A Different Kitchen*, vinyl studio album, United Artists Records, 1978
[m] The Velvet Underground, "I'm Waiting For The Man", track 2 on *The Velvet Underground & Nico*, vinyl studio album, Verve, 1967
[n] Talking Heads, "Crosseyed And Painless", track 2 on *Remain In Light*, vinyl studio album, Sire, 1980.
[o] The Phosphorus Bombs, "Chain of Command", track 1 on *Chain of Command*, digital album, Bandcamp.com, 2015.

[p] Shonen Knife, "Burning Farm", track 8 on *Burning Farm*, vinyl studio album, Zero Records, 1983.

[q] Motörhead, "Ace Of Spades", track 1 on *Ace Of Spades*, vinyl studio album, Bronze, 1980.

[r] Dadabots, "Brain Bricks," track 6 on *Bot Prownies*, mp3 download, self-released on Bandcamp.com, 2018. Video at

[s] Terveet Kädet, "Minä Haluan Paljon Rahaa", track 3 on *Terveet Kädet*, vinyl studio album, Propaganda, 1983.

[t] The Undertones, "My Perfect Cousin", track 9 on *Hypnotized*, vinyl studio album, Sire, 1980.

[u] The Pixies, "Debaser", track 1 on Doolittle, compact disc studio album, 4AD, 1989.

[v] Doe Maar, "De Bom", track 12 on *Lijf Aan Lijf*, vinyl studio album, Sky, 1983.

[w] The Sex Pistols, outro to "No Fun", Live At Winterland, San Fransisco, 1978

[x] The Fall, "How I Wrote 'Elastic Man'", track 1 on *How I Wrote 'Elastic Man'*, 7" vinyl single, Rought Trade, 1980.

[y] Green Day, "At The Library", track 1 on *39/Smooth*, vinyl studio album, Lookout! Records, 1990.

[z] The Ramones, "Blitzkrieg Bop", track 1 on *Ramones*, vinyl studio album, Sire, 1976.

THIS PAGE UNINTENTIONALLY
LEFT BLANK

About the Author

> I'm eternally grateful
> To my past influences
> *Mark E. Smith, 1980[x]*

Hi, it's Keir Finlow-Bates here! I'm currently an inventor of blockchain-based technologies and an entrepreneur, living in Finland with my wife and our large family. I was born in Australia but grew up in Austria, Germany, and the Netherlands. And I also have a New Zealand passport even though I'm English.

I first found out about blockchain in late 2009 when a work colleague pointed me at the seminal Nakamoto paper. Unfortunately, I spent my time studying the technology rather than buying lots of cheap bitcoin, which is why I'm still working for a living and writing books like the one you've just read.

I've spent most of my career as a software test engineer and used to have hobbies such as making cheese, brewing beer, reading pretentious literature, and writing bad poetry, but these days I split my time equally between working on new blockchain concepts, looking after my kids, repairing the things they break, and sleeping.

You can find a collection of my short videos on blockchain concepts at www.youtube.com/thinklair if you want to learn more.